MW00618977

INTERNATIONAL CRIMINAL LAW

IN A NUTSHELL

by

DAVID P. STEWART
Visiting Professor of Law
Georgetown University Law Center
Member, Inter-American Juridical Committee

WEST
ACADEMIC
PUBLISHING

Mat #40177836

This publication was created to provide you with accurate and authoritative information concerning the subject matter covered; however, this publication was not necessarily prepared by persons licensed to practice law in a particular jurisdiction. The publisher is not engaged in rendering legal or other professional advice and this publication is not a substitute for the advice of an attorney. If you require legal or other expert advice, you should seek the services of a competent attorney or other professional.

PREFACE

The purpose of this book is to provide a self-contained introduction to the emergent field of international criminal law. It is aimed primarily at the beginning student and to complement the growing number of textbooks and treatises now in use in U.S. law schools. However, it may also serve as a helpful "field guide" for practitioners and others new to the topic.

Although its origins extend far back in history, international criminal law has taken definitive shape only in the past two decades. The war crimes trials at Nuremberg and Tokyo following World War II marked the first time that the international community acted to punish former high-level government officials for violations of international law. At the time, they seemed to offer the prospect of a truly international system of justice.

Yet the Cold War intervened, and it was nearly half a century before the international community again acted. The establishment of the *ad hoc* tribunals for the former Yugoslavia and Rwanda and the subsequent creation of a permanent International Criminal Court, along with the exercise by some national courts of jurisdiction over individuals accused of the most serious violations of human rights, like former Chilean Head of State Augusto Pinochet, indicate new emphasis on the individual responsibility of State agents for their actions.

The field of international criminal law continues to evolve, institutionally and normatively. It now boasts a number of international and hybrid tribunals as well as an increasing array of treaties and agreements articulating international crimes and providing a basis for international cooperation such as extradition and mutual legal assistance. National authorities more frequently prosecute individuals for transnational or international offenses, and domestic courts are more often empowered to exercise extraterritorial criminal jurisdiction. Victims of widespread atrocities seek to recover compensation in the courts of foreign States under theories of universal jurisdiction.

More and more attorneys have had relevant experience in the field, either though work at one of the *ad hoc* or hybrid courts, at one of the human rights bodies, or as domestic prosecutors. And practitioners increasingly encounter issues of international criminal law. In short, while it was once the purview of a few academics and scholars, international criminal law is more and more a "main stream" topic.

This first edition of the Nutshell focuses on the core concepts, institutions, and principles in an effort to make the field accessible to students and practitioners alike.

DAVID P. STEWART

July 2013

ACKNOWLEDGMENTS

I am indebted to a number of wonderful student assistants at Georgetown University Law Center who provided invaluable research and writing contributions to this small volume, among them Adam Coady, Garrett Traub, Abhimanyu George Jain, Arielle N. Greenbaum, Meg Parker, and John Michael Allen. My sincere thanks to each of them.

GENERAL REFERENCES

An enormous literature is available today in the field of international criminal law. For purposes of simplicity and clarity, I have chosen to keep references in the text of this Nutshell to a minimum. For those wishing to delve deeper, the following may be helpful.

Textbooks. Quite a few law schools now teach courses on international criminal law, and the various textbooks in use offer a useful source of additional information. Naturally, I am strongly partial to Luban, O'Sullivan and Stewart, *International and Transnational Criminal Law* (Aspen 2010) (2nd ed. forthcoming). Other textbooks currently in use are Paust, Scharf, Sadat, Grulé & Zagaris, *International Criminal Law: Cases and Materials* (Carolina, 4th ed. 2013); Cassese, Aquaviva, Fan & Whitley, *International Criminal Law: Cases and Commentary* (Oxford 2011); Van Schaack and Slye, *International Criminal Law and Its Enforcement: Cases and Materials* (Foundation, 2nd ed., 2010); and Podgor and Clark, *International Criminal Law: Cases and Materials* (3rd ed., LexisNexis, 2010). For a basic introduction, see Van Schaack and Slye, *International Criminal Law: The Essentials* (Kluwer 2008).

Treatises. In addition, a significant number of treaties have been published in the field over the past few years, each with varying orientations and emphases. For further reading or research, I recommend the following:

Bassiouni, *Introduction to International Criminal Law*, 2nd Revised Ed. (M.Nijhoff 2013); Cassese, Gaeta, Baig, Fan, Gosnell & Whiting, eds., *Cassese's International Criminal Law* (Oxford, 3rd ed. 2013); Findlay, *International and Comparative Criminal Justice: A Critical Introduction* (Routledge 2013); Carter & Pocar, eds., *International Criminal Procedure: The Interface of Civil Law and Common Law Legal Systems* (Elgar 2013); Van Den Herik and Stahn, eds., *The Diversification and Fragmentation of International Criminal Law* (M.Nijhoff 2012); Schabas & Bernaz, *Routledge Handlook of International Criminal Law* (Routledge 2012); Steinke, *The Politics of International Criminal Justice* (Oxford 2012); Meron, *The Making of International Criminal Justice: A View from the Bench* (Oxford 2011); Fisher, *Moral Accountability and International Criminal Law: Holding Agents of Atrocity Accountable to the World* (Routledge 2011); Ilias Bantekas, *International Criminal Law* (Hart, 4th ed. 2010); Cryer, Friman, Robinson, Wilmshurst, *An Introduction to International Criminal Law and Procedure* (Cambridge, 2nd ed. 2010); May and Hoskins, *International Criminal Law and Philosophy* (Cambridge 2009); Antonio Cassese, ed., *Oxford Companion to International Criminal Justice* (Oxford 2009); Bassiouni, *International Criminal Law* (M.Nijhoff, 3rd ed., 2008); and Zahar & Sluiter, *International Criminal Law: A Critical Introduction* (Oxford 2008).

Research Assistance. Several excellent electronic resources are available. Among them, one can recommend in particular the Electronic Resource Guide of the American Society of International Law, in particular its Electronic Information System for International Law, at *www.eisil.org.* See also the ICJ's Library on-line tools at *www. peacepalacelibrary.nl.*

The research guides at various law school libraries can be very useful, including the Georgetown University Law Center at *http://www.law. georgetown.edu/library/*, Columbia University Law School's Arthur Diamond Law Library at *http:// web.law.columbia.edu/library*; the NYU Law Library at *http://julius.law.nyu.edu/*, the Duke Law Library at *http://law.duke.edu/lib/*, and the Harvard University Law Library at *http:// www.law.harvard.edu/library/.*

You may also wish to consult Schabas, McDermott, Hayes, eds., *Ashgate Research Companion to International Criminal Law* (Ashgate 2013), and Brown, *Research Handbook on International Criminal Law* (Elgar 2011).

OUTLINE

TABLE OF CASES

References are to Pages

TABLE OF CONVENTIONS

SOURCES BY CHAPTER

CHAPTER 1

Antonio Cassese, *International Criminal Law* 3 (2d ed. 2008). **Part II.**

Thomas Buergenthal and Sean D. Murphy, *Public International Law in a Nutshell* (5th ed. 2013). **Part III.**

Application of Convention on Prevention and Punishment of Crime of Genocide (Bosn. & Herz. v. Serb. & Montenegro), 1996 I.C.J. 595. **§1-14.**

Valesquez Rodriguez, Inter-Am. Ct. H.R. (ser.C) No. 4, 951. L.R. 232 (29 July 1988). **§1-14.**

CHAPTER 2

Manley O. Hudson, The Proposed International Criminal Court, 32 Am. J. Int'l L. 549 1938). G.A. Res. 95(1), U.N. GAOR, 1st Sess., U.N.Doc. A/ 236 (Dec. 11, 1946). **Part I.**

G.A. Res. 260(III)B, U.N. Doc. A/810 (Dec. 9, 1948). **§2-2.**

U.N. Doc. A/RES/29/3314 (Dec. 14, 1974). **§2-5.**

Rome Statute of the International Criminal Court, art. 27 U.N. Doc.A/CONF.183/9* (July 17, 1998). **§2-5.**

Rep. of the In'tl Law Comm'n, 2d Sess., June 5-29, 1950, U.N. doc. A/1316 (A/5/12) part III, GAOR,

5th Sess., Supp. No. 12 (1950) (extracted from the *Yearbook of the International Law Commission,* vol. II, 1950). **§2-6.**

Gov't of Israel v. Eichmann, 36 I.L.R. 5 (Supreme Ct. 1968) (Israel). **§2-7.**

Attorney-Gen. of Israel v. Eichmann, 361 I.L.R. 277 (Dist. Ct. 1968) (Israel). **§2-7.**

R. v. Finta, [1994] 1 S.C.R. 701 (Can.). **§2-7.**

CHAPTER 3

The S.S. "Lotus" (Fr. v. Turk.), 1927 P.C.I.J. (ser. A) No. 10 (Sept. 7). **§3-2 (1).**

Case Concerning the *Arrest Warrant of 11 April 2000* (Dem. Rep. Congo v. Belg.) (Int'l Ct. Justice, Feb.14, 2002).41 I.L.M. 536 (2002) (separate opinion of Judges Higgins, Buergenthal, and Kooijmans). **§3-2 (1), §3-3, §3-7.**

1982 UN Convention on the Law of the Sea, 21 I.L.M. 261 (1982). **§3-2 (5).**

The Antelope, 23 U.S. 66 (1825). **§3-2 (1) (A).**

Pasquantino v. United States, 544 U.S. 349 (2005). **§3-2 (1) (A).**

Special maritime and territorial jurisdiction, 18 U.S.C. §7 (2013). **§3-2 (1) (D).**

Blackmer v. United States, 284 U.S. 421 (1932). **§3-2 (2).**

Skiriotes v. United States, 313 U.S. 69 (1941). **§3-2 (2).**

United States v. Clark, 315 F. Supp. 2d 1127 (W.D. Wash. 2004), aff'd 435 F.3d 1100 (9th Cir. 2006). §3-2 (2), **§3-6 (3).**

Geoffrey R. Watson, *Offenders Abroad: The Case for Nationality-Based Criminal Jurisdiction,* 17 Yale J. Int'l L. 41 (1992). **§3-2 (2).**

United States v. Cutting, 70 U.S. 441 (1865). **§3-2 (3).**

United States v. Zehe, 601 F. Supp. 196 (D. Mass. 1985). **§3-2 (4).**

United States v. Pizzarusso, 388 F.2d 8 (2d Cir.1968). **§3-2 (4), §3-6 (2).**

Attorney-Gen. of Israel v. Eichmann, 361 I.L.R. 277 (Dist. Ct. 1968) (Israel). **§3-2 (4).**

Jones v. Ministry of the Interior of Saudi Arabia, [2006] UKHL 26, (appeal taken from Eng.) (per Lord Bingham). **§3-2 (5).**

Charles Doyle, *Extraterritorial Application of American Criminal Law,* Cong. Research Serv. Report, RS22497 (Feb. 12, 2012). **§3-6.**

Murray v. Schooner Charming Betsy, 6 U.S. (2 Cranch) 64 (1804). **§3-6 (1).**

McCulloch v. Sociedad Nacional de Marineros de Honduras, 372 U.S. 10 (1963). **§3-6 (1).**

United States v. Vasquez-Velasco, 15 F.3d 833 (9th Cir. 1994). **§3-6 (1).**

Sale v. Haitian Ctrs. Council, Inc., 509 U.S. 155, 176 (1993). **§3-6 (2).**

United States v. Bowman, 260 U.S. 94 (1922). **§3-6 (2).**

United States v. Layton, 855 F.2d 1388 (9th Cir. 1988). **§3-6 (2).**

Regina v. Bartle and the Comm'n of Police for the Metropolis and Others, ex parte Pinochet, [2000] 1 A.C. 119 (H.L.) **§3-2 (5), §3-7.**

Al-Adsani v. United Kingdom, App. No. 3576/97, 34 Eur. H.R. Rep. 11 (2002). **§3-2 (4), §3-7.**

Office of Chief of Counsel for Prosecution of Axis Crimes, *Nazi Conspiracy and Aggression: Final Opinion and Judgment of the International Military Tribunal* (1947). **§3-8.**

Principles of International Law Recognized in the Charter of the Nürnberg Tribunal and in the Judgment of the Tribunal, Y.B. Int'l Law Comm., vol. II (1950). **§3-8.**

Application of Convention on Prevention and Punishment of Crime of Genocide (Bosn. & Herz. v. Serb. & Montenegro), 2007 I.C.J. 43. **§3-10.**

Alain Pellet, *Can a State Commit a Crime? Definitely, Yes!*, 10 Eur. J. Int'l L. 425 (1999). **§3-10.**

Advisory Opinion on Consistency of Certain Danzig Legislative Decrees with Constitution of Free City, 1935 P.C.I.J. (ser. A/B) No. 65 (Dec. 4). **§3-11.**

United States v. Flemming, 677 F.3d 252 (3d Cir. 2010). **§3-11.**

United States v. Altstötter et al. (Justice Case), 3-4 December 1947, III Trials of War Criminals Before the Nuremberg Military Tribunals Under Control Council Law No. 10, 1946-1949. **§3-11.**

R. v. Finta, [1994] 1 S.C.R. 701 (Can.). **§3-11.**

Court de Cassation [Cass.] [supreme court for judicial matters] crim., Jan. 26, 1984, J.C.P. 1984 II G, No. 20197 (note Ruzié), J.D.I. 308 (1984) (Fr.) (Barbie No. 2, *see* English text in 78 I.L.R. 132-136). **§3-11.**

R. v. Bow St. Metro. Stipendiary Magistrate and Others ex parte Pinochet Ugarte (No. 3), [2000] 1 A.C. 147 (H.L.) (Eng.) (In Re: Pinochet, Opinion of the Lords of Appeal for Judgment in the Cause). **§3-11.**

Prosecutor v. Karemera et al., Case No. ICTR 98-44-T, Judgment, (Mar. 19, 2008). **§3-13.**

Prosecutor v. Bagilishema, Case No. ICTR 95-1A-A, Judgment, (July 3, 2002). **§3-13.**

Prosecutor v. Delalić, Case No. IT-96-21-A, Judgment, (Feb. 20, 2001). **§3-13.**

Prosecutor v. Prlić et al., Case No. IT-04-74-PT, Judgment, (Sept. 26, 2005). **§3-13.**

Prosecutor v. Halilović, Case No. IT-01-48-A, Judgment, (Oct. 16, 2007). **§3-13.**

Prosecutor v. Ntagerura et al., Case No. ICTR 99-46-A, Judgment, (July 7, 2006). **§3-13.**

CHAPTER 4

Celebici Appeals Judgment, Case No. IT-96-21-1, Judgment, (Feb. 20, 2001). **§4-1 (3).**

Prosecutor v. Dusko Tadić a/k/a "Dule," Case No. IT 94-I-AR72, Judgment, (Int'l Crim. Trib. for the Former Yugoslavia Oct. 2, 1995). **§4-1 (5).**

Prosecutor v. Erdemović, Case No. IT-96-22-A, Judgment, (Oct. 7, 1997). **§4-1 (7).**

Gow, Kerr & Pajic, *Prosecuting War Crimes: Lessons and Legacies of the International Criminal Tribunal for the Former Yugoslavia* (Routledge 2013) **§4-1 (9).**

Swart, Zahar & Sluiter, *The Legacy of the International Criminal Tribunal for the Former Yugoslavia* (Oxford 2011). **§4-1 (9).**

U.N.S.C. Res. 955 (1994). **§4-2.**

Prosecutor v. Jean-Paul Akayesu, Case No. ICTR 96-4-T2, Judgment, (Sept. 2, 1998). **§4-2 (1).**

Prosecutor v. Nahimana et al., Case No. ICTR 99-52-A, Judgment, (Nov. 28, 2007). **§4-2 (3).**

Prosecutor v. Karemera et al., Case No. ICTR 98-44-T, Judgment, (Mar. 19, 2008). **§4-2 (3).**

Jean Kambanda v. The Prosecutor, Case No. ICTR 97-23-A, Judgment, (Oct. 19, 2000). **§4-2 (4).**

Prosecutor v. Ngirabatware, Case No. ICTR 99-54-T, Judgment, (Dec. 20, 2012). **§4-2 (4).**

Prosecutor v. Ndindiliymana, Case No. ICTR 00-56-T, Judgment, May (17, 2011). **§4-2 (5).**

Gahima, *Transitional Justice in Rwanda: Accountability for Atrocity* (Routledge 2012). **§4-2 (7).**

Cruvellier and Voss, *Court of Remorse: Inside the International Criminal Tribunal for Rwanda* (Wisconsin 2010). **§4-2 (7).**

Rep.of the Int'l Law Comm'n, 46th sess., May 2–22, 1994, UN Doc. A/49/10; U.N. GAOR, 49th Sess., Supp. No. 10 (1994). **§4-5.**

Prosecutor v. Katanga and Chui, Case No. ICC-01/04-01/07-T-ENG, (Sept. 26, 2008). **§4-13 (5).**

Prosecutor v. Lubanga, Case No. ICC-01/04-01/06 Judgment, Trial Chamber, (Aug. 7, 2012). **§4-17 (2).**

S.C. Res. 748, U.N. Doc. S/RES/748 (Mar. 31, 1992). **§4-22.**

S.C. Res. 883, U.N. Doc. S/RES/883 (Nov. 11, 1993). **§4-22.**

Al Megrahi v. HM Advocate, (2002) J.C. 38 (Scot.). **§4-22.**

Prosecutor v. Noonan, Case No. SCSL-2004-14-AR72(E), Decision on Preliminary Motion Based on Lack of Jurisdiction (Child Recruitment), (May 31, 2004). **§4-23.**

Prosecutor v. Alex Tamba Brima, Brima Bazzy Kamara and Santigie Borbor Kanu, Case No.

SCSL-2004-16-A, Judgment, (Feb. 22, 2008). **§4-23.**

Valerie Oosterveld, *Gender and the Charles Taylor Case at the Special Court for Sierra Leone*, 19 Wm & Mary J. Women & the Law 7 (2012). **§4-23.**

Rep. of the Secretary-General on the establishment of a Special Tribunal for Lebanon, U.N. Doc. S/2006/893 (Nov. 15, 2006). **§4-27.**

U.N.S.C. Res. 1757 (2007). **§4-27.**

Ben Saul, *Legislating from a Radical Hague: The United Nations Special Tribunal for Lebanon Invents an International Crime of Transnational Terrorism*, 24 Leiden J. Int'l L. 677 (2011). **§4-27.**

Questions Relating to the Obligation to Prosecute or Extradite (Belg. v. Sen.), Judgment, 2012 I.C.J. Rep. 1 (July 20, 2012). **§4-30.**

CHAPTER 5

Reservations to Convention on Prevention and Punishment of Crime of Genocide, Advisory Opinion, 1951 I.C.J. 15, 3 (May 28). **§5-1.**

Prosecutor v. Akayesu, Case No. ICTR 96-4-T, Judgment, (Sept. 2, 1998). **§5-1, §5-1 (1) (D), §5-2 (1) (B).**

Prosecutor v. Kambanda, Case No. ICTR 97-23-S, Judgment and Sentence, (Sept. 4, 1998). **§5-1.**

Prosecutor v. Krstić, Case No. IT-98-33-A, Judgment, (Aug. 2, 2001). **§5-1, §5-1 (1) (C).**

Prosecutor v. Popović, Beara et al., Case No. IT-05-88, Judgment, (June 10, 2010). **§5-1.**

Prosecutor v. Seromba, Case No. ICTR 2001-66-A, Judgment, (Mar. 12, 2008). **§5-1 (1) (A) (ii).**

Prosecutor v. Tolimir, Case No. IT-05-88/2-T, Judgment, (Dec. 12, 2012). **§5-1 (1) (A) (iv), §5-1 (1) (A) (v), §5- (1) (A) (i), §5-2 (2), §5-2 (3), §5-3 (5).**

Prosecutor v. Kayishema and Ruzindana, Case No. ICTR 95-1-T, Trial Judgment, (May 21, 1999). **§5-1 (1) (B), §5-2 (2).**

Prosecutor v. Semanza, Case No. ICTR 97-20-T, Judgment, (May 15, 2003). **§5-1 (1) (B), §5-2 (1) (A) (i), §5-2 (1) (A) (ii), §5-2 (1) (B)**.

Prosecutor v. Mugenzi and Mugiraneza, Case No. ICTR 99-50-A, Judgment, (Feb. 4, 2013). **§5-1 (1) (D).**

Prosecutor v. Brdanin, Case No. IT-99-36-A, Judgment, (Apr. 3, 2007). **§5-1 (1) (D)**.

Prosecutor v. Blagojević and Jović, Case No. IT-02-60-T, Judgment, (Jan. 17, 2005). **§5-1 (2).**

Prosecutor v. Nzabonimana, Case No. ICTR 98-44D-T, Judgment, (May 31, 2012). **§5-1 (3).**

Genocide, 18 U.S.C. § 1091 (2009). **§5-1 (4).**

Definitions of Genocide, 18 U.S.C. § 1093 (2012). **§5-1 (4).**

Schabas, *Genocide in International Law: The Crime of Crimes* (Cambridge, 2nd ed. 2009). **§5-1 (4).**

Prosecutor v. Blašić, Case No. IT-95-14-T, Judgment, (Mar. 3, 2000). **§5-2 (1) (B) (i).**

Situation in the Republic of Kenya, Case No. ICC-01/09, Decision, (Mar. 31, 2010). **§5-2 (1) (B) (i).**

Prosecutor v. Kunarac, Kovac and Vukovic, Case No. IT-96-23 and IT-96-23/1-A, Judgment, (June 12, 2002). **§5-2 (1) (C), §5-2 (2).**

Prosecutor v. Lukić, Case No. IT-98-32/1-A, Judgment, (Dec. 4, 2012). **§5-2 (2).**

Leila Sadat, *Forging a Convention for Crimes Against Humanity* (Cambridge 2013). **§5-2 (2).**

Leila Sadat, *Crimes Against Humanity in the Modern Age*, 107 Am. J. Int'l L. 334 (2013). **§5-2 (2).**

David Luban, *A Theory of Crimes Against Humanity*, 29 Yale J. Int'l. L. 85 (2004). **§5-2 (2).**

Prosecutor v. Boškoski and Tarčulovski, Case No. IT-04-82-A, Judgment, (May 19, 2010). **§5-3 (3).**

Detter, *The Law of War* (Ashgate, 3rd ed. 2013); Solis, *The Law of Armed Conflict: International Humanitarian Law in War* (Cambridge 2010). **§5-3 (13).**

Opinion and Judgment of the International Military Tribunal at Nuremberg (1946). **§5-4.**

Definition of Aggression, G.A. Res 3314 (XXIX) U.N. GAOR, 29th Sess., U.N. Doc A/1732 (Dec. 14, 1974). **§5-4.**

Review Conference of the Rome Statute of the International Criminal Court, RC/9/11 of June 11, 2010. http://www.icc-cpi.int/iccdocs/asp_docs/ASP9/OR/RC-11-ENG.pdf. §5-4, §5-4 (1) (C), §5-4 (2) (B).

Carrie McDougall, *The Crime of Aggression Under the Rome Statute* (Cambridge 2013). §5-4 (3).

Michael Scharf, *Universal Jurisdiction and the Crime of Aggression*, 53 Harv. Int'l L.J. 357 (2012). §5-4 (3).

Jennifer Trahan, *A Meaningful Definition of the Crime of Aggression: A Response to Michael Glennon*, 33 U. Pa. Int'l L. J. 907 (2012). §5-4 (3).

CHAPTER 6:

Rome Statute of the International Criminal Court, art. 25 U.N. Doc.A/CONF.183/9* (July 17, 1998) **Part II, § 6-1**.

Prosecutor v. Natelić and Martinović, IT-98-34A, Judgment, (May 3, 2006). **Part II.**

Rome Statute of the International Criminal Court, art. 30, U.N. Doc.A/CONF.183/9* (July 17, 1998). **Part II, § 6-1.**

Prosecutor v. Seromba, ICTR 2001-66-A, Judgment, (Mar. 12, 2008). **§ 6-1.**

Prosecutor v. Boškoski and Tarčulovski, IT-04-82-A, Judgment, (May 19, 2010). **§ 6-2.**

Rome Statute of the International Criminal Court, art. 28 U.N. Doc.A/CONF.183/9* (July 17, 1998). **§ 6-2.**

Prosecutor v. Blašić, IT-95-14-5T, Judgment, (Mar. 3, 2000). **§ 6-2.**

Prosecutor v. Lukić, IT-9-32/1-A, Judgment, (Dec. 12, 2012). **§ 6-3.**

Prosecutor v. Perišić, IT-04-81-A, Judgment, (Feb. 28, 2013). **§ 6-3.**

Prosecutor v. Akayesu, ICTR 96-4-T, Judgment, (Sept. 22, 1988). **§ 6-5.**

Prosecutor v. Tadić, IT-94-1-A, Judgment, (July 15, 1999). **§ 6-8.**

Prosecutor v. Brdanin, IT-99-36-A, Judgment, (Apr. 3, 2007). **§ 6-8.**

Prosecutor v. Gotovina, IT-06-90-A, Judgment, (Nov. 16, 2012). **§ 6-8.**

Prosecutor v. Stanišić and Simatović, IT-03-69-T, Judgment, (May 30, 2013). **§ 6-8.**

Prosecutor v. Prlić, IT-04-74T, Judgment, (May 29, 2013). **§ 6-8.**

Situation in the Democratic Republic of the Congo (Prosecutor v. Katanga), ICC-01/04-01/07, April 15, 2013. **§ 6-8.**

Prosecutor v Karemera and Ngirumpatse, ICTR 98-44-T, Judgment, (Feb. 2, 2012). **§ 6-11.**

Prosecutor v. Musema, ICTR 96-13-T, Judgment, (Jan. 27, 2000). **§ 6-11.**

In re Yamashita, 327 U.S. 1 (1946). **Part V.**

UN Supplementary Convention on the Abolition of Slavery, the Slave Trade, and Institutions and Practices Similar to Slavery, 226 U.N.T.S. 3 (1956). **§ 7-3.**

Convention on the Suppression and Punishment of the Crime of Apartheid, 1015 U.N.T.S. 243 (1966). **§ 7-4.**

Convention against Torture and Other Cruel, Inhuman or Degrading Treatment or Punishment, 1465 U.N.T.S. 85 (1984). **§ 7-5.**

International Convention for the Protection of All Persons from Enforced Disappearance, G.A. Res. 61/177, U.N. Doc. A/RES/61/177 (Dec. 20, 2006). **§ 7-6.**

UN Convention Against Transnational Organised Crime, 2237 U.N.T.S. 319 (2000). **§ 7-7.**

OECD Convention on Combating Bribery of Foreign Public Officials in International Business Transactions, reprinted at 37 I.L.M. 1 (1997). **§ 7-8.**

UN Convention Against Corruption, 2349 U.N.T.S. 1 (2003). **§ 7-8.**

Money Laundering Control Act, 18 U.S.C. § 1956 (1986). **§ 7-9.**

UN Convention against Illicit Traffic in Narcotic Drugs and Psychotropic Substances, 1582 U.N.T.S. 95 (1988). **§ 7-9, 7-10.**

UN Convention on Psychotropic Substances, 1019 U.N.T.S. 175 (1971). **§ 7-10.**

UNG.A. Res. 60/158, (Feb. 28, 2006). **§ 8-2.**

Interlocutory Decision on the Applicable Law: Terrorism, Conspiracy, Homicide, Perpetration, Cumulative Charging, STL-11-01/I (Feb. 16, 2011). **§ 8-2.**

U.N. Sec. Coun. Res. 1566 (Oct. 4, 2004). **§ 8-2.**

Convention on Offences and Certain Other Acts Committed on Board Aircraft, 704 UNTS 219, 20 UST 2941, TIAS 6768, 2 I.L.M. 1048 (1963). **§ 8-5.**

Aircraft Piracy (Destruction of Aircraft) Act, 18 U.S.C. § 32 (2006). **§ 8-5, 8-6.**

UN Convention for the Suppression of Unlawful Seizure of Aircraft, 12325 UNTS 860, 22 U.S.T. 1641, TIAS 7192, 10 I.L.M. (1970). **§ 8-6.**

Anti-Hijacking Act, 49 U.S.C. § 1301 (1974). **§ 8-6.**

UN Convention for the Suppression of Unlawful Acts Against the Safety of Civil Aviation, 974 UNTS 178, 24 U.S.T. 564, TIAS 7570, 10 I.L.M. 1151 (1971). **§ 8-7.**

Aircraft Piracy, 49 U.S.C. § 46502 (1996). **§ 8-7.**

Protocol for the Suppression of Unlawful Acts of Violence at Airports Serving International Civil Aviation, 14118 U.N.T.S. 1589, 27 I.L.M. 627 (1989). **§ 8-7.**

Convention on the Suppression of Unlawful Acts Relating to International Civil Aviation, 50 I.L.M. 141 (2011). **§ 8-7.**

UN Convention on the Prevention and Punishment of Crimes Against Internationally Protected Persons, 1035 UNTS 167, 28 U.S.T 1975, TIAS 8532, 13 I.L.M. 41 (1974). **§ 8-8.**

UN Convention Against the Taking of Hostages, 21931 UNTS 1316, TIAS 11081, 18 I.L.M. 1456 (1979). **§ 8-9.**

Hostage Taking Act, 18 U.S.C. § 1203 (1996). **§ 8-9.**

Convention on the Physical Protection of Nuclear Materials, 1456 UNTS 101, TIAS 11080; 18 I.L.M. 1419 (1980). **§ 8-10.**

18 U.S.C. §§ 128, 831. **§ 8-10.**

UN Convention for the Suppression of Unlawful Acts Against the Safety of Maritime Navigation, 1678 UNTS 201, TIAS 11080 (1988). **§ 8-11.**

Protocol for the Suppression of Unlawful Acts Against the Safety of Fixed Platforms Located on the Continental Shelf, 1678 U.N.T.S. 304 (1988). **§ 8-11.**

18 U.S.C. §§ 2280, 2281 (1996). **§ 8-11.**

UN Convention for the Suppression of Terrorist Bombings, 2149 UNTS 256, 37 I.L.M. 249. **§ 8-12.**

18 U.S.C. § 2332 (1996). **§ 8-12.**

International Convention for the Suppression of the Financing of Terrorism, Dec. 9, 1999, 2178 U.N.T.S. 197, T.I.A.S. 13075, 39 I.L.M. 270. **§ 8-13.**

18 U.S.C. § 2339 (2002). **§ 8-13.**

Second Additional Protocol to the 1957 European Convention on Extradition, Dec. 13, 1957, E.T.S. 24. **§ 9-6.**

Council of Europe Convention on Laundering, Search, Seizure and Confiscation of Proceeds of Crime, C.E.T.S. 141, reprinted at 30 ILM 148 (1991). **§ 9-6.**

Valentine v. U.S. ex rel. Neidecker, 299 U.S. 5 (1936). **§ 9-7.**

Elcock v. United States, 80 F. Supp. 2d 70 (E.D.N.Y. 2000). **§ 9-8.**

European Convention on Extradition, E.T.S. 24 (1960). **§ 9-8.**

Inter-American Extradition Convention (1981). **§ 9-8.**

Soering v. United Kingdom, 161 Eur. Ct. H.R. (Ser. A.) 1, 11 EHRR 439 (1989). **§ 9-8.**

Mironescu v. Costner, 480 F.3d 664 (4th Cir. 2007), *cert. denied*, 552 U.S. 1135 (Jan. 9, 2008). **§ 9-8.**

Trinidad y Garcia v. Thomas, 683 F.3d 952 (9th Cir. 2012), *cert. denied*, 133 S.Ct. 845 (Jan. 7, 2013). **§ 9-8.**

United States v. Puentes, 50 F.3d 1567 (11th Cir. 1995), *cert denied*, 516 U.S. 933 (Oct. 16, 1995). **§ 9-9.**

United States v. Burke, 425 F.3d 400 (5th Cir. 2005), *cert. denied*, 547 U.S. 1208 (2006). **§ 9-9.**

United States v Valencia-Trujillo, 573 F.3d 1171 (11th Cir. 2009). **§ 9-9.**

United States v. Kaufman, 858 F.2d 994 (5th Cir. 1988). **§ 9-9.**

*Terlinden v. Ames,*184 U.S. 270, 289 (1902). **Part III.**

Eain v. Wilkes, 641 F.2d 504, 508 (7th Cir. 1981). **§ 9-12.**

United States v. Kin-Hong, 83 F.3d 523 (1st Cir. 1996). **§ 9-12.**

In re Extradition of Beresford-Redman, 753 F.Supp.2d 1078 (C.D.Cal. 2010). **§ 9-12.**

United States v. Castaneda-Castillo, 739 F.Supp.2d 49 (D.Mass. 2010). **§ 9-12.**

Skaftourous v. United States, 667 F.3d 144 (2d Cir. 2011). **§ 9-14.**

In re Extradition of Azra Basic, --- F.Supp.2d ---, 2012 WL 3067466 (E.D. KY, July 27, 2012). **§ 9-14.**

Fed. R. Crim. P. 1(a)(5)(A). **§ 9-14.**

Fed. R. Evid. 1101(d)(3). **§ 9-14.**

18 U.S.C. § 3190 (1948). **§ 9-14.**

Hoxha v. Levi, 465 F.3d 554, 561 (3d Cir. 2006). **§ 9-15, 9-16.**

Prasoprat v. Benov, 421 F.3d 1009, 1012 (9th Cir. 2005), *cert. denied*, 546 U.S. 1171 (2006). **§ 9-15.**

The Antelope, 23 U.S. 66, 123 (1825). **§ 9-29.**

Restatement (Third) of Foreign Relations Law of the United States § 483, Reporters' Note 3 (1987). **§ 9-29.**

Pasquantino v. United States, 544 U.S. 349 (2005). **§9-29.**

CHAPTER 10:

Linde v. Arab Bank P.L.C., 706 F. 3d 92, 114-115 (2d Cir. 2013). **Part II.**

In re Grand Jury Subpoena, 696 F. 3d 428 (5th Cir. 2012). **Part II.**

In re Grand Jury Proceedings (Bank of Nova Scotia), 691 F.2d 1384 (11th Cir. 1982), *cert. denied,* 103 S.Ct. 3086 (June 13, 1983). **Part II.**

28 U.S.C. § 1781 (1948). **Part III.**

28 U.S.C. § 1696 (1964). **Part III.**

18 U.S.C. §3512 (2009). **Part III.**

In re Premises Located at 840 140th Ave. NE, Bellevue, Washington, 634 F.3d 557 (9th Cir. 2011). **Part III.**

UN Convention Against Illicit Traffic in Narcotic Drugs and Psychotropic Substances (1988). Part IV, **§ 10-2.**

UN Transnational Organized Crime Convention (2000). **Part IV.**

UN Convention against Corruption. **Part IV.**

International Convention for the Suppression of Act of Nuclear Terrorism Convention. **Part IV.**

Agreement with the People's Republic of China on Judicial Assistance, June 19, 2000, TIAS 13102. **§ 10-2.**

UN doc. A/RES/45/117 (Dec. 14, 1990). **§ 10-3.**

28 U.S.C. § 2467 (2010). **§ 10-4.**

28 U.S.C. § 1782 (1996). **§ 10-4.**

28 U.S.C. § 1783. **§ 10-4.**

In re Premises Located at 840 140th Ave. NE, Bellevue, Washington, 634 F.3d 557 (9th Cir. 2011). **§ 10-4.**

United States v. Trustees of Boston College, 831 F. Supp. 2d 436, 452 (D. Mass., 2011). **§ 10-4.**

In re Request from the United Kingdom, __ F.3d __, 2013 WL 2364165 *6 (1st Cir. May 31, 2013). **§ 10-4.**

In re Request from the United Kingdom, 685 F.3d 1 (1st Cir. 2012). **§ 10-4.**

Reid v. Covert, 354 U.S. 1 (1957). **Part VI.**

United States v. Cotroni, 527 F.2d 708 (2d Cir 1975). **§ 10-5.**

United States v. Verdugo-Urquidez, 494 U.S. 259 (1990). **§ 10-5.**

In re Terrorist Bombings of U.S. Embassies in East Africa (Fourth Amendment Challenges), 552 F.3d 157 , 168-176 (2d Cir. 2008), *cert. denied sub nom.*

El-Hage v United States, 130 S. Ct. 1050 (Jan. 11. 2010). **§ 10-5.**

United States v. Stokes, 710 F. Supp. 2d 689 (N.D. Ill. 2009). **§ 10-5.**

United States v. Barona, 56 F. 3d 1087 (9th Cir 1995). **§ 10-5.**

United States v. Peterson, 812 DF.2d 486 (9th Cir. 1987). **§ 10-5.**

United States v. Lee, 723 F.3d 134, (2d Cir. 2013). **§ 10-5.**

United States v. Flores-Montano, 541 U.S. 149 (2004). **§ 10-6.**

United States v. Cotterman, 709 F.3d 951 (9th Cir. 2013). **§ 10-6.**

United States v. Frank, 599 F3d 1221 (11th Cir. 2010), *cert. denied*, 131 S.Ct. 186 (Oct. 4, 2010). **§ 10-7.**

United States v. Yousef, 327 F.3d 56 (2d Cir. 2003). **§ 10-7.**

United States v. Bin Laden, 132 F. Supp. 2d 168 (S.D.N.Y. 2001), aff'd sub nom. *In re Terrorist Bombings of U.S. Embassies in East Africa*, 552 F. 3d 177 (2d Cir. 2008), *cert. denied sub. nom. Al 'Owhali v. United States*, 129 S.Ct. 2778 (June 8, 2009). **§ 10-7.**

David Henek, *Ensuring Miranda's Right to Counsel in U.S. Interrogations Abroad*, 57 N.Y.L. Sch. L. Rev. 557 (2012/13). **§ 10-7.**

INTERNATIONAL CRIMINAL LAW

IN A NUTSHELL

CHAPTER 1

WHAT IS INTERNATIONAL CRIMINAL LAW?

I. INTRODUCTION

Throughout history, criminal law has been almost exclusively a matter of national (or domestic) law. In the traditional view, each State in the international community has exclusive sovereign authority to define, prosecute, and punish crimes under its own law and procedures, especially when those crimes take place within its territorial boundaries.

Of course, some exceptions have long existed. For centuries, international law has authorized States to punish the perpetrators of certain crimes which cross national boundaries or which occur outside the sovereign territory of any one State. The classic examples are piracy on the high seas and slave trading. Since ancient times, States have made bilateral agreements to return (or extradite) fugitives who have escaped from one country to another date. International law has long prohibited certain conduct during armed conflict which could be punished by anyone who had custody of the offender.

Yet for the most part, criminal law has been a matter of the exclusive competence of individual States and their domestic laws and courts. Since World War II, however, three broad and related developments have fundamentally changed this situation.

First, crime has become increasingly transnational. In activities as diverse as drug trafficking, money laundering, credit card fraud and terrorism, criminals today operate with little regard for national boundaries or political borders. In fact, criminal organizations often use these boundaries to great advantage. In short, as the economy has become "globalized," so has crime.

In response, States have entered into a growing network of treaties and other agreements aimed at combating these new forms of transnational crime and facilitating cross-border cooperation between law enforcement authorities. These have included agreements defining new types of transnational crime (such as corruption, drug trafficking, and acts of terrorism) and implementing new forms of information sharing and cooperation between law enforcement authorities (such as through mutual legal assistance treaties).

Second, beginning with the massive atrocities committed during the Second World War, the international community has worked to criminalize the most atrocious kinds of violent conduct and abuse and to establish international courts to prosecute and punish those who commit the most serious offenses.[1] The Nuremberg and Tokyo War

---

[1] Although some international sources use the spelling "offences," for consistency this Nutshell will use the American spelling "offenses" unless quoting an original source.

Crimes Tribunals created at the end of World War II marked the beginning of this effort. The crime of genocide was codified by treaty in 1948. In the 1990s, the United Nations created two special tribunals to deal with the widespread atrocities which occurred in the former Yugoslavia and in Rwanda. In 1998, the Rome Statute created the International Criminal Court to prosecute those individuals who commit genocide, crimes against humanity, and war crimes. Since then, a number of hybrid or specialized courts have also been established (dealing, for example, with Lebanon, East Timor, and Sierra Leone).

Third, the international human rights revolution has required all governments to respect and promote fundamental rights and freedoms, in particular to protect individuals in every country from the most serious kinds of abuse and exploitation (including by prosecuting those who commit such abuses whether they are foreign nationals or domestic criminals).

Taken together, these developments have brought about significant changes in the way the international community deals with crime. They have come to constitute the substance of the relatively new (and continually evolving) field known broadly as international criminal law.

II. DEFINITION OF INTERNATIONAL CRIMINAL LAW

There is no single agreed definition of the term "international criminal law." The scope of the topic—which particular subjects are included within the term—depends on the perspective of the persons providing the definition. One definition describes "a body of international rules designed both to proscribe certain categories of conduct (war crimes, crimes against humanity, genocide, torture, aggression, terrorism) and to make those persons who engage in such conduct criminally liable." *See* Antonio Cassese, *International Criminal Law 3* (2d ed. 2008). Generally, one can identify three different approaches.

§ 1–1   THE NARROWEST VIEW

In its most technical sense, the term is used to refer only to those few crimes established directly by international law and subject to the jurisdiction and practice of international courts created for the specific purpose of prosecuting individuals for those crimes.

From this perspective, the subject matter of international criminal law properly focuses on the International Criminal Court and its predecessors (the *ad hoc* tribunals for the former Yugoslavia and Rwanda) and on the so-called "core crimes" of genocide, war crimes, and crimes against humanity, as well as the crime of aggression (the definition of which has only recently been agreed). In other words, it involves only situations where individual perpetrators are prosecuted before international tribunals for violations of crimes established by international law. Their criminal responsibility is determined under, and their punishment imposed by, international law both substantively and procedurally.

§ 1–2   A BROADER VIEW

A more expansive definition includes *transnational crimes*—crimes which have been agreed to by the international community and defined in multilateral treaties but which are prosecuted by domestic authorities under domestic laws giving effect to those treaties, rather than before international courts or tribunals. Because prosecutions carried out in domestic courts are based on domestic implementation of international norms, they are sometimes said to represent the *indirect* enforcement of international criminal law. Some scholars describe them as *hybrid* crimes because, strictly speaking, they are neither entirely international nor entirely domestic.

Transnational crimes concern the international community because they involve significant cross-border activities and require a common and coordinated response by all States. For various reasons, however, they have not been included within the jurisdiction of the International Criminal Court or other supranational tribunals. The list of these transnational crimes is long and growing rapidly. It includes trafficking in people or drugs, acts of terrorism, cyber-crime, organized crime, money laundering and corruption, among others.

Of course, there is some overlap between this category and the narrower group of "core crimes," since both are defined by international law and the "core crimes" can be prosecuted in national courts as well as before the international tribunals. Domestic courts can prosecute a much larger range of international crimes than the international tribunals can. In practice, most international criminal law prosecutions fall within this broader "transnational" definition.

§ 1–3   THE INCLUSIVE VIEW

A third approach recognizes the term "international criminal law" as encompassing not only (i) the "core crimes" within the jurisdiction of the international criminal tribunals, as well as (ii) the "transnational crimes" of within the jurisdiction of domestic courts, but also (iii) the many other substantive and procedural issues that arise when domestic criminal law is applied to transnational activities.

This view acknowledges that States use their own criminal laws and procedures to regulate actions that take place outside their national boundaries, including with respect to people, entities, activities, or evidence in other countries. Doing so can create problems at the international level, for example on issues of jurisdiction, apprehension of suspects, taking of testimony and collecting evidence abroad, assisting foreign and international law enforcement authorities, and enforcing criminal judgments. In this sense, the term "international criminal law" includes both the international aspects of domestic law and the domestic effect of international law, in their procedural as well as substantive criminal applications.

The issues which arise at this intersection of international and domestic law (sometimes referred to as the *law of international judicial assistance and cooperation in criminal matters*) are increasingly important in a world of ever-more rapid movement of people, goods, money and information. Most practicing lawyers are likely to encounter issues of international criminal law in this third dimension.

Because it is important for students to understand the overall context in which these issues arise, this book adopts the third and most comprehensive approach to defining international criminal law. The following chapters accordingly address questions involving the transnational application of domestic criminal law (for example, the extraterritorial reach of substantive crimes), international cooperation in criminal matters (including extradition and mutual legal assistance), international treaties and conventions addressing transnational crimes (such as torture, corruption, trafficking), and the jurisdiction and practice of international tribunals in cases of genocide, crimes against humanity and war crimes.

III. CREATION OF INTERNATIONAL CRIMINAL LAW

A basic understanding of the nature and sources of international law is important for any student of the field of international criminal law.

In its classic (some scholars might say increasingly outmoded) formulation, international law governs only the relations among sovereign States at the international level. It deals with issues such as the definition of national boundaries, the "recognition" of States and the establishment of diplomatic relations between them, the formation and interpretation of treaties, the law of the sea, the use of force, the laws of war, and issues of war and peace.

These classic issues of "public international law" have traditionally had only limited application in domestic courts. Until recently, only a few international tribunals have existed with competence to issue binding decisions with which States must comply. With just a few exceptions, international law in this sense did not address questions involving how a State treated its own citizens and had very little to say about the prosecution of crimes. Crime remained almost entirely a matter of domestic law, and the tribunals that did exist (such as the International Court of Justice) lacked jurisdiction over individuals.

Today the situation is quite different, mostly as a result of the emergence of international criminal law as well as international human rights and humanitarian law over the last sixty years. All of the questions of public international law mentioned above continue to be important to lawyers in foreign ministries and international organizations. What has changed is that international law is increasingly relevant to the treatment of individuals by their own governments as well as those of foreign countries. In limited situations, it can even be the basis on which criminal prosecutions can be initiated against individuals for their own conduct. The number of tribunals charged with interpreting and applying international law has grown significantly, in part due to the creation of specialized international criminal tribunals.

The following sections highlight only a few issues directly relevant to the subject matter of this book. Students desiring a more complete introduction to international law should refer to Thomas Buergenthal and Sean D. Murphy, *Public International Law in a Nutshell* (5th ed. 2013).

§ 1–4   THE ROLE OF CONSENT

In traditional theory, which still provides the basis for most applications of international law today, sovereign States play the central role in creating the international legal principles to which they must adhere. In other words, they are both the "subjects" and the "objects" of international law. This reflects the fact that the international system lacks a real legislature authorized to adopt binding rules. Thus, the fundamental norm is the consent of the individual community "members:" a sovereign State cannot be bound to a rule which it has not accepted.

§ 1–5   SOURCES OF INTERNATIONAL LAW

The specific rules of international law are not codified in any single legislative code or enactment. Under article 38 of the Statute of the International Court of Justice (ICJ), which is appended to the Charter of the United Nations, international law derives from three main sources:

(1) international treaties or conventions "establishing rules expressly recognized by the contesting states;"

(2) international custom "as evidence of a general practice accepted as law"; and

(3) the general principles of law "recognized by civilized nations."

In addition, under article 38, the Court may look to "judicial decisions and the teachings of the most highly qualified publicists of the various nations, as subsidiary means for the determination of rules of law."

§ 1–6   TREATIES

Treaties are the primary source of rules and obligations in contemporary international criminal law. (As used here, the term "treaty" means the same thing as an international convention, agreement or protocol, and includes both bilateral and multilateral agreements.) They are almost always written agreements, negotiated by States with the intention of imposing legally binding commitments as a matter of international law.

Generally speaking, however, treaties do not become binding and enforceable until they have been formally accepted by individual States (by ratification or accession), and each State has its own domestic processes for doing so. In the United States, for example, once a treaty has been negotiated and completed, and once it has been signed by someone authorized to do so, the

President may transmit it to the U.S. Senate for advice and consent to ratification. After the Senate has given its advice and consent, and subject in most cases to the adoption of any necessary implementing legislation by the U.S. Congress, the President may ratify the treaty. Only at that stage does the treaty become formally binding on the United States.

Perhaps the most important international treaty in the field of international criminal law today is the one that created the International Criminal Court. Known as the Rome Statute, it was negotiated at and adopted by a diplomatic conference convened under the auspices of the United Nations. While the Rome Statute is legally binding only on those States that have ratified or acceded to it, many of its provisions contain definitions, statements of principle and procedural norms reflecting the views of a majority of the international community. For that reason, this book will frequently refer to those provisions for purposes of illustration.

As of June 2013, the Rome Statute had been ratified by 122 States, well over half of the 194 Member States of the United Nations. Another 17 States (including the United States) have signed but not ratified or acceded. For the authoritative list of parties and signatories to the Rome Statute and other criminal law treaties, visit the UN Treaty Collection Database at *http://treaties.un.org/ pages/ParticipationStatus.aspx* (search under Chapter 18 "penal matters").

§ 1–7   CUSTOMARY INTERNATIONAL LAW

Binding legal obligations may also arise from customary international law. As opposed to the formal, written provisions of an international treaty or agreement, customary international law obligations derive from the general and consistent practice of States over a substantial period of time based on a sense of legal obligation. It is important to consider the two main elements of this definition: (i) an "objective" component involving the *actual conduct or practice* of States and (ii) a "subjective" component reflecting a *sense of legal obligation* by those States (referred to *opinio juris sive necessitates* or simply *opinio juris*).

Both requirements must be satisfied. Thus, a rule of customary international law may be said to exist where it can be demonstrated that a substantial number of States in the international community have in fact behaved in a certain way, generally and consistently for a substantial period, out of a belief that they are legally obligated to do so. Conduct alone, without the "subjective" sense of legal obligation, is not sufficient to establish a rule of customary international law. It is equally insufficient (from this classic perspective) to rely only on statements (such as UN General Assembly speeches or resolutions) as demonstrating the existence of an established rule of customary international law without also undertaking actual conduct which reflects that rule.

Although customary international law is still accepted as one of the primary sources of substantive international law, it can be difficult to establish a factual record of consistent State practice coupled with the necessary *opinio juris*. In relatively new fields such as international criminal law, the practice of States tends to be dynamic and changing, creating difficulties of clarity and precision. There is some question about whether the practice of non-State entities (such as international tribunals) can itself give rise to norms of customary international law. It can also be argued that statements by government representatives about international law (for example, in speeches to the UN General Assembly or even resolutions adopted by that body) may reflect authoritative views about international legal obligations but cannot by themselves create rules of customary international law. Unless supported by evidence of actual State practice, such statements may only reflect political expectations or normative aspirations.

In theory, an established rule of customary international law binds all States except those that have consistently and openly objected to the formation of the rule from its inception (the so-called "persistent objectors"). But it is not possible to be a "persistent objector" to a rule which reflects a "peremptory norm" from which no State may derogate (or opt out). Such a norm is said to constitute *jus cogens*, binding on all States regardless of their consent. Thus, States may not, by treaty, agree to something which contravenes a *jus cogens* norm. Although the term *jus cogens* is frequently employed, there is no general agreement on which specific norms it covers. However, few would disagree that the prohibition against genocide is such a norm.

§ 1–8   GENERAL PRINCIPLES OF LAW

Common principles of law recognized and applied by the world's major legal systems supply the third main source of international law. Here, the element of State consent derives from the fact that, by adopting and enforcing a given rule, national legislatures and courts reflect the State's acceptance of the rule in question. When that rule has been adopted and enforced in a similar way by a substantial number of States among the world's various legal systems and traditions, it can be said to have achieved an international character. This is, in effect, a third way by which States, through their actions, can create binding law—here by taking action in their domestic legal systems (as opposed to negotiating and ratifying treaties or through consistent practice at the international level from a sense of legal obligation).

In practice, courts and tribunals resort to consideration of general principles only when the norm in question cannot be clearly identified in an applicable treaty or as part of customary international law. In other words, general principles tend to be invoked as a supplementary source to buttress or complement descriptions of the normative content of international law.

§ 1–9   SUBSIDIARY SOURCES

Article 38 of the ICJ Statute also provides that "judicial decisions and the teachings of the most highly qualified publicists of the various nations" may be considered as *subsidiary* means for the determination of relevant rules of law. In the international legal system, there is no rule of *stare decisis*, meaning that even in the International Court of Justice, prior decisions are typically accorded appropriate consideration but not binding effect. The same is true in many national legal systems, especially those based on the civil (as opposed to common) law. Until recently, principles of criminal law have mostly been articulated in national (rather than international) courts, so it has been difficult to consider the decisions of one State's courts as authoritative with respect to issues before the courts of another State. With the advent of international criminal courts, the importance of decisional law has clearly increased.

This secondary status is also given to the views of experts in the field (the "publicists"). This reflects the prominent role that academics and commentators have long played in the international legal system. Since international law is not codified, and considering the difficulties that can arise in uncovering actual State practice for purposes of customary international law and general principles, judges have often relied on the treatises and analyses of learned scholars who devote their careers to determining such things. In many civil law systems, academic commentaries or treatises have traditionally been given a far more persuasive role than they play in the U.S. system. The same has been true at the international level. However compelling their substantive contributions may be, the views and opinions of "the most highly qualified publicists" do not themselves constitute a source of law, under article 38 at least, but only provide a subsidiary means for ascertaining the content of the law.

§ 1–10   IN PRACTICE

The interplay between treaty law, customary international law, and general principles can be complicated and confusing. For example, new multilateral treaties are sometimes adopted on the basis that they merely codify pre-existing principles of customary international law or even general principles of law. At the same time, it is sometimes argued that a widely ratified multilateral treaty can give rise to a new norm of customary international law, or even *jus cogens*, which in turn binds even those States which have not ratified the treaty in question. The circularity of this approach is obvious.

Consider the crime of genocide. Following World War II and the Nuremberg Tribunal, the international community concluded a treaty defining the crime of genocide and requiring all States Parties to prosecute and punish those guilty of committing that offense. As of June 2013, 142 States are party to the Convention on the Prevention and Punishment of the Crime of Genocide, adopted by the UN General Assembly on

December 9, 1948. The treaty crime of genocide has been incorporated into the Rome Statute (as well as the statutes of the *ad hoc* tribunals for the former Yugoslavia and Rwanda) without substantive change. Even though genocide continues to occur around the globe, most international lawyers and scholars would agree that genocide is now prohibited by customary international law and in fact constitutes a peremptory norm of international law (*jus cogens*). Moreover, because genocide is also a crime under the domestic law of many States with differing legal systems, its prosecution and punishment arguably constitutes a general principle of law.

On the other hand, it is much more difficult to contend that international law clearly prohibits the application of the death penalty for the most serious crimes. Some widely ratified regional treaties do contain restrictions or outright prohibions on capital punishment, but those provisions do not bind non-parties. No explicit prohibition exists in any global treaty, although some argue that the practice is inherently precluded by provisions prohibiting torture or cruel, inhuman or degrading treatment or punishment (even where the relevant treaty expressly exempts "official sanctions"). The second optional protocol to the International Covenant on Civil and Political Rights, adopted in 1989, calls for the abolition of the death penalty but permits States Parties to retain the death penalty in time of war, and many of its 76 States Parties have taken such a reservation.

It is true that a majority of States have abolished capital punishment domestically, either wholly or in part. Only about one-third of the States in the international community today continue to have the death penalty, and the trend certainly appears to be in the direction of abolishing capital punishment. Perhaps as a result, none of the international criminal tribunals is empowered to impose that sanction. But it can certainly be debated whether that fact establishes a general principle of law, a binding rule of customary international law, or a rule of *jus cogens* compelling all States to do what the majority have done. Some States (including the United States) expressly reject such a rule, in part to preserve their options to be "persistent objectors" and to reserve the decision to the duly elected representatives of the people in their respective legislatures.

IV.   THE PURPOSES OF INTERNATIONAL CRIMINAL LAW

The questions of genocide and capital punishment also raise an important issue about the nature and future development of international criminal law, namely what functions it serves, or should serve, in the global community. This issue can be approached from several perspectives.

§ 1–11   PEACE, ORDER, STABILITY, AND DETERRENCE

In the international system, as in most human communities, criminal law and the threat of prosecution and punishment for its violation serve primarily to deter future violations. From this perspective, it may make little difference to the individual perpetrator whether the prosecution and punishment take place in a domestic court under domestic law or at the international level. What matters is the likelihood that an illegal act will in fact entail serious consequences, thereby deterring potential violators from acting on their plans or impulses.

In a decentralized legal system consisting of independent States with differing jurisdictional approaches, the certainty of punishment is obviously diminished. One State may have differing rules than another about exactly what criminal behavior is prohibited, and jurisdictional hurdles may prevent prosecution of perpetrators for acts committed in the territory of other States. From this perspective, the creation of supranational courts for the prosecution of the most serious crimes makes it more likely that those who break the rules will in fact be called to account and thus strengthens the deterrence factor.

Another important goal of international criminal law is to help keep the peace. Maintaining good order is a function of law in general. International law serves to enhance peace and security in the world community, in part by constraining the use and abuse of power. By providing a forum for the prosecution of those who commit the most serious abuses—the "core crimes" of genocide, crimes against humanity, war crimes and aggression—the

International Criminal Court helps deter those who would commit such acts, not just for humanitarian reasons or because those crimes violate fundamentally shared values of the world community, but also because those acts tend to threaten the very fabric and structure of the international system. Demonstrating that there can be no impunity for these major crimes helps to create trust and respect for the developing system of international criminal justice. The prospect of prosecution and punishment thus serves a preventive and stabilizing purpose.

§ 1–12   RETRIBUTION

At the same time, some people justify punishing those responsible for the most horrific crimes simply on the basis of retribution—making the guilty pay for the terrible wrongs they have committed. International criminal law deals largely (but not exclusively) with various kinds of organized violence committed in situations of widespread abuse, where prosecutions under domestic law may not be viable. Prosecution before international tribunals may be the only alternative to allowing the guilty to go unpunished. In contrast to those interested in deterring future misconduct, the proponents of retributive justice tend to look backwards and to see punishment for past deeds as a fundamental requirement of an organized community.

One criticism often leveled at international criminal law is that historically, and especially in post-war contexts, it has represented "victors' justice." Some of the most important developments in the field of international criminal law have in fact taken place after horrendous conflicts and in response to widespread atrocities. For example, the landmark tribunals created at the end of World War II—the Nuremberg Tribunal in Germany and the Tokyo Tribunal in Japan—were created by the victorious Allied Powers to punish war crimes and other offenses committed by their enemies during the war. In a few instances, defendants were convicted and punished for conduct in which the victorious Allies also engaged (for example, conducting unrestricted submarine warfare).

In such situations, is the charge of "victor's justice" a legitimate criticism? Few would argue that those who committed genocide and crimes against humanity should escape prosecution and punishment simply because they were defeated. Does the problem lie in the fact that prosecutions have taken place before a court created only after the conflict has ended? Like the Nuremberg and Tokyo courts, the two *ad hoc* tribunals established by the UN Security Council in 1993 and 1994 represent *ex post* reactions to the abuses which took place during the conflicts in the former Yugoslavia and in Rwanda. By contrast, the International Criminal Court has only prospective jurisdiction.

Does a more serious concern arise when the specific crimes being prosecuted had not previously been clearly agreed upon or articulated by the international community? Or, that the defendants were acting under the authority of their own governments? Defendants at Nuremberg made such contentions—that what they had done violated no clearly established pre-existing norm of international law but had been required by their domestic law. They also contended that the composition of the Tribunal did not reflect independence and impartiality (it included no German judges) and that the trial was a sham and based on vengeance rather than legal principles. Are *ex post facto* prosecutions ever justified?

§ 1–13 RESTORATIVE OR TRANSITIONAL JUSTICE

Some scholars discount punishment-as-retribution and *ex post facto* vengeance as legitimate aims of a modern criminal law system. Others argue that confronting and punishing the abusers is essential to overcoming the damage they have caused, particularly in situations of widespread atrocities. The purpose, they say, is not just "truth-telling" or public condemnation but to acknowledge and learn from the past in order to create a clear path to the future. This thought is sometimes captured by the phrase "no peace without justice." The emphasis here is on *restorative* justice, on rebuilding societies in the wake of conflict.

Another term that has gained currency is *transitional justice*. It reflects the concern that purely vengeful or retributive responses to past atrocities have the potential to do more harm than good, by hardening and perpetuating the same societal antagonisms that gave rise to the conflict in the first place. In some situations, justice for the victims and deterrence of future violations must take second seat to the more important goal of post-conflict reconciliation and rebuilding—even to the point of granting amnesties and pardons to those who committed atrocities.

In recent years, some States have established post-conflict "truth and reconciliation" commissions to help heal their wounds (for example, South Africa, Peru, Liberia, and Sierra Leone). These commissions may include highly qualified people (not limited to judges and lawyers) who take evidence, hear witnesses, and present a report describing what occurred and perhaps even assigning individual responsibility. Generally, they do not function as courts and do not sentence the guilty. In Rwanda, however, a system of communal courts (known as *gacaca*) served much the same purpose. Do these alternative approaches constitute acceptable ways of "doing justice," even if they allow perpetrators to escape trial and punishment?

§ 1–14   A DUTY TO PROSECUTE?

Some experts argue that impunity is unacceptable in any situation and that under international law there is (or should be) a clear duty to prosecute those who have committed the most serious crimes. Arguably, there is growing textual support for this proposition. For example, the preamble to the Rome Statute affirms "that the most serious crimes of concern to the international community as a whole must not go unpunished and that their effective prosecution must be ensured by taking measures at the national level and by enhancing international cooperation" and recalls "that it is the duty of every State to exercise its criminal jurisdiction over those responsible for international crimes."

Under the 1948 Genocide Convention, as interpreted by the International Court of Justice, States Parties to that treaty are obligated to prosecute perpetrators of genocide even when it was not committed within their territories. *See Case Concerning Application of the Convention on the Prevention and Punishment of the Crime of Genocide* (Bosnia-Herzegovina v. Yugoslavia), Preliminary Objections, 11 July 1996, para. 31 ("the obligation . . . to prevent and to punish the crime of genocide is not territorially limited by the Convention"). The same is true for grave breaches of the Geneva Conventions of 1949. Most of the multilateral criminal treaties require States Parties to "extradite or prosecute" the specific crimes defined in those treaties.

Under human rights law, States are said to have an affirmative duty to prevent, investigate and punish human rights violations. *See*, for example, the decision of the Inter–American Court of Human Rights in *Velasquez Rodriguez*, 29 July 1988, 95 I.L.R. 232, para. 166.

On the other hand, it is doubtful whether customary international law can truly be said today to impose a duty on States to prosecute all violations of international criminal law, or even just "core crimes" committed within their jurisdiction. While acknowledging the gravity of mass atrocities, the injustices and the suffering of victims, one can argue that mandatory prosecutions (regardless of circumstances) do not always serve broader societal interests and goals such as those pursued in a truth and reconciliation context.

§ 1–15   HARMONIZATION AND PROGRESSIVE DEVELOPMENT

The international community today is still premised on the principle of the sovereign equality and political independence of States. There is no global legislature, no universal law enforcement mechanism, and no single international court with compulsory jurisdiction. So the international system remains more diffuse (one can say "horizontal") than most domestic legal systems. In this context, international criminal law serves an important function in progressively articulating the standard, goals, and values of the world community as a whole.

This is true both of how international crimes are defined and of the evidentiary and procedural rules by which prosecutions may be conducted. While national legal systems increasingly share some fundamental concepts (such as a presumption of innocence), they continue to vary widely on some basic principles (for example, the legitimacy of trials *in absentia* or representation by qualified legal counsel). It may still be too early to proclaim the existence of a universally-accepted body of procedural rules. Still, the decisions of the various supranational criminal courts (as well as the growing body of human rights norms) provide a growing source of principles and practices from which a universal code of criminal procedure may one day emerge.

§ 1–16   A NOTE ON HUMAN RIGHTS AND HUMANITARIAN LAW

As this discussion illustrates, international criminal law is closely connected to international human rights law. Most of the core crimes at the heart of international criminal law also constitute the most serious violations of human rights law. The "due process" principles of human rights (especially those set forth in Article 14 of the International Covenant on Civil and Political Rights) guide the conduct of prosecutions before international tribunals. Clearly, international human rights law exerts an increasingly powerful and pervasive force on domestic criminal procedure. Decisions by the European Court of Human Rights, the Inter-American Human Rights Commission and Court, and the UN Human Rights Committee (established to oversee implementation of the International Covenant on Civil and Political Rights) all push States in the direction of procedural fairness and recognition of defendants' rights, forcing modifications in domestic rules to conform to regional and universal norms.

There is of course a fundamental difference between the two fields. International human rights law imposes obligations on governments in the way they treat individuals (in particular, people who are within the territory and subject to the jurisdiction of the State concerned). International criminal law imposes criminal responsibility on individual perpetrators. Both are aimed at protecting the interests of people, but they do so in different ways. International criminal law aims to deter the commission of the gravest atrocities and to provide those charged with such offenses with a fair trial within a reasonable time before an impartial and independent tribunal. These aspects are discussed in greater detail in Chapter 4.

International criminal law is also closely related to another field, commonly referred to as international humanitarian law. The latter term covers the body of international rules and principles intended to limit the effects of armed conflict, in particular by protecting persons who are not (or are no longer) participating in the fighting. It also seeks to regulate the means and methods by which warfare is conducted. For example, the Geneva Conventions of 1949 (and their two Additional Protocols of 1977) provide protections to specified categories of individuals (civilian non-combatants, the wounded, prisoners of war, and the shipwrecked). Other instruments and principles of customary international law impose obligations on the combatants not to cause superfluous injury or unnecessary suffering, to avoid severe or long-term damage to the environment, and not to use certain kinds of weapons (such as exploding bullets, chemical and biological weapons, blinding laser weapons, and anti-personnel mines). *See* Chapter 5.

The most serious violations of international humanitarian law may be prosecuted as war crimes and thus constitute one of the "core crimes" within the jurisdiction of the International Criminal Court (as well as the two *ad hoc* tribunals for the former Yugoslavia and Rwanda).

§ 1–17   FURTHER READING

Yuval Shany, *Assessing the Effectiveness of International Courts: A Goal-Based Approach*, 106 Am J. Int'l L. 225 (2012).

CHAPTER 2

A BRIEF HISTORY OF
INTERNATIONAL CRIMINAL LAW

To appreciate the significance of recent developments in the field, especially the creation of true international criminal tribunals, a basic understanding of the historical background and most significant antecedents of the contemporary system is useful.

I. ORIGINS AND EVOLUTION

The deepest historical roots of substantive international criminal law lie in the law of war, and more precisely in the once-prevalent distinction between "just" and "unjust" wars. Centuries ago, when the idea of sovereignty was personified in the King or Queen, some uses of force by one monarch or ruler against another were considered entirely legitimate while others were prohibited. Violations of these rules might be punishable by the party that won the conflict in a kind of "victor's justice." The first prosecution for initiating an "unjust war" may have occurred as long ago as 1268, when Count von Hohenstaufen was executed for starting an unlawful war.

The distinction between just and unjust wars has long since been abandoned. Today, the prohibition against the use of force by States in international relations is clearly enshrined in the United Nations Charter, art. 2(4). The UN Security Council can

authorize the use of force under Chapter VII of the
Charter, and article 51 recognizes that States have
an inherent right of self-defense. With respect to
individuals, evolving concepts of international
humanitarian law have gradually endorsed the need
to punish those who violate the most important
rules governing the conduct of armed conflict. For
example, individual criminal liability was
established by the Brussels Conference of 1874,
which prohibited unnecessary cruelty and acts of
barbarism committed against the enemy.

International mechanisms for this purpose were
slow to develop. After World War I ended in 1918,
the victorious Allies attempted to establish an
international tribunal, under article 227 of the
Versailles Treaty, to prosecute the German Kaiser
Wilhelm II for "a supreme offence against
international morality and the sanctity of treaties."
However, the Kaiser succeeded in evading arrest
and was eventually granted asylum in the
Netherlands. Articles 228 and 229 of the Versailles
Treaty also provided for prosecution of German
nationals before special Allied courts, but German
authorities refused to surrender the individuals in
question. Some were prosecuted before domestic
German tribunals, but few were convicted. Two of
these trials, held in Leipzig before the German
Reichsgericht or Supreme Court during this period,
involved the sinking of two Allied hospital ships (the
Dover Castle and the *Llandovery Castle*) and
established important precedents on the defense of
superior orders.

In subsequent years, the League of Nations (predecessor to the United Nations) mounted an ultimately unsuccessful effort to gain agreement on the establishment of an international court for these purposes. A treaty to create such a court was actually concluded in 1937 but never gained the necessary support. See Manley O. Hudson, *The Proposed International Criminal Court*, 32 Am. J. Int'l L. 549 (1938).

II. THE NUREMBERG TRIBUNAL

Atrocities committed by Hitler's Nazi Germany before and during World War II (including the Holocaust) resulted in the first successful effort to prosecute individuals before an international court for violations of international law.

In August 1945, several months after the war in Europe had effectively ended, the four principal Allied nations (the United States, France, the United Kingdom and the Soviet Union) reached an agreement to create a tribunal for "the just and prompt trial and punishment of the major war criminals of the European Axis countries." This so-called London (or Nuremberg) Charter established an International Military Tribunal (IMT) consisting of only four judges, one appointed by each of the four signatory countries (backed up by four alternates). The Tribunal, which subsequently took its seat in the German city of Nuremberg, had jurisdiction over three main categories of offenses: crimes against the peace, war crimes, and crimes against humanity.

More specifically, under article 6(a) of the London Charter, the term "crimes against the peace" included both (i) the planning, preparation, initiation or waging of a war of aggression, or a war in violation of international treaties, agreements or assurances, as well as (ii) participation in a common plan or conspiracy for the accomplishment of "any of the foregoing."

As defined by article 6(b), "war crimes" included violations of the laws or customs of war, such as the murder, ill-treatment, or deportation of civilians in occupied territories and prisoners of war, as well as the killing of hostages or "wanton destruction" of cities, towns and villages, and devastation "not justified by military necessity."

By contrast, article 6(c) defined "crimes against humanity" to include murder, extermination, enslavement, deportation, and other inhumane acts committed against any civilian population, before or during the war; or persecutions on political, racial or religious grounds in execution of or in connection with any crime within the jurisdiction of the Tribunal, whether or not in violation of the domestic law of the country where perpetrated.

Importantly, article 6 also provided that "leaders, organizers, instigators, and accomplices participating in the formulation or execution of a common plan or conspiracy to commit any of the foregoing crimes are responsible for all acts performed by any persons in execution of such plan." It was this provision that formed the basis for the most serious allegations against the individual defendants. Most were charged with participation in the formulation and execution of a "common plan" or "conspiracy" to commit crimes against the peace, war crimes, and crimes against humanity, centered on the National Socialist or "Nazi" Party.

Among its other notable features, the London Charter stated, in article 7, that the official position of individual defendants, whether Heads of State or responsible government officials, neither relieved them from criminal responsibility nor mitigated punishment. Further, the defendants could not escape criminal responsibility on the grounds that they had acted pursuant to governmental or superior orders, although such facts could be considered in mitigation of punishment (article 8). The Charter also provided that the IMT was not bound by "technical rules of evidence" but could "admit any evidence which it deems to be of probative value" (article 19).

Twenty-four Nazi leaders were indicted and tried before the IMT. The main charges were all based on article 6 of the Charter. The first count of the indictment described the overall conspiracy, the second concerned crimes against peace, the third charged war crimes, and the fourth focused on crimes against humanity. One defendant was too ill to go to trial; one committed suicide; and one was tried *in absentia*, convicted and sentenced to death (Martin Bormann). Of the other twenty-one defendants, three were acquitted and all others were convicted. Eleven were sentenced to death; all were executed except Hermann Göring, who committed suicide. The other seven defendants received prison sentences ranging from ten years to life. The last remaining prisoner (Rudolf Hess) committed suicide in 1987.

In addition, four groups were declared to be criminal organizations, including the Nazi Party's political leadership corps and their staffs, the Gestapo (or Secret Police), the Sicherheitsdienst (or Security Service), and the regular and "Waffen SS" (components of the Nazi Party).

§ 2–1   CONTROL COUNCIL LAW NO. 10

The Nuremberg Tribunal was not the only court to prosecute war crimes in Europe following World War II. Under an order promulgated in December 1945, known as Allied Control Council Law No. 10, each of the four Powers occupying Germany (the United States, United Kingdom, France and the Soviet Union) was authorized to establish military tribunals to prosecute suspects found in its respective zone of occupation.

CCL No. 10 generally followed the London Charter in focusing on crimes against the peace, war crimes and crimes against humanity. However, it expanded the tribunals' jurisdiction in several ways, *inter alia* by including torture, imprisonment and rape within the scope of crimes against humanity. It also eliminated the requirement that crimes against humanity could only be prosecuted if they had been committed "in execution of or in connection with" another crime within the jurisdiction of the Tribunal, meaning a war crime or crime against the peace. Thus, in these tribunals (unlike in the IMT), individuals could be prosecuted for crimes against humanity which did not occur during actual armed conflict, such as atrocities committed against civilians in Germany prior to the war.

Counting those prosecuted by the four Allied Powers, many more cases were brought before the CCL No. 10 tribunals (often called the "subsequent proceedings") than came before the IMT itself. Within the American zone alone, after the conclusion of the IMT proceedings, twelve major trials were held at Nuremberg involving some 185 defendants. The judgments in a number of these trials contained significant statements of legal principles (for example establishing the criminal liability of top officials of the Nazi Party and the High Command of the German Army, of civilian officials for directing Germany's pre-World War II rearmament program, for the administration of concentration camps, and of particular note for the atrocities committed by the so-called *Einsatzgruppen* or 'special action groups').

Many other cases (generally for less serious violations of the laws of war) were prosecuted before military commissions established by the occupying powers (for example, 489 cases involving 1672 defendants were pursued by the U.S. military at Dachau).

In an important sense, then, the IMT itself represented only the top level of an extensive system of post-war criminal prosecutions for atrocities and violations of the law of war in the

European Theater. Still, it marked the real beginnings of modern international criminal law and was the first tribunal to hold individuals personally responsible for their crimes under international law.

III. THE TOKYO TRIALS

The post-war trials in the Pacific Theater (commonly referred to as the Tokyo Trials) took place before the International Military Tribunal for the Far East (the IMTFE). It consisted of eleven judges, one from each of the victorious Allied powers in the war against Japan (United States, United Kingdom, Soviet Union, Republic of China, the Netherlands, Australia, New Zealand, Canada, France, British India, and the Philippines).

Unlike the Nuremberg Tribunal, the IMTFE was established unilaterally by the proclamation of the Supreme Allied Commander, U.S. General Douglas MacArthur, following the Japanese surrender. However, its Charter followed the London Charter closely and provided for jurisdiction over (a) crimes against the peace (including "the planning, preparation, initiation or waging of a declared or undeclared war of aggression, or a war in violation of international law, treaties, agreements or assurances, or participation in a common plan or conspiracy for the accomplishment of any of the foregoing"), (b) conventional war crimes (specifically, "violations of the laws or customs of war") and (c) crimes against humanity (namely, "murder, extermination, enslavement, deportation, and other inhumane acts committed against any civilian population, before or during the war, or persecutions on political or racial grounds in execution of or in connection with any crime within the jurisdiction of the Tribunal, whether or not in violation of the domestic law of the country where perpetrated").

The IMTFE's Charter also specified that "[l]eaders, organizers, instigators and accomplices participating in the formulation or execution of a common plan or conspiracy to commit any of the foregoing crimes are responsible for all acts performed by any person in execution of such plan."

Between 1946 and 1948, the Tribunal considered charges against some eighty of Japan's senior wartime leadership, including four former premiers, three foreign ministers, four war ministers, generals, ambassadors, and others who were variously accused variously of carrying out a "war of conquest" and of murdering, maiming and ill-treating civilians and prisoners of war, plunder, rape, and other atrocities and "barbaric cruelties."

Only twenty-eight defendants were actually tried, mostly military and political leaders. Two died of natural causes during the trial, and another suffered a nervous breakdown during the trial and was removed. All the others were convicted. Seven were hanged, sixteen were sentenced to life imprisonment (most were paroled in 1955), and two received lesser sentences.

Perhaps the best-known case decided by the IMTFE concerned General Yamashita, who was found guilty of war crimes committed by soldiers under his command on the basis of his responsibility as their superior officer. In its judgment in this case, the Tokyo IMT discussed the principle of "command responsibility" in considerable detail and applied it to civilian and military defendants alike.

Often overlooked is the fact that two judges dissented from the Tribunal's judgment. Judge Röling from the Netherlands argued that no individual liability could be imposed under international law for aggression. Judge Pal from India also challenged the conceptual basis for prosecutions of crimes against the peace, contending that the prohibition on aggressive war reflected a desire by colonial powers to preserve their interests in the status quo. He also criticized the fairness of the trial proceedings themselves.

As in Europe, many hundreds of other war crimes trials were held at various locations in Asia and across the Pacific following the Japanese surrender, many before U.S. military tribunals. Some lasted into the 1950s. Perhaps the largest effort occurred on Guam, where 148 Japanese and Pacific Islanders were prosecuted; thirty received death sentences (some were commuted to life in prison) and ten were hanged. All told, over 5000 Japanese soldiers and officials were indicted for war crimes; most were convicted. Additionally, the Soviet Union held a number of trials of Japanese war criminals, notably for the members of a special Japanese bacteriological and chemical warfare unit ("Unit 731") at Khabarovsk. China also conducted its own trials, resulting in over 500 convictions and many executions.

IV. SUBSEQUENT DEVELOPMENTS

The Nuremberg and Tokyo Trials were the first real international criminal tribunals and laid the groundwork for the development of a new field of international law. Largely because of Cold War tensions, however, no other international criminal tribunals were established until 1993, nearly a half century later.

Still, several significant developments did take place. These included (1) the adoption of the Genocide and Geneva Conventions, (2) efforts within the International Law Commission to write a "code of crimes" and a statute for a global criminal tribunal, and (3) domestic efforts to prosecute war criminals.

§ 2–2   THE GENOCIDE CONVENTION

One of the first accomplishments of the new United Nations (created in October 1945) was to affirm the Nuremberg Charter and the Judgment of the IMT. This was done by a unanimous vote of the very first UN General Assembly. *See* UN G.A. Res. 95(1) (Dec. 11, 1946).

Thereafter, work began on a new multilateral treaty to clarify and codify the prohibition in international law against the kind of widespread abuses which had been perpetrated by the Nazi regime against civilian populations. Neither the Nuremberg nor Tokyo Tribunals included the term "genocide" within their jurisdictional mandates, but a concerted effort by a Polish lawyer, Raphaél Lemkin, convinced the world community that a new formulation was necessary to focus global condemnation.

On December 9, 1948 (the day before it adopted the Universal Declaration of Human Rights), the UN General Assembly completed work on the Convention on the Prevention and Punishment of the Crime of Genocide. *See* UN G.A. Res. 260(III)(B) (Dec. 9, 1948). The treaty entered into force on January 12, 1951, 78 U.N.T.S. 277 (text available at *http://treaties.un.org/*) It remains one of the foundational treaties in the field of international criminal law. As of June 2013, 142 States were parties to the Convention.

The Convention proclaims that "genocide, whether committed in time of peace or in time of war, is a crime under international law." Art. 1. It defines the term "genocide" as including "any of the following acts committed with intent to destroy, in whole or in part, a national, ethnical, racial or religious group, as such: (a) Killing members of the group; (b) Causing serious bodily or mental harm to members of the group; (c) Deliberately inflicting on the group conditions of life calculated to bring about its physical destruction in whole or in part; (d) Imposing measures intended to prevent births within the group; (e) Forcibly transferring children of the group to another group." Art. 2.

The definition thus contains three distinct elements: (1) commission of one or more of the specifically prohibited acts (2) against a "national, ethnical, racial or religious group" (3) with the intent to destroy that group "as such" and "in whole or in part."

In addition to genocide itself, the Convention prohibits conspiracy to commit genocide, direct and public incitement to commit genocide, attempt to commit genocide, and complicity in genocide. Art. 3. Persons committing genocide or any of the other acts enumerated in article III shall be punished, whether they are constitutionally responsible rulers, public officials or private individuals. Art. 4.

Article 6 provides for two methods of enforcement. First, it contemplates domestic prosecutions before the national courts of the country where the genocide occurred ("[p]ersons charged with genocide or any of the other acts enumerated in article III shall be tried by a competent tribunal of the State in the territory of which the act was committed"). Second, it says that those persons could be tried before "such international penal tribunal as may have jurisdiction with respect to those Contracting Parties which shall have accepted its jurisdiction." The Convention itself did not, however, establish such a tribunal.

§ 2–3   THE 1949 GENEVA CONVENTIONS

A second major development took place in August 1949, when four new multilateral conventions concerning the protection of victims of war were adopted by a diplomatic conference. Like the Genocide Convention, these treaties were intended to clarify and strengthen international rules in response to the abuses and atrocities of World War II. They are universally accepted (as of June 2013, 194 States had ratified or acceded to them) and they constitute the cornerstone of what is generally called "international humanitarian law."

The four treaties deal separately with different groups of persons not actively engaged in combat or who can no longer fight. Thus, Convention I protects the wounded and sick in land warfare; Convention II protects wounded, sick and ship-wrecked in sea warfare; Convention III protects prisoners of war; and Convention IV protects civilians. A basic premise of the Conventions is that parties engaged in an armed conflict must distinguish between legitimate combatants, on the one hand, and non-combatants on the other, since the latter are deserving of special protections.

The Conventions were drafted to apply primarily to conflicts between States ("international armed conflicts") although one increasingly important provision (known as "Common Article 3") applies to conflicts "not of an international character," which originally referred to conflicts taking place within a single State. This distinction was further elaborated in 1977 with the adoption of two Additional

Protocols to the Geneva Conventions, one of which was designed specifically for "non-international" conflicts. Today, the terms are used somewhat differently to differentiate conflicts between the organized military forces of two States, on the one hand, from those between a State and non-State groups such as terrorist organizations, even when the conflict in question crosses international boundaries.

Violations of the Conventions constitute "war crimes," for which individual criminal responsibility attaches. The most serious war crimes, called "grave breaches," must be punished. The term "grave breach" is defined slightly differently in each convention, but includes such acts as willful killing, torture or inhumane treatment.

§ 2–4   EFFORTS OF THE INTERNATIONAL LAW COMMISSION

Apart from the Genocide and Geneva Conventions, much of the post-war efforts to elaborate new principles and mechanisms of international criminal law took place within the International Law Commission (or "ILC"). Created in 1948, the ILC is a body of thirty-four experts elected by the UN General Assembly and charged with the codification and progressive development of international law. Over much of the next fifty years, the Commission worked on two related projects—drafting a "statute" for creation of a new international criminal court, and preparing a codification of the substantive rules of international criminal law. Both efforts encountered substantial difficulties.

§ 2–5   PROPOSALS FOR A NEW COURT

As part of the same resolution by which it adopted the Genocide Convention in 1948, the UN General Assembly invited the International Law Commission to study "the desirability and possibility of establishing an international judicial organ for the trial of persons charged with genocide or other crimes." As described above, such a body had been explicitly contemplated, but not created, by the Genocide Convention. Some early progress was made within the ILC and in a separate UN committee, and a draft "statute" was submitted to the General Assembly in 1954. But thereafter the General Assembly decided that this work should be deferred until after debate on a definition of "aggression" was completed. That did not occur until 1974. *See* Definition of Aggression, U.N. Doc. A/RES/29/3314 (Dec. 14, 1974) (text and background information available at *http://untreaty.un.org/ cod/avl/ha/da/da.html*).

After intermittent consideration of the topic, the ILC completed a revision of the draft statute in 1994. Spurred by the catastrophic situations in the former Yugoslavia and then Rwanda, the UN General Assembly appointed a special *Ad Hoc* Committee on the Establishment of International Criminal Court. Eventually, this effort formed the basis for the international convention establishing the International Criminal Court. *See* the Rome

Statute of the International Criminal Court, art. 27, U.N. Doc. A/CONF.183/9* (July 17, 1998). For the text of the Convention and related information, *see* the website of the International Criminal Court at *http://www.icc-cpi.int/Pages/default.aspx.*

§ 2–6   CODIFYING SUBSTANTIVE PRINCIPLES

The second part of the ILC's efforts involved trying to codify the substantive law of the Nuremberg and Tokyo Tribunals. In 1950, the ILC adopted a statement of the Principles of International Law Recognized in the Charter and the Judgment. *See* Report of the International Law Commission, U.N. Doc. A/1316 (A/5/12) part III, paras. 95–127. It incorporated the IMT's definition of war crimes, crimes against humanity, and crimes against peace, and it enshrined the principle of individual criminal liability for their commission. It included provisions on complicity and precluded the defense of immunity as Head of State or Government. It also stated that the defense of superior orders could not relieve an individual from responsibility under international law "provided a moral choice was in fact possible to him."

Four years later, in 1954, the Commission produced a broader "draft code of offences against the peace and security of mankind." That text proved controversial, however, and work was suspended for twenty years while attention focused instead on efforts to define the notion of "aggression." The question was again referred to the Commission in

1978, and a draft code was provisionally adopted on first reading in 1991. The text was completed in July 1996. It is available at *http://untreaty.un.org/ilc/texts/instruments/english/draft%20articles/7_4_1996.pdf*.

§ 2–7 NATIONAL PROSECUTIONS

The third major aspect of post-war developments involved sporadic and only sometimes successful efforts by individual States to prosecute war criminals under their domestic laws. After the closure of the IMT, IMTFE and related courts, and prior to the establishment of the *ad hoc* tribunals for the former Yugoslavia and Rwanda in 1993 and 1994 respectively, no international tribunal existed with jurisdiction over international criminal defendants. Consequently, national courts offered the only place where persons charged with war crimes, genocide and crimes against humanity could be pursued. In fact, such prosecutions were specifically contemplated by the Genocide and Geneva Conventions. They often proved difficult and politically sensitive.

By way of illustration, six of the most well-known cases are briefly described here.

1. Klaus Barbie

Barbie headed the Nazi Gestapo in Lyon, France, from November 1942 to August 1944. Because of his involvement in torture and other atrocities, including the deportation of large numbers of French Jews and partisans to death camps, he was called the "Butcher of Lyon." After the war, he fled to Argentina. He was tried *in absentia* by French authorities for war crimes and crimes against humanity, and sentenced to death. Eventually he moved to Bolivia, where he lived under a false name. In 1983, he was extradited to France and prosecuted a second time, convicted again, and sentenced to life imprisonment. He died in 1991.

2. Paul Touvier

A colleague of Barbie and a senior officer of a paramilitary unit of the Vichy Government (the "Milice"), Touvier was prosecuted in absentia for treason by French authorities after the war and sentenced to death. In 1971, he was pardoned, but was subsequently charged with crimes against humanity arising out of a massacre of Jewish hostages in 1944. Finally arrested in 1989, he was tried in 1994, convicted, and sentenced to life imprisonment. He died in prison two years later.

3. Maurice Papon

Another a high-ranking official of the French Vichy Government, Maurice Papon was convicted in 1998 of complicity in Nazi crimes against humanity during the German occupation, in particular for his role in deporting hundreds of Jews from southwestern France to their deaths in German concentration camps. His participation in those crimes was not revealed until 1981, after he had had a successful career in the French Government (including service as prefect of police in Paris and as

France's budget minister). Tried, convicted and sentenced to ten years in prison, he served less than three years. According to his obituary, he always protested that he had done only what the Germans had made him do.

4. Adolf Eichmann

Sometimes called the "architect of the Holocaust," Eichmann was a senior officer in the *Schutzstaffel* (or "SS"), the elite force under Heinrich Himmler which was primarily responsible for the crimes against humanity perpetrated by the Nazis. Eichmann played a central role in organizing the mass deportation of Jews to extermination camps in Nazi-occupied Eastern Europe. He escaped at war's end and lived under an assumed name in Argentina. He was eventually captured by Israeli agents and returned to Israel, where he was convicted of crimes against humanity and war crimes. *See* Government of Israel v. Eichmann, 36 ILR 5 (1968) and Attorney-General of Israel v. Eichmann 36 1LR 277 (1968). *See also* Hannah Arendt, *Eichmann in Jerusalem* (1963). Eichmann was hanged in 1962. The Government of Argentina protested his apprehension as a "violation of the sovereign rights of the Argentine Republic" and the UN Security Council asked Israel to make appropriate reparations. This diplomatic dispute was settled by a joint communiqué.

5. Imre Finta

Finta, a senior Hungarian police officer during World War II, immigrated to Canada in 1948, settled in Toronto, and became a Canadian citizen in 1956. He was accused of war crimes and crimes against humanity for having assisting in the forced deportation of Jews from Budapest during the Holocaust. He was charged under Canadian war crimes legislation which allowed prosecution of any person who committed a war crime or crime against humanity outside Canada that, if it had been committed in Canada, would constitute an offense against Canadian law. His defense was that he had only been following orders. He was acquitted because the jury could not conclude that, in the violent anti-Semitic climate of the time, he was aware he had been assisting in an illegal policy of persecution; in other words, the jury felt he lacked the specific intent (*mens rea*) required by the statute. The acquittal was upheld by the Ontario Court of Appeal in 1992 and the Canadian Supreme Court two years later. The Supreme Court accepted his defense of superior orders, noting *inter alia* that "[e]ven where the orders are manifestly unlawful, the defense ... will be available in those circumstances where the accused had no moral choice as to whether to follow the order." *R. v. Finta*, [1994] 1 S.C.R. 701. Finta died in Canada in December 2003.

6. John Demjanjuk

Beginning in 1977, U.S. authorities accused John Demjanjuk of having served as an SS guard at several German extermination camps during World War II. Following the war, he immigrated to the United States, became a naturalized citizen, and worked as a diesel engine mechanic in Ohio. The U.S. government acted to revoke his citizenship on the grounds that he had concealed his wartime activities on his immigration application. After a district court granted that request, the Government of Israel successfully sought his extradition and prosecuted him under its Nazis and Nazi Collaborators (Punishment) Law, which gave jurisdiction over crimes committed against Jews in Germany during the war. The principal allegation was that Demjanjuk was in fact "Ivan the Terrible," the notorious guard who operated the diesel engines at the Gas Chambers at Treblinka extermination camp. He was convicted and sentenced to death, but five years later the Israeli Supreme Court overturned that judgment, finding reasonable doubt about his identification, and ordered his release.

Demjanjuk returned to the United States and in 1998, won a court ruling restoring his citizenship. However, the Justice Department filed a new complaint alleging that Demjanjuk had served at other death camps in Poland and Germany and was part of an SS-run unit involved in capturing nearly two million Jews in Poland. The government prevailed, and in 2004, that decision was upheld on the basis that the government had presented "clear, unequivocal, and convincing evidence" of Demjanjuk's service in Nazi death camps. The following year, an immigration judge ordered Demjanjuk deported and the decision was upheld on appeal. Deported to Germany in 2009, he was tried, convicted and sentenced to five years in prison on some 28,000 counts of acting as an accessory to murder, one count for each person who died at Sobibor during the time he was alleged to have served as a guard. He was later released and lived at a nursing home where he died in March 2012.

§ 2–8   FURTHER READING

The text of the London Charter, formally known as the Agreement for the Prosecution and Punishment of Major War Criminals of the European Axis and Establishing the Charter of the International Military Tribunal (IMT), August 8, 1945, 82 U.N.T.S. 279 (1951), is available at *http://www. icrc.org/ihl*. For the Tribunal's official records, *see The Trial of German Major War Criminals, Proceedings of the International Military Tribunal Sitting at Nuremberg, Germany* (1950).

See also Telford Taylor, *The Anatomy of the Nuremberg Trials* (1993); Kevin John Heller, *The Nuremberg Military Tribunals and the Origins of International Criminal Law* (Cambridge 2011); Allan Ryan, *Yamashita's Ghost: War Crimes, MacArthur's Justice, and Command Accountability* (Kansas 2012); Tanaka, McCormack & Simpson, eds., *Beyond Victor's Justice: The Tokyo War Crimes Trials Revisited* (M. Nijhoff 2011).

CHAPTER 3
BASIC CONCEPTS AND PRINCIPLES

I. INTRODUCTION

In addition to an appreciation of previous international efforts to hold people accountable for the most serious violations of international law, an understanding of the contemporary field of international criminal law requires a grasp of the fundamental principles on which the system rests today. They include jurisdictional concepts as well as norms governing the actual exercise of authority to prosecute international crimes.

II. CONCEPTS OF JURISDICTION

The new international courts and tribunals are the most visible and important feature of the contemporary international criminal law system. Their jurisdiction is specified in the instrument which established them (Security Council resolution, treaty, or other agreement). But the vast majority of cases involving international or transnational crimes are still prosecuted under national law in domestic courts. The reason is simple: since most crimes take place within one or more States and are committed by or against nationals of those States, those States have the greatest interest in prosecuting the perpetrators. What does international law have to say about when a State can prosecute or punish criminal conduct taking place outside its borders?

§ 3–1   TYPES OF JURISDICTION

International lawyers typically use the term "jurisdiction" to describe the overall authority of each State to determine when and how its national law applies with respect to people, property and conduct outside its territorial borders. For students in American law schools, this differs from the jurisdictional concepts normally encountered in courses on domestic law, such as those distinguishing between personal and subject-matter jurisdiction or describing the relationship between federal and state courts. The reason is that it reflects the structure and principles of the international system, which lacks a global government and still consists mostly of independent States. It can sometimes be useful to think about three different ways in which national jurisdiction can be applied.

1. *Prescriptive Jurisdiction*

First, the term can be used to refer to the ability of one State's national legislature to determine when and how its laws will apply to people and conduct outside its borders—in other words, to prescribe the extraterritorial application of its domestic law. This is known as legislative or prescriptive jurisdiction. For our purposes, the question concerns the scope of a State's authority, under international law, to adopt substantive criminal laws and regulations laws that regulate conduct occurring outside its national boundaries.

2. *Adjudicative Jurisdiction*

Second, "jurisdiction" can describe the authority of national courts (or other adjudicative bodies such as administrative agencies) to apply their law in determining the outcome of particular cases brought before them. This is referred to as judicial or adjudicative jurisdiction. In the criminal context, this would normally involve prosecution of an individual for activities undertaken outside the national boundaries of the country concerned. The fact of prosecution is an exercise of adjudicative jurisdiction, conceptually distinct from the extraterritorial reach of laws which is an exercise of prescriptive jurisdiction. The two are related in practice but theoretically distinct.

3. *Enforcement Jurisdiction*

Third, the term can also be used to describe the ability of governmental authorities (courts, administrative agencies, ministries, police, etc.) to compel compliance with the provisions of national law. We refer to this as enforcement jurisdiction. Examples might include the imposition of criminal penalties, fines for contempt or trade sanctions resulting from violations of the relevant domestic law.

By themselves, these terms do not tell much about the legitimacy of any particular exercise of jurisdiction. In the first instance, the question has to be answered by reference to national law. The national laws of every State are likely to differ on these points.

From the international criminal law perspective, the important question is what, if anything, international law has to say about the legitimacy of the application of national law to persons, property and conduct beyond the territorial boundaries of the State in question. To continue with the example of the United States, even if the Congress has authority under the Constitution to enact a law with extraterritorial effect, does international law limit the exercise of such authority? Could another State, or an individual defendant, challenge such a law on the basis that it contravened principles of international law? As a matter of international law, can States do anything which is not forbidden, or can they only exercise jurisdiction when it is expressly permitted? What limits, if any, does international law impose on "extraterritorial jurisdiction?"

§ 3–2   PERMISSIVE GROUNDS OF EXTRATERRITORIAL JURISDICTION

Customary international law currently recognizes a number of bases or doctrines that justify the exercise of a State's domestic jurisdiction (prescriptive, adjudicative or enforcement) over people, property and activities inside and outside its territory. They are generally grouped under five headings: territoriality, nationality, passive personality, protective and universal. This section also discusses two other types of jurisdiction: the so-called "extradite or prosecute" obligation under various international criminal law treaties and the specialized "international" jurisdiction of international courts and tribunals.

1. *The Lotus Principle*

Before turning to the details of these principles, it is important to note that they are permissive (not required) grounds. In other words, no State is under an obligation to apply its law extraterritorially or to use any or all of these principles to the maximum extent. As a matter of international law, however, it has been less clear whether these principles operate as limitations, that is, whether a State can exercise extraterritorial jurisdiction *only if* affirmatively permitted by one of these principles. This question was addressed nearly a century ago in the famous decision of the Permanent Court of International Justice (PCIJ) in *The S.S. "Lotus"* (France v. Turkey), 1927 P.C.I.J. (ser. A) No. 10, at 13 (Sept. 7).

The case arose as a result of a collision on the high seas between a French vessel (the S.S. *Lotus*) and a Turkish vessel (the *Boz-Kourt*). The Turkish vessel sank and eight Turkish sailors died. After the S.S. *Lotus* arrived in Constantinople, Turkish authorities arrested its first officer, Lt. Demons, who had been on watch when the collision occurred. Even though he was not a Turkish citizen and the collision took place on the high seas, Lt. Demons was prosecuted, convicted of manslaughter, and sentenced to a fine and eighty days' imprisonment.

The French government protested, arguing that under international law, jurisdiction in such cases rests exclusively with the State under whose flag the vessel sails. Since Lt. Demons had been aboard a French vessel, they argued, his culpability was a matter for French authorities. France challenged Turkey before the PCIJ, arguing that Turkey could point to no rule of international law affirmatively permitting it to exercise criminal jurisdiction in such situations. In response, Turkey argued that no rule of international law prohibited it from doing so and that in any event jurisdiction was justified under Turkish law by the fact that the collision had produced effects on the *Boz-Kourt*, which was properly treated as if it were Turkish territory.

The PCIJ agreed with Turkey. It acknowledged that under international law, jurisdiction is primarily territorial but said that a State may also exercise jurisdiction over acts taking place outside its borders which have an effect within its territory. Acknowledging that all States have jurisdiction over acts taking place within their territories, the Court said that restrictions on the independence of States (and their jurisdictional reach) cannot be presumed. Thus, States need not rely on a permissive rule and have the right to exercise extraterritorial jurisdiction unless explicitly prohibited by a treaty provision or rule of customary international law.

The so-called *Lotus* "freedom principle" has never been explicitly reversed. As a matter of international practice, however, few States today argue in favor of unrestricted freedom to exercise extraterritorial jurisdiction. To the contrary, most situations are judged or justified by reference to one of the established jurisdictional principles described below. In effect, States today have adopted the French view, and in practice they ground jurisdictional assertions on one of the recognized principles. Indeed, several judges of the International Court of Justice have referred to the *S.S. Lotus* as "the high water mark of laissez-faire in international relations." *See Arrest Warrant of April 11, 2000* (Democratic Republic of Congo v. Belgium), Judgment, ICJ Reports 2002, joint separate opinion of Judges Higgins, Buergenthal and Kooijmans at para. 51, 41 I.L.M. 536, 585 (2002).

In practice, the assertion of extraterritorial jurisdiction in any given situation may well be justified on the basis of several principles. For example, the kind of jurisdiction asserted by the Turkish government in *S.S. Lotus* might readily be justified today under the "passive personality" principle discussed below (since the victims were Turkish nationals) or as a kind of "objective territorial" or "effects" jurisdiction (*see* discussion in § 3–2 (1)(B–C)). In any event, it would clearly be a matter of "concurrent jurisdiction," since France could also legitimately prosecute Lt. Demons on the basis of his French citizenship nationality or because his negligence, if any, occurred on board a French-flagged vessel (*see* discussion in § 3–2 (2) below).

This is an important point: no rule of customary international law gives preference to one type of jurisdictional assertion or the other. Overlapping or competing claims are entirely possible. There is today no hierarchy of jurisdictional norms. Some limiting principles (such as the "reasonableness" criterion) have emerged (*see* § 3–7 (3) on 'reasonableness' below). In the event of conflicting assertions of jurisdiction, the States themselves must agree on the resolution.

Today jurisdictional competence is often a matter of treaty law. This is the case, for example, with many of the multilateral law treaties discussed below in Chapter 7 on transnational criminal law. In the case of the *S.S. Lotus*, the matter would actually be governed by article 97(1) of the 1982 U.N. Convention on the Law of the Sea, 1833 U.N.T.S. 396 (entered into force Nov. 16, 1994), 21 I.L.M. 261 (1982), and its predecessor article 11(1) of the 1958 Convention on the High Seas, 13 U.S.T. 2312. The rule in those treaties effectively reversed the PCIJ's decision and explicitly provides that in the event of a high-seas collision, no proceedings can be instituted against individuals who might be responsible except before the judicial or administrative authorities of either the vessel's flag State or the State of which that individual is a national.

§ 3–3   THE FIVE TRADITIONAL BASES

1. *The Territoriality Principle*

A basic consequence of sovereignty is that a State has jurisdiction over all crimes occurring within its territory. International lawyers actually distinguish two types of jurisdiction based on territoriality. When the criminal conduct itself occurs within the State's territory, that State is said to be exercising "subjective territorial" jurisdiction. By contrast, when jurisdiction is based on the fact that conduct committed outside the territory has a substantial impact within the territory, the State is said to be exercising "objective territorial" jurisdiction.

An easy way to see the difference is to consider a hypothetical in which an individual on one side of an international border fires a weapon across that border which injures or kills someone on the other side. Which State can exercise jurisdiction over the crime? Most lawyers would say both, of course. The State from which the person fired the weapon would be asserting jurisdiction based on *subjective territoriality*, and the State into which the person fired would be asserting jurisdiction based on *objective territoriality*.

A. Subjective Territoriality

As a matter of traditional international law, a State has plenary jurisdiction to prescribe, adjudicate and enforce criminal law regarding conduct that takes place within its own territory. In general, it can do so without regard to the nationality of the perpetrator or the victim or the interests of other States.

That principle flows from the concept of sovereignty, perhaps more precisely from principles of political independence, territorial integrity and sovereign equality of States. At one time, this authority was considered exclusive, meaning that an attempt by one State to prosecute actions occurring within another State's territory would be deemed an impermissible interference. *Cf.* Chief Justice Marshall's opinion in *The Antelope* (the "perfect equality of nations" means that "no one [State] can rightfully impose a rule on another," "[e]ach legislates only for itself," and "[t]he Courts of no country execute the penal laws of another.") This absolutist view is no longer followed in practice. *See Pasquantino v. United States*, 544 U.S. 349 (2005).

B. Objective Territoriality

This type of jurisdictional assertion is sometimes described as resting on the harmful "effects" of an extraterritorial act on the territory of the State in question. In U.S. law, for example, it underlies the exercise of certain kinds of regulatory as well as criminal jurisdiction, such as in antitrust law. *Cf. Hartford Fire Ins. Co, v. California*, 509 U.S. 764 (1993). It has also been relied upon by U.S. courts in upholding prosecutions for smuggling drugs and other contraband, on the ground that acts in foreign countries had consequential effects on the United States. *See, e.g., United States v. MacAllister*, 160 F.3d 1304 (11th Cir. 1998).

C. Intended Effects

In a narrow set of circumstances, U.S. courts have gone a step farther and upheld criminal jurisdiction based on the "intended effects" of extraterritorial conduct. For example, in *United States v. Noriega*,

746 F. Supp. 1506, 1513 (S.D. Fla. 1990), aff'd 117 F.3d 1206 (11th Cir. 1997), where the prosecution was based on a conspiracy to import narcotics, the court said that: "The fact that no act was committed and no repercussions were felt within the United States did not preclude jurisdiction over the conduct that was clearly directed at the United States." The Restatement (Third), *Foreign Relations Law of the United States*, § 402, comment d, provides: "[c]ases involving intended but unrealized effects are rare, but international law does not preclude jurisdiction in such instances, subject to the principle of reasonableness." The importance of objective territoriality-based jurisdiction is illustrated by cases where vessels carrying narcotics intended for distribution and sale within the United States are intercepted in international waters and successful prosecution hinges on whether the statutory requirement of intent can be met.

D. Assimilation

In addition to objective and subjective territoriality, a third type of territoriality may be described as *assimilation*. It has long been customary for States to treat certain locations as if they were part of its territory. Under the law of the sea, for example, vessels flying the flag of a State are generally treated, for purposes of criminal law, as if they were part of the territory of that State, so that crimes committed on board those vessels can be prosecuted under that State's law even when committed on the high seas or in another country's jurisdiction. The same is true of aircraft registered in that State. Diplomatic or consular missions abroad may also fall into this category.

In U.S. law, the assimilation concept finds its clearest expression in the notion of *special maritime and territorial jurisdiction* codified at 18 U.S.C. § 7. This statute makes specified acts violations of federal criminal law when committed within the "special maritime and territorial jurisdiction" even if those acts are not in fact committed on United States territory strictly speaking. Special maritime and territorial jurisdiction extends to, *inter alia*, marine waters within U.S. jurisdiction, marine, aeronautical and space vessels owned by or in possession of the U.S. government, citizens or corporations, and U.S. diplomatic and consular buildings in foreign countries. In *United States v. Corey*, 232 F.3d 1166 (9th Cir. 2000), cert. denied, 534 U.S. 887 (2001), the Ninth Circuit Court of Appeals upheld criminal jurisdiction over charges of sexual abuse relating to acts committed on a U.S. Air Force base in Japan and in an apartment in the Philippines rented by the U.S. Embassy in the Philippines for use by U.S. Embassy employees.

Along the same lines, the United States recognizes the concept of *special aircraft jurisdiction* covering *inter alia* foreign aircraft whose next scheduled destination is in the United States, as well as aircraft which land on U.S. territory and have on board persons accused of terrorist offenses against that aircraft. *See* 49 U.S.C. § 46501. For instance, in *United States v. Georgescu*, 723 F. Supp. 912 (E.D.N.Y. 1989), the court allowed the prosecution of an alien for physically abusing a foreign national on board a foreign-registered aircraft over the Atlantic Ocean while on its way to a U.S. destination, because it fell within the "special aircraft jurisdiction."

The special maritime and territorial jurisdiction concept has been applied to cover felony offenses committed outside the United States by anyone (1) employed by or accompanying the Armed Forces outside the United States or (2) while a member of the Armed Forces subject to the Uniform Code of Military Justice. *See* the Military Extraterritorial Jurisdiction Act of 2000 ("MEJA"), 8 U.S.C. § 3261. The statute actually criminalizes conduct outside the United States which would have been an offense if it had been engaged in within the special maritime and territorial jurisdiction. The term "employed by the Armed Forces outside the United States" includes not only Department of Defense contractors but also employees of contractors of "any other Federal agency, or any provisional authority, to the extent such employment relates to supporting the mission of the Department of Defense overseas." 18 U.S.C. § 3267.

2. *Nationality*

Many States assert criminal jurisdiction based on nationality. This form of jurisdiction is based on the allegiance that is owed to one's country and the responsibility a State may have, in certain circumstances, for acts of its citizens. International lawyers distinguish two types of nationality jurisdiction: active personality and passive personality. The former rests on the nationality of the *perpetrator*, which the latter rests on the nationality of the *victim*.

Active personality jurisdiction normally rests on the citizenship of the individual committing the offense, but in some instances it may be based on that individual's formal domicile or even residence. A number of States, for example, assert jurisdiction over the activities of their permanent residents even when they are abroad.

Different States invoke the active personality principle to different extents. Civil law countries frequently make more vigorous use of active personality jurisdiction by criminalizing a wide range of activities by their nationals outside their territory. France, for example, asserts extraterritorial jurisdiction over French nationals in all felony cases. *See* Code de Procedure Penale, art. 689. In consequence, many such States refuse to extradite their nationals and instead prosecute them domestically for offenses committed abroad.

By distinction, common law countries have generally relied on territorial concepts and been less willing to assert active personality jurisdiction. But that has begun to change. Today, for instance, the United Kingdom applies nationality-based jurisdiction for a limited number of offenses such as murder, manslaughter, bigamy, offenses on board foreign merchant vessels, sexual offenses against children, etc.

The United States makes limited use of active personality jurisdiction, though a few examples are available. For example, in *Blackmer v. United States*, 284 U.S. 421 (1932), the Court upheld a criminal contempt conviction against a U.S. citizen living in Paris for ignoring subpoenas to testify in a proceeding in the District of Columbia. In *Skiriotes v. United States*, 313 U.S. 69 (1941), the Court affirmed the conviction of a U.S. national who violated a law against sponge-diving even though he was outside U.S. territorial waters at the time. In the case of *United States v. Clark*, 315 F. Supp. 2d 1127 (W.D. Wash. 2004), aff'd 435 F.3d 1100 (9th Cir. 2006), cert. denied 127 S. Ct. 2029 (2007), Clark was indicted and convicted under 18 U.S.C. § 2423(c), which criminalizes the illicit sexual conduct of American citizens or admitted aliens who travel in foreign commerce.

See generally Geoffrey R. Watson, "Offenders Abroad: The Case for Nationality-Based Criminal Jurisdiction," 17 Yale J. Int'l L. 41 (1992).

3. *Passive Personality*

Passive personality jurisdiction is the other aspect of nationality jurisdiction. It justifies the assertion of domestic criminal jurisdiction over acts in violation of the State's laws committed outside the State *against* its nationals. The concept reflects the interest of every State in protecting the safety of its citizens.

Passive personality jurisdiction has traditionally been controversial. One of the most famous examples is the venerable *Cutting* case. It involved a U.S. citizen arrested in Mexico, in 1886, on charges of having criminally libeled a Mexican national. The allegedly libelous statement had been published while its author was in the United States, but his arrest took place much later in Mexico. The relevant Mexican statute asserted jurisdiction over offenses committed in a foreign country by a foreigner against Mexican citizens. The U.S. Government vigorously opposed Mexico's exercise of jurisdiction (and contended that penal laws could not be applied extraterritorially). The case was eventually discontinued.

While initially resisted by many States, the passive personality principle has found increasing acceptance in the face of international terrorism. In 1986, for example, the U.S. Congress enacted the Omnibus Diplomatic Security and Anti-Terrorism Act, which among things grants U.S. courts jurisdiction over persons charged with the extraterritorial murder of U.S. nationals, where the intention of the perpetrator was to intimidate, coerce, or retaliate against the U.S. government. *See* 18 U.S.C. §§ 2331, 2332. Similarly, the Hostage Taking Statute, codified at 18 U.S.C. § 1203, asserts jurisdiction on the basis of the victim's U.S. nationality.

Passive personality jurisdiction is expressly permitted under several international treaties and conventions, including the 1973 Convention on the Prevention and Punishment of Crimes Against Internationally Protected Persons, Including

Diplomatic Agents, 1035 U.N.T.S. 167, 13 I.L.M. 42 (1974); the 1984 UN Torture Convention, 1465 U.N.T.S. 85; the 1988 UN Convention for the Suppression of Unlawful Acts Against the Safety of Maritime Navigation, 1678 U.N.T.S. 221; and the 1979 International Convention against the Taking of Hostages, 1316 U.N.T.S. 205.

See generally Watson, "The Passive Personality Principle," 28 Texas Int'l L. J. 1 (1993).

4. *Protective Jurisdiction*

The protective principle permits the exercise of jurisdiction over a narrow range of conduct that threatens the most vital interests of the State in question. State sovereignty is the basis for the protective principle. The underlying idea is that all States are entitled to exercise jurisdiction over acts which threaten their security, integrity or core governmental interests.

The Restatement (Third), *Foreign Relations Law of the United States* § 402(3) provides that "a state has jurisdiction to prescribe law with respect to . . . (3) certain conduct outside its territory by persons not its nationals that is directed against the security of the state or against a limited class of other state interests." Commonly-cited examples include espionage, counterfeiting the State's currency or official seal, falsification of official documents, perjury before consular officials, and conspiracy to violate the immigration or customs laws. *See*, *e.g.*, *United States v. Zehe*, 601 F. Supp. 196 (D. Mass. 1985), and 18 U.S.C. §§ 792–799 (involving acts of espionage, including providing sensitive information to hostile forces, with no reference to the *locus* of the crime or nationality of the perpetrator).

The exercise of protective jurisdiction need not be justified by actual or intended effects within the State's territory but must involve a genuine threat to vital State interests. These interests are not implicated by mere violation of criminal laws. *See, e.g., United States v. Pizzarusso*, 388 F.2d 8 (2d Cir.), cert. denied 88 S.Ct. 2306 (1968), which only involved visa fraud (lying under oath to a consular officer in the course of a visa application to enter the United States).

Perhaps the most famous and controversial instance of the exercise of protective jurisdiction was the trial of Adolf Eichmann in Israel, in 1961. Eichmann was prosecuted and convicted in an Israeli court for crimes relating to the Holocaust during the Second World War. The alleged crimes were neither committed on Israeli territory, nor targeted at Israeli citizens, nor even directed at Israel, given that the State of Israel came into existence after the Second World War. Nonetheless, the Israeli courts exercised jurisdiction by invoking the protective principle and referring to the interests of the Jewish 'people' which were correlated to the Jewish State. See *Attorney-Gen. of Israel v. Eichmann*, 361 I.L.R. 277 (Dist. Ct. 1968).

5. *Universal Jurisdiction*

The "universality principle" permits any State to prosecute the perpetrators of a small class of the most serious violations of international law (*delicta juris gentium*) regardless of the nationality of the perpetrator or the victim, the place of commission, or any other connection to that particular State. Unlike the other principles discussed above, "universal jurisdiction" is not justified by the interests of particular States in prosecuting certain crimes. It is instead based on the idea that certain international crimes are so heinous that they affect the international legal order as a whole, that the perpetrators are therefore enemies of all mankind (*hostes humani generis*), and that accordingly, all members of the international community have the right (perhaps even the obligation) to bring those individuals to justice.

This begs the question of which specific crimes fall into this select category. Universal jurisdiction is, in theory, a matter of customary international law; no existing convention or treaty defines its scope. The earliest examples of crimes attracting universal jurisdiction were piracy and slave trading. Today, most lawyers and advocates might agree that the list also ought to include genocide, crimes against humanity, and torture.

The Restatement (Third), *Foreign Relations Law of the United States*, § 404 takes a somewhat broader view: "A state has jurisdiction to define and prescribe punishment for certain offenses recognized by the community of nations as of universal concern, such as piracy, slave trade, attacks on or hijacking of aircraft, genocide, war crimes, and perhaps certain acts of terrorism, even where none of the bases of jurisdiction indicated in § 402 is present." However, the "community of nations" has not yet specified which offenses meet that criterion. In point of fact, there are only two clear examples of treaties specifically recognizing universal jurisdiction—piracy (under art. 105 of the 1982 UN Convention on the Law of the Sea) and certain war crimes (under the grave breaches provisions of the 1949 Geneva Conventions).

Some contend that any crime of a peremptory nature (for example, any violation of a *jus cogens* norm) necessarily justifies the exercise of universal jurisdiction and can be prosecuted by any member of the international community. *See, e.g., R. v. Bow St. Metro. Stipendiary Magistrate and Others ex parte Pinochet Ugarte (No. 3)*, [2000] 1 A.C. 147 (H.L.) (Eng.).

In the case of *Jones v. Saudi Arabia*, however, Lord Bingham took the contrary view, that no principle exists whereby States recognize an international obligation to exercise universal jurisdiction over crimes arising from breaches of peremptory norms, nor is there any judicial opinion at they should. *See Jones v. Ministry of the Interior of Saudi Arabia*, [2006] UKHL 26, per Lord Bingham, para. 27.

Universal criminal jurisdiction, while acknowledged in theory, today remains controversial in practice. For instance, in 1999 Belgium introduced legislation which allowed any person to initiate criminal proceedings against any other person, regardless of their nationality, domicile or location, for grave breaches of international law. The presence of the suspect in Belgium was not required for the initiation of proceedings.

§ 3–4   QUESTIONS ABOUT UNIVERSAL JURISDICTION

Universal jurisdiction poses a number of theoretical and practical questions. Is universal jurisdiction incompatible with sovereignty because it permits States with no connections to the crime, the offender, or the victim, to prosecute without regard to interests of other States with clearer interest? Or is it an important, even essential method for ensuring that those who commit the most grievous offenses under international law do not go unpunished because of the inability of the territorial State, or the State of nationality, to bring the offenders to justice?

Do States have an obligation to prosecute violations of peremptory norms? Must they have custody of the alleged offender or may they prosecute *in absentia*? Can multiple States pursue prosecutions of the same crimes simultaneously or sequentially? Are other (non-prosecuting) States obliged to cooperate, for example by providing evidence or enforcing judgments? Does the possibility of unilateral assertions of universal jurisdiction favor powerful States with the means, methods and political will to pursue particular individuals for committing particular crimes which those States find objectionable?

The International Court of Justice had occasion to consider the issues of universal jurisdiction in the so-called "Arrest Warrant Case" (Case Concerning the Arrest Warrant of 11 Apr. 2000 (*Democratic Republic of the Congo v. Belgium*), Judgment, 2002 I.C.J. Rep. 3, 41 I.L.M. 536, 560 (2002)).

The views of the members of the Court differed. In a joint separate opinion, Judges Higgins, Kooijmans, and Buergenthal noted that while no established practice of exercising universal jurisdiction exists today (since virtually all national legislation envisages some sort of link to the prosecuting State), that does not mean such an exercise would be unlawful, and in fact, they saw a trend in favor of universality. Moreover, in their view, a State could choose to exercise universal criminal jurisdiction *in absentia* as long as sufficient safeguards were in place to prevent abuse and "to ensure that the rejection of impunity does not jeopardize stable relations between States."

Judge *ad hoc* Van den Wyngaert (in a dissenting opinion) agreed that no prohibition existed under international law to enacting legislation to allow a State to investigate and prosecute war crimes and crimes against humanity abroad, no matter who had committed them. No rule of conventional or customary international law, Judge Van den Wyngaert said, prohibits universal jurisdiction *in absentia*. In her view, jurisdictional limitations lie at "the core of the problem of impunity" in the sense that where the relevant national authorities are not willing or able to investigate or prosecute, the crime goes unpunished.

The President of the Court, Judge Guillaume, took a different approach. In his view, only one true case of universal jurisdiction exists: piracy. In classic international law, States normally have jurisdiction in respect of extraterritorial offenses only if the offender, or at least the victim, is of their nationality, or if the crime threatens their internal or external security. While some international courts have been created to prosecute particularly heinous crimes, the international community has never "envisaged that jurisdiction should be conferred upon the courts of every State in the world to prosecute such crimes, whoever their authors and victims and irrespective of the place where the offender is to be found." Doing so would, in his view, "risk creating total judicial chaos." It would also "encourage the arbitrary for the benefit of the powerful, purportedly acting as agents for an ill-defined 'international community.' " Such a development, he said, "would represent not an advance in the law but a step backward." Para. 15.

§ 3–5   EXTRADITE OR PROSECUTE

Judge Guillaume made a useful distinction between (i) true universal jurisdiction (in the sense described above) and (ii) a contingent form of jurisdiction based on the "extradite or prosecute" provisions found in many modern international criminal law treaties. He called this "subsidiary universal jurisdiction."

Most multilateral conventions dealing with international crimes contain a special clause, which obligates the apprehending country either to prosecute or to extradite individuals who are suspected of having committed the proscribed offenses. Technically, these are known as *aut dedere aut judicare* clauses. For instance, art. 4(1) of the Hague Convention for the Suppression of Unlawful Seizure of Aircraft requires States Parties to take such measures as may be necessary to establish jurisdiction over these offenses where the offender is present in its territory and it does not extradite him or her. To the same effect, art. 5 of the 1984 UN Torture Convention obligates each State Party to take such measures as may be necessary to establish its domestic jurisdiction "over such offences in cases where the alleged offender is present in any territory under its jurisdiction and it does not extradite him."

The *aut dedere aut judicare* principle is, itself, subject to the conventional and customary limitations attached to extradition and also allows the apprehending State the discretion to extradite and to choose between competing extradition requests.

The difference between pure universal jurisdiction and "extradite or prosecute" jurisdiction is that the former is said to apply to all States as a matter of customary international law and to impose an obligation to prosecute (under domestic law) alleged perpetrators of an as-yet-undefined category of international crimes regardless of their contacts with the State in question. By contrast, the latter applies only to the crime specified in the treaty in question, and to the States Parties to that treaty, and is conditional on their having apprehended the individual in question and, for some reason, declined to extradite him to another State with a traditional jurisdictional claim.

§ 3–6   THE JURISDICTION OF INTERNATIONAL COURTS

A distinction must also be made between (i) the extraterritorial jurisdiction exercised by the domestic authorities of particular States under any of the theories described above and (ii) the "international" jurisdiction exercised by international courts or tribunals. In the latter instance, the international community has conferred a specific jurisdictional grant on an international court by some affirmative act (for example, through a treaty or UN Security Council decision). The court or tribunal in question is therefore exercising a very different form of jurisdictional authority, as to which it would make no sense to require the link of territoriality or nationality or another sovereign interest.

For example, the Rome Statute gives the International Criminal Court jurisdiction over a limited set of crimes committed after a specific date, on the territory of, or by a national of, a State Party to the Statute. This jurisdictional grant is further circumscribed by several "admissibility" criteria. *See* Chapter 5 *infra*. The jurisdictional competence of the various other international tribunals is limited substantively, temporally and procedurally. To date, none of the international courts and tribunals has been vested with anything like true "universal" competence.

§ 3–7   ARE THERE ANY LIMITATIONS?

As noted above, the various bases of jurisdiction recognized by customary international law are permissive and in practice can lead to competing claims of competence, but no rule of customary international law currently exists about resolving those competing claims or giving priority to one over the other.

In U.S. law, no constitutional prohibition prevents the extraterritorial application of U.S. criminal law. Of course, Congress must have constitutional authority to adopt the provision in question. Typically that means the authority to regulate interstate or foreign commerce or to "define and punish Piracies and Felonies committed on the high seas, and Offences against the Law of Nations" in article I, § 8. *See generally* Charles Doyle, Extraterritorial Application of American Criminal Law, Cong. Research Serv. Report RS22497 (Feb. 12, 2012). However, several important doctrines are frequently applied by U.S. courts in respect of extraterritorial criminal jurisdiction.

1. *Charming Betsy Canon*

In U.S. law, a longstanding canon of statutory interpretation states that "an act of Congress ought never to be construed to violate the law of nations if any other possible construction remains." *Murray v.*

Schooner Charming Betsy, 6 U.S. (2 Cranch) 64 (1804); *McCulloch v. Sociedad Nacional de Marineros de Honduras*. 372 U.S. 10, 21 (1963); *cf.* Restatement (Third), *Foreign Relations Law of the United States* § 114: "[W]here fairly possible, a United States statute is to be construed so as not to conflict with international law or with an international agreement of the United States." The rule is based on a presumption that Congress knows, and does not intend to violate, applicable principles of international law. *Cf. United States v. Vasquez-Velasco*, 15 F.3d 833, 839 (9th Cir. 1994).

2. Presumption Against Extraterritoriality

Another long-standing common law presumption in U.S. law is that, unless specifically stated, the Congress does not intend a statute to apply to conduct outside the territorial jurisdiction of the United States. To overcome this presumption, there must be "affirmative evidence of intended extraterritorial application." *Sale v. Haitian Ctrs. Council, Inc.*, 509 U.S. 155, 176 (1993). In the first instance, the issue is what the relevant statute actually says.

However, this presumption does not apply to those particular criminal statutes "which are, as a class, not logically dependent on their locality for the Government's jurisdiction." *United States v. Bowman*, 260 U.S. 94, 98 (1922). In those circumstances, the Supreme Court said that Congress can be presumed to intend the extraterritorial application of criminal statutes which are "as a class, not logically dependent on their locality for the government's jurisdiction, but are enacted because of the right of the government to defend itself against obstruction, or fraud wherever perpetrated, especially if committed by its own citizens, officers, or agents." In such instances, "to limit their locus to the strictly territorial jurisdiction would be greatly to curtail the scope and usefulness of the statute and leave open a large immunity for frauds as easily committed by citizens on the high seas and in foreign countries as at home." *Id.*

Some courts have applied the *Bowman* analysis even when the alleged perpetrator of the crime was a foreign national abroad. *See, e.g., United States v. Pizzarusso*, 388 F.2d 8 (2d Cir. 1968); *United States v. Layton*, 855 F.2d 1388 (9th Cir. 1988).

3. *Reasonableness*

In the United States, some courts have identified a "reasonableness" criterion to the exercise of extraterritorial jurisdiction. See, for example, *United States v. Clark*, 315 F. Supp. 2d 1127 (W.D. Wash. 2004) (even if principles of international law serve as bases for extraterritorial application of a law, international law also requires that such application of the law must be reasonable).

To the same effect, the Restatement (Third), *Foreign Relations Law of the United States* § 403 states clearly that "[e]ven when one of the bases for jurisdiction under § 402 is present, a State may not exercise jurisdiction to prescribe law with respect to a person or activity having connections with another State when the exercise of such jurisdiction is unreasonable. The reasonableness criterion is also applied under 412 to the exercise of jurisdiction to adjudicate." That section articulates criteria for evaluating reasonableness, including *inter alia* the existence of justified expectations that might be protected or hurt by the regulation, the importance of the regulation to the international political, legal, or economic system, the extent to which the regulation is consistent with the traditions of the international system, the extent to which another State may have an interest in regulating the activity, and the likelihood of conflict with regulation by another State.

§ 3–8   INTERNATIONAL IMMUNITIES

In specific cases, domestic prosecutions of foreign governmental officials may be precluded by the application of internationally-recognized doctrines of immunity. For example, as a matter of long-standing customary international law, current (sitting) Heads of State or Government are afforded absolute immunity from the civil and criminal jurisdiction of foreign courts. Some senior officials representing a foreign State, such as foreign ministers, may also benefit from this rule. *See* the ICJ's decision in the *Belgian Arrest Warrant Case*, Judgment of 14 February 2002, paras. 47–55.

By comparison, former Heads of State and Government have traditionally been entitled to a more limited form of immunity for actions taken within the scope of their official duties, but some controversy over this rule has arisen in respect of certain international crimes. See, for example, *Regina v. Bartle and the Comm'n of Police for the Metropolis and Others, ex parte Pinochet*, [2000] 1 A.C. 119 (H.L.); *al-Adsani v. United Kingdom*, App. No. 3576/97, 34 Eur. H.R. Rep. 11 (2002) (paras. 55–66).

As a matter of treaty law, ambassadors and other diplomatic representatives who have been duly accredited to the forum State are entitled to broad immunities under the Vienna Convention on Diplomatic Relations (art. 39(2)). Consular officers may be entitled to protection under the Vienna Convention on Consular Relations. In specific circumstances, immunities may also extend to foreign officials on "special missions" and to senior officials of international organizations (such as the United Nations, the OAS, the World Bank, etc.) as well as to representatives from Member States of those organizations.

When it comes to international criminal tribunals, however, the rules are different. Generally speaking, no immunity is accorded to either sitting or former Heads of State or government or other governmental officials by virtue of their official positions. *See*, for example, art. 7 of the London Charter, and arts. 7(2) and 6(2) of the Statutes of the ICTY and ICTR respectively. Article 27(2) of the Rome Statute provides that "[i]mmunities or special procedural rules which may attach to the official capacity of a person, whether under national or international law, shall not bar the Court from exercising its jurisdiction over such a person."

III. BASIC PRINCIPLES

The following provides a preliminary overview of the most important basic principles on which international criminal law is founded.

§ 3–9   INDIVIDUAL CRIMINAL RESPONSIBILITY

The most fundamental principle is *individual criminal responsibility*—the idea that an individual who commits a crime under international law is personally responsible for that act and is liable to trial and punishment directly under international law, including by an international court or tribunal.

The Judgment of the Nuremberg Tribunal stated that "crimes against international law are committed by men, not by abstract entities, and only by punishing individuals who commit such crimes can the provisions of international law be enforced." Office of Chief of Counsel for Prosecution of Axis Crimes, Nazi Conspiracy and Aggression: Final Opinion and Judgment of the International Military Tribunal, at 53 (1947).

This principle was articulated in the 1945 London Charter, applied in the Nuremberg and Tokyo war crimes tribunals, and adopted by the International Law Commission as Principle I: "Any person who commits an act which constitutes a crime under international law is responsible therefor and liable to punishment." *See* ILC's *Principles of International Law Recognized in the Charter of the Nürnberg Tribunal and in the Judgment of the Tribunal,* 1950 Y.B. Int'l Law Comm., vol. II, para. 97.

Individual criminal responsibility extends not just to the commission of proscribed acts, but also various inchoate crimes including their planning, instigation, ordering, aiding and abetting and preparation. These are discussed *infra* in Chapter 6, part II.

§ 3–10   NOTE ON CRIMINAL LIABILITY OF ORGANIZATIONS

The direct responsibility of individuals for international crimes is well-established. Much more controversial, and much less clear, is the proposition that organizations and other "legal persons" (such as political parties and corporations) can commit international crimes, or that membership in such organizations can be declared criminal.

Article 9 of the 1945 London Charter permitted the trial of any individual member of any group or organization that the tribunal might declare a "criminal organization." Some organizations were in fact named as criminal by the IMT, including the SS and the Leadership Corps of the Nazi Party. Similarly, Allied Control Council Law No. 10 provided that organizations (and membership in such organizations) could be declared criminal. However, in neither case was membership alone sufficient to hold individuals responsible for the acts of the organization. Individuals having no knowledge of the criminal purposes or acts of the organization could not be convicted without some measure of proof that they were personally implicated in the criminal acts themselves. In point of fact, no international criminal tribunal after the International Military Tribunal has exercised jurisdiction over legal persons, nor is the notion of corporate criminal liability universally recognized.

§ 3–11   NOTE ON STATE RESPONSIBILITY

It is commonly accepted that States cannot subjected to criminal liability. The "State" (like the "Government") is a legal fiction that does not act apart from the individuals who constitute it. It cannot be imprisoned, and while it can be punished in some ways (for example, through monetary fines or other sanctions), doing so is often seen as simply shifting the consequences of illegal conduct from the responsible individuals to the organizational entity.

Saying that States cannot commit crimes is certainly not the same thing as saying that States have no obligations to prevent and refrain from acts which constitute international crimes or to make reparations in particular cases. Clearly, all States have a responsibility not to engage in international criminal acts. States may incur responsibility for breaching international law norms, and this responsibility may result in liability to pay damages, reparations or other compensation. For instance, in the Genocide Convention case, the ICJ considered the Srebrenica massacre and found that although Serbia was neither responsible nor liable for the particular circumstances of that case, States could indeed be responsible for not preventing genocide. *See* Case Concerning the Application of the Convention on the Prevention and Punishment of the Crime of Genocide (*Bosnia and Herzegovina v. Serbia and Montenegro*), ICJ Judgment (Feb. 26, 2007).

The responsibility of States may also extend to acts of individuals or groups acting under its instructions or control, or whose actions are attributable to it. *See* the International Law Commission's Draft Articles on the Responsibility of States for Internationally Wrongful Acts, arts. 4–11 (completed in 2001). *See generally,* Alain Pellet, *Can a State Commit a Crime? Definitely, Yes!,* 10 Eur. J. Int'l L. 425 (1999).

§ 3–12   LEGALITY

Under the principle of "legality," individuals may not be prosecuted for conduct that was not unlawful at the time it was committed. Nor should they be held liable for an act which they did not know, or could not reasonably have been expected to know, was in fact prohibited. The principle is premised on the ideas of non-retroactivity and fair notice.

Put differently, a criminal prosecution must be based on the alleged violation of a legal norm that existed at the time of the offense, was accessible to the accused, and was clear enough to make the possibility of prosecution and punishment foreseeable. Some scholars consider that the principle of legality also requires a sufficient indication of the applicable penalties.

The general principle of legality was recognized long ago by the Permanent Court of International Justice in its *Advisory Opinion on Consistency of Certain Danzig Legislative Decrees with Constitution of Free City*, 1935 P.C.I.J. (ser. A/B) No. 65 (Dec. 4).

Today, the principle is reflected in most international human rights instruments, including the International Covenant on Civil and Political Rights (art. 15), the European Convention of Human Rights (art. 7), the Charter of Fundamental Rights of the European Union (art. 49), and the African Convention on Human and Peoples' Rights (art. 9).

The proscription against non-retroactivity in criminal matters is frequently referred to by two separate Latin maxims: *nullem crimen sine lege* (no crime outside the law) and *nulla poena sine lege* (no punishment outside the law). The first is incorporated in article 22(1) of the Rome Statute, which states: "A person shall not be criminally responsible under this Statute unless the conduct in question constitutes, at the time it takes place, a crime within the jurisdiction of the Court." The second is reflected in article 23: "A person convicted by the Court may be punished only in accordance with this Statute."

Nulla poena sine lege is properly understood to preclude punishment "outside the law" as well as the retroactive application of more severe penalties than would have been applicable at the time when the criminal offense was committed. Thus, if the law is changed *after* the offense has been committed to provide a lighter penalty, the offender is entitled to benefit from that change. This is expressed in article 24(2) of the Rome Statute: "In the event of a change in the law applicable to a given case prior to a final judgment, the law more favourable to the person being investigated, prosecuted or convicted shall apply."

In this application, it is similar to the *"rule of lenity"* found in some common law systems (including the United States). That rule provides that when ambiguity in a criminal statute cannot be clarified by either its legislative history or inferences drawn from the overall statutory scheme, the ambiguity is resolved in favor of the defendant. See, e.g., *United States v. Flemming*, 677 F.3d 252 (3d Cir. 2010). The rule covers criminal prohibitions as well as penalties.

An exception to the principle of legality is generally recognized with regard to the most serious international crimes, such as genocide, crimes against humanity, and grave breaches of international humanitarian law. Since these crimes have been universally condemned by the international community as violations of customary international law, it is implausible to allow an accused to escape responsibility by arguing that at the time of the acts were committed they had not been specifically forbidden by an applicable statute, treaty or convention. *See, e.g., United States v.*

Altstötter et al. (Justice Case), 3–4 December 1947, III Trials of War Criminals Before the Nuremberg Military Tribunals Under Control Council Law No. 10, 1946–1949 at 975.

As Canadian Supreme Court Justice Cory stated in the *Finta* case, "war crimes or crimes against humanity are so repulsive, so reprehensible, and so well understood that it simply cannot be argued that the definition of crimes against humanity and war crimes are vague or uncertain. . . . These crimes, which violate fundamental human values, are vehemently condemned by the citizens of all civilized nations." *See R. v. Finta*, [1994] 1 S.C.R. 701 (Can.).

The International Covenant on Civil and Political Rights recognizes, in article 15(1), the general rule against *ex post facto* criminal law: "no one shall be held guilty of any criminal offence on account of any act or omissions which did not constitute a criminal offence, under national or international law, at the time when it was committed." It also states, in article 15(2), that "[n]othing in this article shall prejudice the trial and punishment of any person for any act or omission which, at the time when it was committed, was criminal according to the general principles of law recognized by the community of nations."

These provisions, and similar language in the European Convention on Human Rights and Fundamental Freedoms, were relied on by the French Cour de Cassation in the *Barbie* case in finding that crimes against humanity are exempted from the principle of legality as formulated in French law. *See* Court de Cassation [Cass.] [Supreme Court for judicial matters] crim., Jan. 26, 1984, Bull. Crim., No. 34 (Fr.) (Barbie No. 2), *see* English text at 78 I.L.R. 132–136).

The invocation of the heinous nature of crimes under international law to justify prosecution and punishment notwithstanding the absence of explicit statutory prohibition at the time of commission is manifest in many principles of international criminal law. It forms part of the justification for the denial of the 'superior orders' defense as discussed above. It formed part of the justification for the denial of Head of State immunity to General Augusto Pinochet by the U.K. House of Lords, on the grounds that the commission of crimes against humanity and torture could not reasonably form a part of the functions of a Head of State. *See R. v. Bow St. Metro. Stipendiary Magistrate and Others ex parte Pinochet Ugarte (No. 3)*, [2000] 1 A.C. 147 (H.L.) (Eng.) (In Re: Pinochet, Opinion of the Lords of Appeal for Judgment in the Cause).

§ 3–13   NON BIS IN IDEM

International criminal law recognizes the principle that no one should be tried or punished more than once for the same offense. This principle (comparable to the principle of double jeopardy) is often expressed as *non bis in idem*. It is rooted in the concepts of fundamental fairness and finality, and finds expression in the major human rights treaties.

It would be misleading, however, to think of *non bis in idem* as constituting a sweeping doctrine prohibiting double jeopardy. As a matter of international law, it applies only to prosecutions within the same legal system. For example, article 14(7) of the ICCPR provides that "[n]o one shall be liable to be tried or punished again for an offence for which he has already been finally convicted or *acquitted in accordance with the law and penal procedure of each country*" (emphasis added). *See also* art. 4 of Protocol 7 to the European Convention on Human Rights and Fundamental Freedoms. It would not be a violation of this doctrine for one State to bring a prosecution against an individual who had been acquitted of the same crime in another State.

The rule has a specific application when applied to international criminal tribunals, because their jurisdiction overlaps that of domestic courts. Reflecting the primacy of their jurisdiction, for example, the statutes of the ICTY and ICTR provide that no one may be tried for the same conduct after he or she has been prosecuted *at the Tribunal*, but a prior prosecution in a national court does not necessarily prevent the Tribunals from undertaking their own prosecution. *See* art. 10 of the ICTY Statute and art. 9 of the ICTR Statute. Thus, national courts cannot prosecute someone who has already been prosecuted in the *ad hoc* tribunals, but the tribunals are not prevented from bringing a second prosecution of someone previously tried in a domestic court. A comparable rule is in articles 8 and 9 of the Statute for the Special Court of Sierra Leone.

The Rome Statute, in art. 20(1), says that "[e]xcept as provided in this Statute, no person shall be tried before the Court with respect to conduct which formed the basis of crimes for which the person has been convicted or acquitted by the Court." In art. 20(2), the Statute provides that "[n]o person shall be tried by another court for a *crime* referred to in article 5 for which that person has already been convicted or acquitted by the Court."

Article 20(3) states that no person who has already been tried by another court for *conduct* falling within the scope of articles 6, 7 or 8 (genocide, crimes against humanity or war crimes) shall be tried by the Court with respect to the same conduct *unless* the proceedings in the other court were (i) "for the purpose of shielding the person concerned from criminal responsibility for crimes within the jurisdiction of the Court" or (ii) "were not conducted independently or impartially in accordance with the norms of due process recognized by international law and were conducted in a manner which, in the circumstances, was inconsistent with an intent to bring the person concerned to justice."

§ 3–14   COMMAND OR SUPERIOR RESPONSIBILITY

A basic tenet of the laws of war, now incorporated into international criminal law, allows the imposition of liability upon a commander (superior officer) for the most serious wrongful acts of his or her subordinates, when he or she ordered those acts to be performed or failed to prevent them from occurring. The commander of course has a duty to refrain himself (or herself) from committing those acts, and from ordering others to commit them, but in addition is required to take whatever action is necessary to prevent people under his or her authority from committing them. This rule was articulated most famously during the Tokyo Trials in the case against Japanese Army General Yamashita.

The ICTY and ICTR have expanded this principle beyond the narrow confines of a military organization. Both have held that civilians may be recognized as superiors for the purposes of command responsibility. *See Prosecutor v. Karemera et al.*, ICTR 98–44–T, Decision on Motions for Judgment of Acquittal, (Mar. 19, 2008) para. 15; *Prosecutor v. Bagilishema*, ICTR 95–1A–A, Judgment, (July 3, 2002), para. 85; *Prosecutor v. Delalić*, IT–96–21–A, Judgment, (Feb. 20, 2001) paras. 195–6; *Prosecutor v. Prlić et al.*, IT–04–74–PT, Decision to Dismiss the Preliminary Objections Against the Tribunal's Jurisdiction, (Sept. 26, 2005) para. 19.

The rule is effectively codified in article 28(1)(a) of the Rome Statute. It states that "[a] military commander or person effectively acting as a military commander shall be criminally responsible for crimes within the jurisdiction of the Court committed by forces under his or her effective command and control, or effective authority and control as the case may be, as a result of his or her failure to exercise control properly over such forces, where: (i) that military commander or person either knew or, owing to the circumstances at the time, should have known that the forces were committing or about to commit such crimes; and (ii) that military commander or person failed to take all necessary and reasonable measures within his or her power to prevent or repress their commission or to submit the matter to the competent authorities for investigation and prosecution."

Article 28(1)(b) states that, "with respect to superior and subordinate relationships not described in paragraph (a), a superior shall be criminally responsible for crimes within the jurisdiction of the Court committed by subordinates under his or her effective authority and control, as a result of his or her failure to exercise control properly over such subordinates, where: (i) The superior either knew, or consciously disregarded information which clearly indicated, that the subordinates were committing or about to commit such crimes; (ii) The crimes concerned activities that were within the effective responsibility and control of the superior; and (iii) The superior failed to take all necessary and reasonable measures within his or her power to prevent or repress their commission or to submit the matter to the competent authorities for investigation and prosecution."

As is evident from the text of art. 28(1), the primary requirement for invocation of command responsibility is the requirement of *effective control*.

See Prosecutor v. Halilović, IT–01–48–A, Judgment, (Oct. 16, 2007) para. 59; *Prosecutor v. Ntagerura et al*, ICTR 99–46–A, Judgment, (July 7, 2006) para. 342.

§ 3–15   NO DEFENSE UNDER DOMESTIC LAW

An individual is still liable for committing an act which is a crime under international law even though that act might be required, permitted, or not prohibited, under the applicable domestic law. Thus, it is no defense to a charge of genocide that the acts constituting that crime were not illegal under the internal law of the country where they took place. That national law does not impose a penalty for an act which constitutes a crime under international law does not relieve the person who committed the act from responsibility under international law.

§ 3–16   NO OFFICIAL POSITION IMMUNITY

The fact that the accused acted as "Head of State" or "Head of Government" (such as a king, president or prime minister) does not shield that person from individual criminal responsibility for the most serious crimes under international law. The same is true for government officials of lesser rank, who sometimes claim they were only acting in a governmental capacity. As stated in article 7 of the London Charter, "[t]he official position of defendants, whether as Heads of State or responsible officials in Government Departments, shall not be considered as freeing them from responsibility or mitigating punishment."

Article 27(1) of the Rome Statute repeats this basic rule by stating that "official capacity as a Head of State or Government, a member of a Government or parliament, an elected representative or a government official shall in no case exempt a person from criminal responsibility under this Statute, nor shall it, in and of itself, constitute a ground for reduction of sentence." Article 27(2) provides that "[i]mmunities or special procedural rules which may attach to the official capacity of a person, whether under national or international law, shall not bar the Court from exercising its jurisdiction over such a person.

Art. 7(2) of the Statute of the ICTY and art. 6(2) of the Statute of the ICTR lay down rules to similar effect.

§ 3–17 NO SUPERIOR ORDERS DEFENSE

An individual cannot avoid personal responsibility for a crime under international law on the basis that he or she was merely carrying out the orders of a superior or the laws and policies of his or her government. This principle was also recognized and endorsed at the Nuremberg and Tokyo Tribunals, and has been reinforced by more recent decisions of the *ad hoc* tribunals. It is no defense to the charge of an international crime that the accused acted pursuant to an order of his government or of a superior official, whether or not that order was lawful. However, mitigation of punishment is possible in some cases where the individual did not know, or could not reasonably be expected to know, that the order in question was unlawful, or had no viable alternative to compliance.

Denial of "superior orders" as a defense to individual criminal responsibility explores a gray moral area. Crimes under international law are often committed by individuals acting in their capacity as members of military organizations or militias. In that context, refusal to obey an order can be construed as a breach of military discipline and can result in severe punishment, including execution, for disobeying the orders of a superior. At the same time carrying out the order will implicate the individual in the commission of a heinous crime. Denying the 'superior orders' defense requires individuals in these circumstances to refuse to participate in the commission of heinous crimes at the risk of their own lives and well-being. This may be defended morally, but in some situations it can be difficult to justify it legally.

Recognizing the burden that denial of this defense can create, the statutes of the ICTY (art. 7(4)) and ICTR (art. 6(4)) allow for the fact that the accused was acting pursuant to superior orders to be taken into account "in mitigation of punishment if . . . justice so requires." As stated in article 33(1) of the Rome Statute, "[t]he fact that a crime within the jurisdiction of the Court has been committed by a person pursuant to an order of a Government or of a superior, whether military or civilian, shall not relieve that person of criminal responsibility unless: (a) The person was under a legal obligation to obey orders of the Government or the superior in question; (b) The person did not know that the order was unlawful; and (c) The order was not manifestly unlawful."

§ 3–18 FAIR TRIAL AND HUMAN RIGHTS

One of the most important consequences of the emergence of new international criminal tribunals has been the articulation of normative principles and protective processes to govern the actual conduct of prosecutions under international law. To a considerable extent, the protections now set forth in the statutes and rules of procedure and evidence of the various tribunals reflect the direct application of well-established principles of international human rights law.

Whether or not these various rules and procedures constitute customary international law is debated. Some contend that because they have been accepted and implemented by the international community, they do constitute a new body of customary international law applicable to criminal proceedings in all courts and tribunals, both international and domestic. Others respond that the rules, practices, and even decisions of a given tribunal do not qualify as customary international law since they do not reflect state practice. Still others suggest that the most basic rules were general principles of law recognized by civilized nations and are therefore properly applicable in any court or tribunal.

Whatever one's views on this issue are, international human rights law has clearly had a profound effect on expectations of fair trial procedures at the international level. The rules may vary in their details between courts, and they continue to evolve through the decisional law of the tribunals themselves. Still, one can identify a set of essential principles that inform this emergent body of law and practice. For ease of reference, we can look in the first instance to the Rome Statute. Some of the more significant provisions are summarized below. (Some of these provisions are also reflected in art. 21 of the ICTY Statute and art. 20 of the ICTR Statute).

1. *Investigative Stage*

Article 55(a) of the Rome Statute acknowledges that at the investigative stage, a person cannot be compelled to incriminate himself or herself or to confess guilt, or subjected to any form of coercion, duress or threat, torture, or any other form of cruel, inhuman or degrading treatment or punishment. Where necessary, he or she is entitled to the assistance of a competent interpreter and such translations as are necessary to meet the requirements of fairness. Importantly, he or she shall "not be subjected to arbitrary arrest or detention" or "deprived of his or her liberty except on such grounds and in accordance with such procedures as are established in this Statute."

Where there are grounds to believe that a person has committed a crime within the Court's jurisdiction and that person is about to be questioned, he or she is entitled, under article 55(b), to be informed that there are grounds to believe that he or she has committed such a crime, to remain silent (without such silence being a consideration in the determination of guilt or innocence), to have legal assistance of his or her own choosing, and to be questioned in the presence of counsel unless the person has voluntarily waived his or her right to counsel.

2. At Trial

Under article 63, the presence of the accused is required during the trial. However, if the accused "continues to disrupt the trial," the Trial Chamber can remove him or her and arrange for him or her to observe the trial and instruct counsel from outside the courtroom.

Article 66 states clearly that "[e]veryone shall be presumed innocent until proved guilty before the Court in accordance with the applicable law." It also states that the onus is on the Prosecutor to prove the guilt of the accused and that, "[i]n order to convict the accused, the Court must be convinced of the guilt of the accused beyond reasonable doubt."

Article 67 guarantees the right to a public hearing, to "a fair hearing conducted impartially," to be informed promptly and in detail of the nature, cause and content of the charge, in a language which the accused fully understands and speaks, to adequate time and facilities for the preparation of the defense and to communicate freely with counsel of the accused's choosing in confidence, and to be tried without undue delay.

The accused is also entitled to examine, or have examined, the witnesses against him or her and to obtain the attendance and examination of witnesses on his or her behalf under the same conditions as witnesses against him or her. (This is similar to, but not precisely the same, as the "right of confrontation" afforded defendants under the U.S. Constitution.) In addition, the Prosecutor is required to disclose to the defense ("as soon as practicable") any evidence in the Prosecutor's possession or control which he or she believes "shows or tends to show the innocence of the accused, or to mitigate the guilt of the accused, or which may affect the credibility of prosecution evidence."

None of these courts allows for application of the death penalty. *See* art. 77, Rome Statute; art. 101, ICTY Rules of Procedure and Evidence; art. 101, ICTR Rules of Procedure and Evidence.

IV. NOTE ON COMPARATIVE CRIMINAL PROCEDURE

The student of international criminal law needs to avoid the assumption that foreign judicial systems work like the domestic systems he or she is most familiar with. Different legal systems provide different judicial structures, pathways, and procedures for different types of criminal prosecutions. For example, single trial courts (combining civil and criminal jurisdiction) such as those found in the United States are rare. Instead, criminal courts may be entirely separate from the civil, commercial, or labor courts. Moreover, legal systems are constantly evolving as a result of both internal and external developments. In fact, the existence of the International Criminal Court has had a direct impact on a number of domestic criminal law systems.

Many scholars tend to classify contemporary legal systems into five or six broad categories. A distinction is often made between those following the "common law" tradition (e.g., the United States, the United Kingdom, and most of the former Commonwealth countries), and those in the "civil law" tradition (e.g., most of Western Europe and Central and South America). Common law systems are characterized by doctrines of separation of powers, the independence of the judiciary, the principle of judicial review, and the prominence of judge-made law (including *stare decisis* or judicial precedent). By distinction, civil law systems are frequently described as based on a more unitary (or even bureaucratic) view of legal authority, resting primarily on comprehensive legal codes reflecting the will of the legislators and permitting for relatively circumscribed roles for the courts.

For most of the twentieth century, one could also identify a "socialist law" tradition, for example in the former Soviet Union and much of Eastern Europe, which combined features of a code-based system, a judiciary with a sharply limited scope, and a system of political supervision ensuring decisional fidelity to the governing principles of Marxism-Leninism. Islamic States and peoples generally follow *Shari'a* law reflecting the divinely-revealed principles and requirements of the Koran (Qur'an). In Africa and elsewhere, the role of custom or indigenous law still exerts profound influence, and local communal values and procedures continue to play an important role in informal systems of justice and accountability. Finally, the legal systems of the People's Republic of China (PRC) and other Asian countries can be said to share certain common elements reflecting the unique historical, cultural, religious, and political traditions of that region.

In terms of criminal procedure, certain broad differences can be identified between the common law "accusatorial" approach and the civil law "inquisitorial" approach. Common law systems usually (but not always) rely on the decision of a jury of "peers" (private citizens) whose job is to decide whether the prosecutor has proved the charges. In contrast, traditional or "classical" civil law systems of criminal justice employ an approach in which the goal is to establish the fact of the defendant's guilt or innocence by means of an official (and, in theory at least, objective or impartial) fact-finding process. The prosecutor is often a professional governmental official and may even have judicial status (both judges and prosecutors are often called "magistrates"). The defendant is expected to cooperate in this quest for the truth and consequently enjoys fewer rights to resist or object to the process.

Once it has been established that a crime has been committed, preliminary investigation is undertaken to determine the facts of the situation, typically under the direction of an investigating magistrate (*juge d'instruction* or *juez instructor*). The trial proceeding itself may be conducted before an entirely different court, and may be relatively brief and informal by common law standards. The duty of the court is to seek the truth; the main examination of the accused (and witnesses, if any) is conducted primarily by the presiding judge. The speed, nature, and formalities of the proceedings also reflect these differences.

These broad distinctions can be misleading. Many legal systems do not fit neatly into the categories described above, nor are the categories themselves entirely accurate descriptors. For instance, codification of both substantive and procedural law is increasingly common in common law countries, and in many civil law systems, decisional law (known in French as *jurisprudence* or in Spanish as *jurisprudencia*) actually plays a significant if not necessarily binding role.

Even within the "Romano-Germanic" civil law tradition, marked differences have long existed between the French approach (which has heavily influenced the legal systems of Italy, Portugal, and Spain) and the German (followed by the Scandinavians, South Korea, and Greece). At the same time, both approaches have long incorporated procedural elements associated with the common law (e.g., public trials and oral testimony). More importantly, many domestic systems embrace or even combine elements of the different approaches.

Few countries today fall neatly into the "accusatorial" or "inquisitorial" camps.

It is as yet too early to know whether one byproduct of the creation of international courts and tribunals will be the harmonization, or perhaps even unification, of criminal law in terms of procedural rights or (eventually) substantive law.

§ 3–19   FURTHER READING

Sluiter, Frinan, Linton, Zappala & Vasiliev, eds., *International Criminal Procedure: Principles and Rules* (Oxford 2013); Dan Stigall, "International Law and Limitations on the Exercise of Extraterritorial Jurisdiction in U.S. Domestic Law," 35 Hastings Int'l & Comp. l. Rev. 323 (2012); Gary Shaw, "Convicting Humanity in Absentia: Holding Trials in Absentia at the International Criminal Court," 44 Geo. Wash. Int'l L. Rev. 107 (2012); Marlies Glasin, "Do International Courts Require Democratic Legitimacy?", 23 Eur. J. Int'l L. 43 (2012); Werle, *Principles of International Criminal Law* (TM Asser, 2nd ed. 2009).

CHAPTER 4

INTERNATIONAL CRIMINAL COURTS

I. INTRODUCTION

The emergence of international criminal courts is a phenomenon of the past twenty years. Historically, most prosecutions for violations of international criminal law, including international humanitarian law, have taken place in domestic courts. The post-World War II tribunals set a precedent that was unique in several respects. Beginning with the establishment of the two *ad hoc* tribunals (one for the former Yugoslavia in 1993, the other for Rwanda in 1994), the new institutions now include the International Criminal Court (which began operating in 2002) as well as a variety of "mixed" or "hybrid" courts.

This chapter summarizes the origins, structure, jurisdiction, and current status of these tribunals. The substantive law on which their decisions have been based is discussed in Chapter 5.

II. THE *AD HOC* TRIBUNALS

The International Criminal Tribunals for the former Yugoslavia ("ICTY") and for Rwanda ("ICTR") were both created by the UN Security Council, acting under Chapter VII of the UN Charter, in response to widespread armed conflict involving massive violations of human rights and humanitarian norms. The first international war crimes tribunals since Nuremberg and Tokyo, they are subsidiary organs of the United Nations, conceived as temporary institutions with limited jurisdiction. They are now advancing into their second decade of existence.

While criticized for their high cost and the slow pace of proceedings, the two tribunals have in fact completed a significant number of trials. Altogether, as of June 2013, some 250 individuals had been indicted, of whom about 115 were convicted and 30 acquitted. For most of the others, indictments were withdrawn or proceedings terminated or transferred to national courts. Only a few of the accused were never brought to trial. The *ad hoc* tribunals have also produced a substantial body of decisional jurisprudence which has contributed to the progressive development of many aspects of international criminal law and procedure. In an important sense, the prosecutions before these two courts served as a developmental laboratory, laying the groundwork for the International Criminal Court.

In December 2010, the Security Council asked the Tribunals to complete their work by the end of 2014 and established an International Residual Mechanism for Criminal Tribunals to assist them in that task. *See* UN Sec. Coun. Res. 1966, discussed *infra* at **§ 4–3**.

§ 4–1   THE ICTY

In 1991, the Socialist Federal Republic of Yugoslavia began to dissolve. First to secede were Slovenia and Croatia. In early 1992, the province of Macedonia declared its independence, followed by Bosnia and Herzegovina. That spring, Serbia and Montenegro formed the Federal Republic of Yugoslavia. In this process, deep-seated ethnic tensions fueled violent conflicts, pitting various groups (such as Muslims, Serbs, Croats, and Bosnians) against each other.

Responding to reports of massive atrocities and fearful that the fighting might spread further, the U.N. Security Council eventually charged a Commission of Experts to investigate serious violations of international humanitarian law in the former Yugoslavia. The following year, acting under its peacekeeping authority, the Security Council created the International Criminal Tribunal for the Former Yugoslavia (the "ICTY").

1. *Jurisdiction*

The ICTY is charged with prosecuting "persons responsible for serious violations of international humanitarian law committed in the territory of the former Yugoslavia since 1991." Specifically, it has jurisdiction over genocide, crimes against humanity, violations of the laws and customs of war, and grave breaches of the 1949 Geneva Conventions (which apply in international armed conflicts). The ICTY's Statute does not include crimes against the peace, and the specific list of crimes against humanity in article 5 is somewhat broader than the London Charter, including imprisonment, rape, and torture "when committed in armed conflict, whether international or internal in character, and directed against any civilian population."

Note that the ICTY's jurisdiction is limited in several ways—by time, location and offense. Moreover, it is "concurrent" with that of the national courts of the various States which today comprise the territory of the former Yugoslavia. In other words, an individual accused of a crime within the ICTY's substantive jurisdiction may also be tried before those national courts. However, the ICTY has "primary" jurisdiction over the latter, meaning that at any stage of proceedings, it may require those national courts to defer any proceedings they had undertaken or were contemplating in favor of the ICTY's prosecution. This arrangement reflected a concern that, given the inter-ethnic nature of the underlying conflict, if the national tribunals could assert primary jurisdiction they might insist on trying their own nationals. In practice, however, the ICTY has not exercised its right of primacy in many cases.

2. *Structure*

The Tribunal consists of three separate organs. First are the *Chambers*. There are three separate Trial Chambers, each consisting of three judges. Their decisions are reviewed by an Appeals Chamber, a seven-member body headed by the President of the Court, which serves as the final authority on matters of law. Judges come from many nations, but no two judges can be nationals of the same State. Second is the *Office of the Prosecutor*. An independent unit, it is responsible for conducting investigations and pursing the cases. Third is the *Registry*. It manages court records, supports the court more generally, and plays an important role in assigning defense counsel.

3. *Applicable Law*

The ICTY Statute provided essential definitions of the various crimes over which the Tribunal has jurisdiction (grave breaches of the Geneva Conventions, violations of the laws or customs of war, genocide and crimes against humanity) but left the ICTY to interpret and apply those definitions in light of what it considered to be the rules of customary international law. In its decision in the *Celebici* case, the Appeals Chamber pointed out that the Security Council, when establishing the ICTR, was not creating new law but had (among other things) codified existing customary rules for the purposes of the Court's jurisdiction. *See Celebici Appeals Judgment*, IT–96–21–1 (Feb. 20, 2001) at para. 170.

4. *Issues*

The ICTY has rendered a number of significant decisions which have influenced the development of international criminal law. Technically, these decisions have no binding effect beyond the particular case in which they are rendered, since strictly speaking, the principle of *stare decisis* does not apply either in the Tribunal or more generally in international criminal law. In practice, the need for certainty, stability, and predictability in the administration of justice does produce a kind of *de facto* precedential system.

5. *Legitimacy*

One of the first issues litigated in the ICTY involved a direct challenge to the legitimacy of the tribunal itself. Dusko Tadić, a Bosnian Serb accused of crimes against humanity, grave breaches of the 1949 Geneva Conventions, and violations of the laws or customs of war, argued that the UN Security Council lacked the authority under Chapter VII of the UN Charter to create subsidiary bodies with judicial powers. He also argued that the ICTY lacked authority to judge its own validity. Unsurprisingly, the Tribunal ruled against him on both points, finding that (i) once the Security Council determines the existence of a "threat to the peace" it has "a wide margin of discretion" in choosing the appropriate response, including the creation of a criminal tribunal, and (ii) the ability to determine the scope and validity of its own competence is "a major part of the incidental or inherent jurisdiction of any judicial or arbitral tribunal." *See Prosecutor v. Dusko Tadić a/k/a "Dule,"* IT 94–I–AR72, Decision on the Defense Motion for an Interlocutory Appeal on Jurisdiction (Oct. 2, 1995), paras. 18, 31, 32.

6. *Joint Criminal Enterprise*

One of the ICTY's most significant (and controversial) contributions has been the articulation of the concept of "joint criminal enterprise." The Statute contains no provision for convicting joint participants in specific crimes on the basis of conspiracy or related concepts. But many of the atrocities committed during the Balkan conflict were in fact the product of joint activity. In a series of decisions, the Tribunal developed and applied a theory of responsibility based on the notion of a "joint criminal enterprise" ("JCE"). This concept permits a chamber to hold all individuals within a group responsible for the crimes committed by the group. Fundamentally, a joint criminal enterprise consists of a common plan in which a number of individuals participate with the shared aim of committing an international crime or crimes. It was introduced in the Tadić Appeals Judgment, IT–94–1–A (July 15, 1999), paras. 185 ff. The concept is discussed in Chapter 6, part III.

7. *Duress*

The ICTY faced other difficult issues relating to the culpability of defendants. For example, one member of the Bosnian Serb Army, Drazen Erdemović, was accused of killing unarmed civilians during the massacre at Srebrenica in 1995. He admitted to killing a number of individuals but invoked the defense of duress, arguing that he had been told by his superior commander either to kill the civilians or be killed himself. The Tribunal rejected that argument, holding that duress cannot be a defense to crimes against humanity or war crimes. *Prosecutor v. Erdemović*, IT–96–22–A, Judgment, (Oct. 7, 1997). (Separately, the ICTY decided that that duress can be considered a mitigating factor in assessing punishment.)

8. *Milošević*

Perhaps the most notorious ICTY proceeding was the prosecution of Slobodan Milošević, former president of Serbia and Yugoslavia and former Supreme Commander of the Yugoslav Army. He was charged with a number of offenses including genocide, complicity in genocide, persecutions, torture, crimes against humanity, grave breaches of the Geneva Conventions and violations of the laws or customs of war involving Common Article 3 (among others). He evaded capture for several years but was eventually arrested by Serbian authorities and surrendered to the Tribunal. Milošević never acknowledged the ICTY's legitimacy. He refused legal counsel and chose to represent himself through most of the proceedings. His abusive approach to the proceedings and his ill-health caused repeatedly delays in the trial. After five years in custody, and only weeks before a verdict was expected, he died in March 2006. His death prompted a wave of public criticism of the ICTY for being too slow.

9. *Evaluation*

The Tribunal has brought to justice many of those most responsible for the violence and abuses that took place during the Balkans conflict. As of June 2013, the Tribunal had indicted 161 persons for crimes committed during the conflict in the former Yugoslavia, of whom sixty-nine were convicted and eighteen acquitted. Only twenty-five remained on trial or in some stage of appeal, including the trials of Ratko Mladić (former commander of the Main Staff of the Bosnian Serb Army) and Radovan Karadžić (former President of Republika Srpska and commander of its armed forces). Thirteen cases had been transferred to national jurisdictions, and thirty-six indictments were withdrawn or terminated (for example by reason of the death of the accused). Some forty accused were in different stages of proceedings.

The ICTY's official website is *http://www.icty.org/*. *See generally* Gow, Kerr & Pajic, *Prosecuting War Crimes: Lessons and Legacies of the International Criminal Tribunal for the Former Yugoslavia* (Routledge 2013); Swart, Zahar & Sluiter, *The Legacy of the International Criminal Tribunal for the Former Yugoslavia* (Oxford 2011).

§ 4–2   THE ICTR

The genocide which took place in Rwanda during the spring and early summer of 1994 is well-known. It occurred in the context of longstanding conflict between the two main ethnic groups, the majority Hutu and the minority Tutsi. While estimate vary, between 800,000 and a million people died and perhaps half a million women were raped during the 100 days of that appalling conflict. Most of the victims were Tutsis, and most of the perpetrators were Hutus.

In November 1994, the UN Security Council acted under Chapter VII to establish an *ad hoc* tribunal. The International Criminal Tribunal for Rwanda (ICTR) was created for "the sole purpose of prosecuting persons responsible for genocide and other serious violations of International Humanitarian Law committed in the territory of Rwanda and Rwandan citizens responsible for genocide and other such violations committed in the territory of neighboring States, between 1 January 1994 and 31 December 1994." *See* UN Sec. Coun. Res. 955 (1994).

Like the ICTY, the substantive jurisdiction of the ICTR covers genocide and crimes against humanity (although the definition of the latter includes an additional element of discrimination). In contrast to the ICTY, however, the ICTR's Statute reaches only serious violations of Common Article 3 and Additional Protocol II of the Geneva Conventions (which apply to internal—or "non-international"— conflicts). The reason is that, unlike the Balkan conflict, the Rwandan genocide occurred primarily within a single country between different ethnic groups of Rwandans and did not involve a significant international dimension.

Like the ICTY, the ICTR has concurrent jurisdiction with Rwandan courts but also has "primacy" meaning that it can require national courts to surrender cases to it. *See* ICTR Statute, art. 8(1).

The Tribunal is headquartered in Arusha, Tanzania, and is thus more distant, both geographically and symbolically, from the people in Rwanda than the ICTY is from the people in the former Yugoslavia. Structurally, the Tribunal is similar to the ICTY, with Trial Chambers, an Appeals Chamber, a Registry, and an independent prosecutor's office. Under article 13(4) of the Statute, the ICTY's Appeals Chamber also serves as the ICTR's Appeals Chamber. In 2002, in an effort to speed up the work of the Tribunal, the Security Council amended the Statute to permit the election of *ad litem* judges to sit in the Chambers. *See* ICTR Statute article 12.

1. *Genocide*

In *Prosecutor v. Akayesu*, ICTR 96–4–T2, Judgment, (Sept. 2, 1998), the Tribunal became the first international tribunal to interpret and apply the definition of genocide as set forth in the 1948 Genocide Convention. The Trial Chamber offered a lengthy factual description of the violence which had occurred in Taba Province in 1994 and of Akayesu's responsibility as communal leader (or *bourgmestre)* in and for those acts, which it found were aimed at "the complete disappearance of the Tutsi people." Akayesu was convicted of (and sentenced to life imprisonment for) committing and being complicit in genocide, for direct and public incitement to commit genocide, and for crimes against humanity.

2. Rape and Sexual Assault as Genocide

In addition, the *Akayesu* judgment held that rape (defined as "a physical invasion of a sexual nature committed on a person under circumstances which are coercive") and other forms of sexual assault can constitute acts of genocide when committed with the necessary genocidal intent. Specifically, it found that sexual assault had formed an integral part of the effort to destroy the Tutsi as an ethnic group and that the rape had been systematically committed against Tutsi women only, manifesting the specific intent required for those acts to constitute genocide.

3. Direct and Public Incitement

In what has come to be known as the "Media Case," the Tribunal convicted three individuals of direct and public incitement to commit genocide. Ferdinand Nahimana and Jean-Bosco Barayagwiz had been deeply involved in Radio Television Libre des Mille Collines, the radio station that effectively branded Tutsis as the enemy. Hassan Ngeze owned and edited a popular newsletter that published anti-Tutsi messages. The Appeals Chamber also determined, *inter alia*, that in certain circumstances hate speech could constitute the "persecution" crime against humanity. *Prosecutor v. Nahimana et al.*, ICTR 99–52–A, Appeals Chamber Judgment, (Nov. 28, 2007). *See Prosecutor v. Karemera et al.*, ICTR 98–44–T, Decision on Motions for Judgment of Acquittal, (Mar. 19, 2008) para. 15.

4. *Government Officials*

In *Kambanda v. The Prosecutor*, ICTR 97–23–A (Oct. 19, 2000), the Appeals Chamber affirmed a judgment against Rwanda's former prime minister Jean Kambanda. In 1998, in what was then the first international decision against a former head of government for genocide, the Trial Chamber had sentenced Kambanda to life imprisonment after he pled guilty to genocide, conspiracy to commit genocide, direct and public incitement to commit genocide, and complicity in genocide, as well as to two counts of crimes against humanity for murder and extermination.

More recently, the Trial Chamber sentenced Augustin Ngirabatware, Rwanda's former Minister of Planning, to thirty-five years imprisonment for genocide, direct and public incitement to commit genocide and rape as a crime against humanity. The Chamber also found him guilty of participating in a joint criminal enterprise with the purpose of destroying, in whole or in part, the Tutsi ethnic group, and more particularly exterminating the Tutsi civilian population in the Nyamyumba commune. *Prosecutor v. Ngirabatware*, ICTR 99–54–T (Dec. 20, 2012).

5. *Crimes Against Humanity*

While many of its judgments have involved genocide, the ICTR has also addressed various aspects of crimes against humanity (including murder, rape, and extermination) and the problem of cumulative charges and convictions. In *Prosecutor v. Ndindiliymana*, ICTR 00–56–T, Judgment, (May 17, 2011), para. 92, for example, it affirmed that an accused can be held responsible for multiple crimes based on the same underlying conduct but "only where each crime may be distinguished by a materially distinct element."

6. *Evaluation*

The ICTR has contributed to the restoration of peace and the process of national reconciliation in Rwanda. One of the most basic, yet most important, achievements is the collection of a historical record of the genocide, including testimony of witnesses, victims, accused, and video and audio recordings. This record proved invaluable to the Appeals Chamber in discrediting and rejecting theories that genocide had not actually occurred in Rwanda.

As of June 2013, it had convicted about fifty individuals and acquitted about twenty. Another seventy-five or so remained on trial. Eight cases had been transferred to national courts.

Like the ICTY, the ICTR has suffered from lack of cooperation even though the Statute requires UN Member States to assist in its investigations and prosecutions. The Tribunal does have an enforcement mechanism under article 7 *bis* of its Rules of Procedure and Evidence, which authorizes the Tribunal's President to report an uncooperative State to the UN Security Council for appropriate action. As the Tribunal has matured, cooperation has progressively increased.

Another significant criticism of both the ICTR and the ICTY is that neither operates at the sites where the crimes being investigated took place. In fact, when the UN Security created the Tribunal, Rwanda actually had a seat on the Council; it cast the only "no" vote, partly because it believed that it was essential for the Tribunal to take place within the country. This criticism was at least one reason for the placement of the ECCC Extraordinary Chambers in the Courts of Cambodia (ECCC) in Cambodia and the Special Court for Sierra Leone (SCSL) in Sierra Leone.

7. *Additional Information*

The ICTR's statute, rules, judgments and other documentation are available at its official website at *http://www.ictr.org*. *See generally* Gahima, *Transitional Justice in Rwanda: Accountability for Atrocity* (Routledge 2012); Cruvellier and Voss, *Court of Remorse: Inside the International Criminal Tribunal for Rwanda* (Wisconsin 2010).

§ 4–3   THE INTERNATIONAL RESIDUAL MECHANISM

For several years, concern built over the slow pace of proceedings in the *ad hoc* tribunals. In 2002, the Security Council endorsed a broad strategy for the transfer of cases to relevant national courts to help the ICTY to complete its work by 2010. The ICTR was given a similar deadline. When it became clear that goal would not be met, the Council established an International Residual Mechanism for Criminal

Tribunals. In UN Sec. Coun. Res. 1966, adopted on December 22, 2010, the Council asked both Tribunals "to expeditiously complete all their remaining work" no later than the end of 2014 and decided that the Mechanism would assume their jurisdiction, rights, obligations and essential functions, effective on July 1, 2012 with respect to the ICTR and on July 1, 2013 for the ICTY. The Mechanism will operate for an initial period of four years.

Under its Statute, this new Mechanism will continue the functions of the ICTY and of the ICTR, including the prosecution of persons already indicted who are "among the most senior leaders suspected of being most responsible for the crimes" within their respective jurisdictions. With minor exceptions, the Mechanism is not authorized to initiate new prosecutions.

The Statute specifies the Mechanism's structure (including its division into separate branches for Rwanda and the former Yugoslavia), the qualification of judges, its rules of evidence and procedure, the rights of the accused, and transitional arrangements governing the completion of trials, referrals and appeals pending before the *ad hoc* tribunals when the respective branches of the Mechanism come into force. Article 28 directs States to cooperate with the Mechanism in its investigations and prosecutions and to comply with its requests for assistance.

§ 4–4   FURTHER READING

The website for the IRM is at *http://www.icty.org/ sid/10874.*

III. THE INTERNATIONAL CRIMINAL COURT

The International Criminal Court ("ICC") is the first permanent or "standing" tribunal to be established expressly for the purpose of prosecuting genocide, war crimes and crimes against humanity. Unlike the ICTY and ICTR, it was not created by the UN Security Council but instead by a multilateral treaty concluded at a diplomatic conference. Concluded on July 17, 1998, the treaty is known as the Rome Statute.

The ICC became operational in 2002. As of June 2013, eighteen separate cases, involving eight different "situations," had been instituted before the ICC (*see* § 4–17 below). Some thirty individuals have been indicted. One (Dyilo) has been convicted and one (Chui) acquitted. Charges have been dismissed in six cases and six more are in pretrial proceedings. Five individuals are currently in custody and eleven more are fugitives or have yet to be surrendered to the Court.

§ 4–5   BACKGROUND

Efforts to create such an institution extend as far back as the League of Nations following World War I. An initial attempt to establish a tribunal to prosecute war crimes failed in 1937. Although efforts continued in the early years of the United Nations, they were stymied mostly by Cold War antagonisms. The issue was raised again by Trinidad and Tobago in 1989, when it proposed an international forum for prosecuting drug traffickers. Eventually, in 1992, the UN General Assembly asked the International Law Commission to prepare a statute for a tribunal with broader jurisdiction. Building on earlier efforts as well as the recently created *ad hoc* tribunals, the ILC adopted a proposed text in 1994. *See* Report of the ILC, 46th sess., May 2–22, 1994, UN Doc. A/49/10; U.N. GAOR, 49th Sess., Supp. No. 10 (1994). That text served as the basis for consideration by a UN preparatory committee held between 1996–98.

The Rome Statute itself was adopted in 1998 at a formal diplomatic conference held in Rome by a final vote of 120-7 (with twenty-one abstentions). The Statute came into force on July 1, 2002. As of June 2013, 122 States had become parties to the Rome Statute (through ratification or accession) and an additional thirty-one had signed (but not ratified or acceded), including the Russian Federation, Egypt, the Islamic Republic of Iran, Israel, Sudan, the Syrian Arab Republic and the United States. Still, a quarter of the UN's 194 Member States have neither signed nor ratified, including the India, Pakistan, Turkey, Sudan, the Philippines and the People's Republic of China.

In July 2010, a review conference of the Assembly of States Parties was held in Kampala, Uganda to review the operation of the Court and its

mechanisms. Perhaps most importantly, the
conference adopted several amendments to the
Rome Statute, one creating the crime of aggression
and another (the so-called Belgian amendment)
criminalizing the use in non-international conflicts
of weapons prohibited by various arms control
treaties (covering, *inter alia*, biological and chemical
weapons and anti-personnel mines).

The Rome Statute is a lengthy, detailed and
complex multilateral treaty, divided into thirteen
parts and 128 articles. It directs the Court to
conduct investigations and prosecutions for crimes
of genocide, crimes against humanity, war crimes
and aggression (as discussed below, the provisions
on aggression are not yet in effect). The operation of
the Court also requires reference to other
instruments, including the Elements of Crimes and
the Rules of Procedure and Evidence.

§ 4–6   THE STRUCTURE OF THE COURT

The International Criminal Court is an independent
entity with its own "international legal personality."
It is composed of four "organs": (1) the Presidency,
(2) the Chambers, (3) the Office of the Prosecutor,
and (4) the Registry. The Assembly of States Parties
also plays a key role.

1. *The Presidency*

consists of the President and the two Vice-
Presidents, who are responsible for the Court's
overall operation and administration. They are
elected by the Court's eighteen judges. In addition to

assigning cases to the Chambers and overseeing the work of the Registry, the Presidency manages the Court's external relations.

The eighteen judges are elected by a two-thirds majority vote of the Assembly of States Parties for non-renewable terms of nine years. The judges must be "persons of high moral character, impartiality and integrity who possess the qualifications required in their respective States for appointment to the highest judicial offices." In making their selection, the States Parties must take into account the need for representation of the principal legal systems of the world, equitable geographical representation; and (iii) a fair representation of female and male judges.

2. *The Chambers* (or *Judicial Division)*

consist of an Appeals Division (four judges), a Trial Division (eight judges) and a Pre-Trial Division (six judges). The judges of each Division sit in Chambers which are responsible for conducting the proceedings of the Court in specific cases. Assignment of judges to Divisions is made on the basis of the nature of the functions each Division performs and the qualifications and experience of the judge.

3. *The Office of the Prosecutor*

("OTP") is responsible for examining allegations about crimes within the Court's jurisdiction, conducting the necessary investigations, and directing prosecutions before the Court. The

Prosecutor is independent from the judges and is elected by an absolute majority of the Assembly of States Parties to a non-renewable nine-year term.

4. *The Registry*

provides support services to the Court, including the administration of legal aid matters, court management, victims and witnesses' matters, defense counsel, detention unit, and other kinds of support such as finance, translation, building management, procurement and personnel.

5. *The Assembly of States Parties*

(or "ASP") also plays an important role in the overall functioning of the Court, although it is not formally one of the ICC's "organs." Comprising representatives of those States that have ratified or acceded to the Rome Statute, it provides overall management oversight with respect to issues related to budget, finance and human resources. The ASP decides such issues such as amendments to the Statute, the adoption of normative texts, approval of the budget, and the election of the judges and of the Prosecutor and the Deputy Prosecutor(s). Each State Party has one vote in the ASP, although every effort has to be made to reach decisions by consensus both in the Assembly and the Bureau.

As of June 2013, the staff of the Court totaled nearly 700 persons in the professional and general services categories. The professional staff included more than seventy-five nationalities. The approved budget exceeded 112 million Euros (roughly USD $147 million). During 2012, the Court held over 123 hearings (representing over 6,000 pages of transcripts) and rendered more than 620 decisions, orders and judgments.

§ 4–7   JURISDICTION

The International Criminal Court is a court of limited and specific jurisdiction. Its authority to hear cases is both enabled and constrained by several fundamental rules. Taken separately, each of these rules is fairly simple, but in the context of any given situation, they produce a rather complicated analysis. The following discussion endeavors to provide a "user friendly roadmap."

1. *Jurisdiction Ratione Materiae*

Substantively, the ICC has jurisdiction only over the four "core" crimes of genocide, war crimes, crimes against humanity and aggression. They are introduced here for clarity, and they are discussed in greater detail in Chapter 5.

A. *Genocide*

The definition of genocide in article 6 of the Rome Statute is drawn directly from the 1948 Convention on the Prevention and Punishment of the Crime of Genocide. It states: "For the purpose of this Statute, 'genocide' means any of the following acts committed with intent to destroy, in whole or in part, a national, ethnical, racial or religious group, as such: (a) Killing members of the group; (b)

Causing serious bodily or mental harm to members of the group; (c) Deliberately inflicting on the group conditions of life calculated to bring about its physical destruction in whole or in part; (d) Imposing measures intended to prevent births within the group; (e) Forcibly transferring children of the group to another group."

B. Crimes Against Humanity

In contrast, no multilateral treaty contains an accepted definition of the term "crimes against humanity." Article 7 of the Rome Statute represents one of the first "codifications" of the term. It defines the term to mean any of a number of specific acts (such as murder, extermination, torture, rape or sexual slavery, or persecution against an identifiable group or collectivity on political, racial, national, ethnic, cultural, religious, gender or other grounds) "when committed as part of a widespread or systematic attack directed against any civilian population, with knowledge of the attack."

C. War Crimes

Article 8 contains a detailed definition of the acts which constitute war crimes within the Court's jurisdiction "in particular when committed as part of a plan or policy or as part of a large-scale commission of such crimes." It draws heavily on the 1949 Geneva Conventions and customary international humanitarian law, including the distinction between international and non-international armed conflicts. As to the former, article 8(a) covers "grave breaches" of the 1949 Geneva Conventions, and article 8(b) lists "other serious violations of the laws and customs applicable in international armed conflict."

Article 8(c) applies "[i]n the case of an armed conflict not of an international character" and covers "serious violations of article 3 common to the four Geneva Conventions of 12 August 1949," listing several particular acts "committed against persons taking no active part in the hostilities, including members of armed forces who have laid down their arms and those placed out of combat (*hors de combat)* by sickness, wounds, detention or any other cause." Article 8(e) lists "[o]ther serious violations of the laws and customs applicable in armed conflicts not of an international character, within the established framework of international law." These two provisions apply to armed conflicts not of an international character but not to "situations of internal disturbances and tensions, such as riots, isolated and sporadic acts of violence or other acts of a similar nature." Arts. 8(d) and (e).

D. Aggression

Initially the crime of aggression was left undefined, but in 2010 the ASP agreed on both a definition and the rules under which the Court will exercise jurisdiction over this crime after (a) at least thirty States Parties have accepted the amendments and (b) a decision is taken by two-thirds of States Parties to activate the jurisdiction after January 1, 2017.

As adopted in article 8(*bis*), the "crime of aggression" means "the planning, preparation, initiation or execution, by a person in a position effectively to exercise control over or to direct the political or military action of a State, of an act of aggression which, by its character, gravity and scale, constitutes a manifest violation of the Charter of the United Nations." In turn, "act of aggression" is defined to include "the use of armed force by a State against the sovereignty, territorial integrity or political independence of another State, or in any other manner inconsistent with the Charter of the United Nations." The article lists a number of acts which, "regardless of a declaration of war," shall qualify as an act of aggression. The definition is drawn largely from UN G.A. res. 3314 (XXIX) (Dec. 14, 1974).

2. *Jurisdiction Ratione Personae*

Article 1 of the Rome Statute gives the Court "jurisdiction over persons for the most serious crimes of international concern." As emphasized in article 25, this jurisdiction *ratione personae* extends only to "natural persons" who can be held "individually responsible and liable for punishment." The ICC's jurisdiction thus rests on the basic concept of individual criminal responsibility. Accordingly, cases cannot be brought against States or governments, or against non-State entities such as organizations, institutions or corporations.

The Statute recognizes no immunity based on an individual's official capacity or position, including that of Head of State or Government. As stated in art. 27(2), "[i]mmunities or special procedural rules which may attach to the official capacity of a person, whether under national or international law, shall not bar the Court from exercising its jurisdiction over such a person."

This aspect of the Court's jurisdiction is subject to an important limitation. In exercising its authority under Chapter VII to refer situations to the Court (described in greater detail below), the UN Security Council has the authority to exclude specific individuals from the Court's jurisdiction. It has in fact done so on two occasions: first, in UN Sec. Coun. Res. 1593 (2005), by which it referred "the situation in Darfur since 1 July 2002" to the Prosecutor, and second, in UN Sec. Coun. Res. 1970 (2011), by which it referred "the situation in the Libyan Arab Jamahiriya since 15 February 2011" to the Prosecutor. These two resolutions contained virtually identical statements that "nationals, current or former officials or personnel from a State outside [Sudan or Libya] which is not a party to the Rome Statute of the International Criminal Court shall be subject to the exclusive jurisdiction of that State for all alleged acts or omissions arising out of or related to operations in [Sudan or Libya] established or authorized by the Council, unless such exclusive jurisdiction has been expressly waived by the State."

A. Nationality and Territoriality

Subject to some important exceptions, the ICC may only consider cases involving allegations of the four "core crimes" which were committed either (a) within the territory of a State Party to the Rome Statute or (b) by a national of a State Party to the Rome Statute. In analyzing the Court's jurisdiction over a particular circumstance or "situation," therefore, the starting point will be to determine whether the crime took place in, or was committed by a national of, a State Party to the Rome Statute.

As a general rule, the Court may not consider cases involving States which are not party to the Rome Statute. There are exceptions, however. The Court may do so for crimes committed on the territory of *non-party* States (i) when they were committed by nationals of a State which is a party, or (ii) when they are part of a "situation" referred by the Security Council acting under Chapter VII, or (iii) when the non-party State "opts in" pursuant to article 12(3).

These jurisdictional concepts differ from the normal rules applicable to States as discussed *supra* in Chapter 3. Generally, international criminal law permits States to exercise domestic jurisdiction over crimes committed within their territory or by their nationals. These two grounds provide the most widely exercised bases for prosecutions of international crimes at the domestic level. Strictly speaking, however, they are not applicable to the International Criminal Court, since it is an international organization, not a State, and has no ties of territoriality or nationality.

Moreover, the Court clearly does not exercise "universal jurisdiction" as that concept is normally used, since its jurisdiction is limited by connections of nationality, territoriality, and action of the UN Security Council or the State concerned.

B. Temporal Jurisdiction

The Court has jurisdiction "only with respect to crimes committed after the entry into force of this Statute." See art. 11 (1). That occurred on July 1, 2002. Thus, in contrast to the ICTY and ICTR, which were established to prosecute individuals for crimes which had already been committed during clearly defined periods, the ICC's temporal jurisdiction (jurisdiction *ratione temporis*) is prospective and open-ended.

The crime must also have taken place after the Statute has entered into force for the particular State in question. See art. 11(2): "If a State becomes a Party to this Statute after its entry into force, the Court may exercise its jurisdiction only with respect to crimes committed after the entry into force of this Statute for that State, unless that State has made a declaration under article 12, paragraph 3." Generally, that will occur on the first day of the month after the sixtieth day following the deposit by such State of its instrument of ratification, acceptance, approval or accession. See art. 126(2). Thus, it is not possible for a State to ratify the

Statute in order to submit to the Court a situation which has already taken place on its territory.

No statute of limitations applies to the crimes within the Court's jurisdiction. *See* Art. 29.

A special rule applies to war crimes. A State may, upon ratification of the Statute, declare that it does not accept the jurisdiction of the Court over war crimes committed on its territory or by its nationals for a period of seven years after the Statute enters into force for it. Art. 124. Only two States, France and Colombia, have made use of this "war crimes opt out," although France withdrew its declaration in 2008. An effort to delete the provision was turned back at the Kampala Review Conference in 2010.

§ 4–8   TRIGGERING THE JURISDICTION

How do specific cases get started? What is the process for initiating proceedings? As indicated above, the Statute provides three separate mechanisms. Which mechanism is used to "trigger" the Court's jurisdiction has an effect on the specific jurisdictional prerequisites.

Under art. 13, the Court's substantive jurisdiction over the four "core crimes" may be invoked in one of three ways: (1) if a State Party to the Statute refers "a situation in which one or more of such crimes appears to have been committed" to the Prosecutor, (2) if the UN Security Council refers such a situation to the Prosecutor by taking a decision under Chapter VII of the Charter, or (3) if the

Prosecutor has initiated an investigation on his or her own authority (*proprio motu*).

In the first two instances, the process begins with specific charges against named individuals but rather by referral of "a situation in which one or more of [the core] crimes appears to have been committed." Art. 13. In the third, the Prosecutor is authorized to initiate "investigations *proprio motu* on the basis of information on crimes within the jurisdiction of the Court." Art. 15(1). That information may be generated by the OTP itself or provided to it by others.

§ 4–9   REFERRAL BY A STATE PARTY

A State Party may refer to the Prosecutor "a situation in which one or more crimes within the jurisdiction of the Court appear to have been committed by requesting the Prosecutor to investigate the situation for the purpose of determining whether one or more specific persons should be charged with the commission of such crimes." Art. 14(1). It also requires that "[a]s far as possible, a referral shall specify the relevant circumstances and be accompanied by such supporting documentation as is available to the State referring the situation." Art. 14(2).

To date, five situations have been presented under this mechanism—all by the concerned States themselves (thus prompting the term "self-referrals"). In December 2003, the Government of Uganda referred the "situation concerning the Lord's Resistance Army in northern and western

Uganda." In March 2004 the Democratic Republic of Congo (DRC) referred the situation of crimes allegedly committed "anywhere in the territory of the DRC" since the Rome Statute entered into force in 2002. In January 2005, the government of the Central African Republic made a similar referral regarding crimes committed anywhere on its territory. In 2012 Mali did likewise. In 2011, the President of Côte d'Ivoire (at the time a signatory but not yet a party to the Statute) invited the Prosecutor to initiate an investigation into crimes committed since 2004.

A referral by a State Party does not necessarily result in an investigation, much less a prosecution. Under article 53, the Prosecutor must initiate an investigation *unless* he determines that there is no "reasonable basis to proceed." Such a determination turns on whether crimes within the Court's jurisdiction appear to have been committed, whether the potential case(s) would be admissible, and where prosecution would be in the interests of justice.

§ 4–10 REFERRAL BY THE SECURITY COUNCIL

Article 13(b) authorizes the UN Security Council to refer situations to the Court by exercising its Chapter VII powers. This provision reflects the need for the international community to address situations quickly and effectively even in the absence of referrals by (or over the objections of) the States directly concerned. Under article 53, such a referral requires the Prosecutor to initiate an investigation *unless* he determines that there is no reasonable basis to proceed.

To date the Security Council has exercised this authority twice. In September 2004, it referred the "situation in Darfur" and in February 2011, it referred the "situation in Libya." *See* UN Sec. Coun. Res. 1593 and 1970. Neither Sudan nor Libya is a party to the Rome Statute.

§ 4–11   PROSECUTORIAL INITIATIVE

The Rome Statute permits the Prosecutor to initiate investigations on his or her own authority (*proprio motu*) on the basis of information provided to the Court, without a referral by a State Party or the Security Council.

This authority is subject to several constraints. Investigations *proprio motu* must be based on an affirmative determination that there is a "reasonable basis" for proceeding. Article 53(1) requires the Prosecutor to consider whether the case would be admissible in accordance with article 17 and whether, "taking into account the gravity of the crime and the interests of victims," there are "substantial reasons to believe that an investigation would not serve the interests of justice." He or she must also seek the approval of the Pretrial Chamber before proceeding. *See* Arts. 13(c), 15(4), and 53(l)(a). The Prosecutor is limited to initiating investigations in cases involving either conduct on the territory of States Parties or acts committed by the nationals of such States. He must also defer to an investigation being conducted by national parties unless the Pretrial Chamber decides that those authorities are either unwilling or unable genuinely to investigate or prosecute. *See* Arts. 12, 17 and 18.

In conducting the investigation, the Prosecutor is required "to cover all facts and evidence relevant to an assessment of whether there is criminal responsibility under this Statute, and, in doing so, investigate incriminating and exonerating circumstances equally." Art 54(1)(a). He or she must "respect the interests and personal circumstances of victims and witnesses, including age, gender . . . and health, and take into account the nature of the crime, in particular where it involves sexual violence, gender violence or violence against children." Art 54(1)(b). He or she has extensive powers to collect and examine evidence, to question suspects, victims and witnesses, and to seek the cooperation of any State or intergovernmental organization.

Giving these *proprio motu* powers to the Prosecutor generated considerable controversy at the 1998 Rome Conference. Some States were concerned about the possibility of investigations by a "rogue" or politically motivated prosecutor. The majority, however, thought it a necessary complement to referrals by the Security Council and States Parties since in given situations States may reluctant to refer cases involving their own nationals or those of another State (especially if doing so might interfere with diplomatic or economic relations) and since action by the Security Council under Chapter VII is subject to the veto power of its five permanent members.

§ 4–12   DEFERRAL BY THE SECURITY COUNCIL

Importantly, under article 16, the Security Council also has the power to instruct the Court to defer any investigation or prosecution for a renewable twelve month period when it is actively considering the particular situation. As in the case of referrals, the Security Council must take such decisions under Chapter VII of the UN Charter.

§ 4–13   COMPLEMENTARITY AND ADMISSIBILITY

Like the two *ad hoc* tribunals, the Court's jurisdiction is "concurrent" or "shared" rather than "exclusive," in the sense that the crimes which it covers can also be prosecuted in the domestic courts of States Parties to the Statute. However, the Rome Statute incorporates a structural preference for prosecution of cases at the national level. This preference is given effect through the related principles of complementarity and admissibility.

1. *Complementarity*

Both the ICTY and the ICTR have *primary* jurisdiction, in the sense that they can require a State to surrender a proceeding even if it is in the process of investigating or prosecuting. In contrast, the ICC's jurisdiction is *complementary,* in the sense that the ICC is required to defer to national courts unless it makes certain determinations. Thus, the Court is not intended to be a substitute for national courts but rather to provide a forum of "last resort" when national criminal jurisdictions fail to do their job.

2. *Admissibility*

Even if a particular situation falling within the Court's temporal and substantive jurisdiction has been properly referred to it, another step remains— the determination of *admissibility*. Under article 17, the Court must determine that a case is *inadmissible* in any of four circumstances: (1) when the case is being investigated or prosecuted by a State which has jurisdiction over it, *unless* the State is unwilling or unable genuinely to carry out the investigation or prosecution; (2) the case has been investigated by a State which has jurisdiction over it and the State has decided not to prosecute the person concerned, *unless* the decision resulted from the unwillingness or inability of the State genuinely to prosecute; (3) the person concerned has already been tried for conduct which is the subject of the complaint, and a trial by the Court is not permitted under article 20, paragraph 3; or (4) the case is not of sufficient gravity to justify further action by the Court. Art. 17(1).

3. *Unwilling or Unable*

The standard for finding "unwillingness" to investigate or prosecute is high. In making this determination, the Court is directed to consider whether the decision by national authorities "was made for the purpose of shielding the person concerned from criminal responsibility," whether there was "unjustified delay in the proceedings," or whether the proceedings "were not or are not being conducted independently or impartially" or "in a manner . . . inconsistent with an intent to bring the person concerned to justice." Art. 17(2). In deciding if the State is "unable" to prosecute, the Court must consider "whether, due to a total or substantial collapse or unavailability of its national judicial system, the State is unable to obtain the accused or the necessary evidence and testimony or otherwise unable to carry out its proceedings." Art. 17(3).

4. *Gravity*

The "gravity threshold" under art. 17(1)(d) has been the subject of considerable analysis and speculation. It remains unclear just what factors might prompt the Court to conclude that a given situation is "not of sufficient gravity to justify further action" and is therefore inadmissible. It is interesting that under article 53 the Prosecutor may similarly determine a case is not in the "interests of justice," taking into account "the gravity of the crime and the interests of victims."

Thus, specific cases are "inadmissible" (even though squarely within the Court's jurisdiction) if they are in fact being investigated or prosecuted by a State Party with jurisdiction. While these decisions obviously require a measure of judgment, they are not discretionary.

5. *Challenges*

While the Court can always consider on its own motion whether it should defer to national proceedings, challenges to the admissibility of a case may be made by an accused, or by a State which has jurisdiction (on the grounds that it is investigating or prosecuting the case or has done so), or by a State from which acceptance of jurisdiction is required under article 12. Art. 19(2).

In this regard, *see Prosecutor v. Katanga and Chui*, ICC–01/04–01/07–T–70–ENG, (Sept. 26, 2008), in which the Appeal Chamber said that the Court is only constrained by the principle of complementarity when domestic proceedings actually have been or are being conducted: "[I]in addressing whether a case is inadmissible under article 17(1)(a) and (b) of the Statute, the initial question to—the initial questions to ask are, one, whether there are ongoing investigations or prosecutions or, two, whether there have been investigations in the past and the State having jurisdiction has decided not to prosecute the person concerned. It is only when the answers to these questions are in the affirmative that one has to examine the question of unwillingness and inability. To do otherwise would be to put the cart before the horse. It follows that in the case of inaction, the question of unwillingness or inability does not arise. Inaction on the part of a State having jurisdiction renders a case admissible before this Court." Decision of Sept. 25, 2009, available at *http://www. icc-cpi.int/iccdocs/doc/doc571253.pdf.*

§ 4–14   APPLICABLE LAW

Article 21(1) of the Statute contains a hierarchy of applicable law. It provides that the Court *shall* apply (a) "in the first place, the Statute, Elements of Crimes and the Rules of Procedure and Evidence;" (b) "in the second place, where appropriate, applicable treaties and the principles and rules of international law, including the established principles of the international law of armed conflict;" and (c) "failing that, general principles of law derived by the Court from national laws of legal systems of the world including, as appropriate, the national laws of States that would normally exercise jurisdiction over the crime, provided that those principles are not inconsistent with this Statute and with international law and internationally recognized norms and standards."

In addition, under article 21(2), the Court *may* apply "principles and rules of law as interpreted in its previous decisions." The Statute thus rejects the strict reliance on decisional precedent (*stare decisis*) which is a hallmark of Anglo-American common law.

Finally, article 21(3) states that "the application and interpretation of law must be consistent with internationally recognized human rights, and be without any adverse distinction founded on grounds such as gender as defined in article 7, paragraph 3, age, race, colour, language, religion or belief, political or other opinion, national, ethnic or social origin, wealth, birth or other status."

§ 4–15 STATE COOPERATION WITH THE ICC

Under article 86, States Parties to the Rome Statute have a treaty obligation to cooperate fully in the investigation and prosecution of crimes within the ICC's jurisdiction. The procedure for requests by the Court is set out in article 87; the obligation of States to surrender persons is contained in article 89; the specific procedures by which the Court may make a request for provisional arrests are indicated in article 92; and the obligations of States Parties with respect to other forms of cooperation are indicated in article 93.

As with the *ad hoc* tribunals, cooperation has posed problems. The Court necessarily relies on assistance from States and international organizations in a number of areas. But in specific cases, States have been less than fully cooperative. Most notably, while the Court has issued arrest warrants for the situation in Uganda, the arrests have not occurred, even though the defendants' locations are generally known. In addition, the Court has had to conclude supplementary arrangements with States on issues concerning witness and enforcement of sentences.

§ 4–16 VICTIM PARTICIPATION AND REPARATIONS

Unlike the *ad hoc* tribunals (which do not permit victim participation except as witnesses), the Rome Statute gives victims an independent right to participate in proceedings. Article 68(3) permits the Court to allow the views and concerns of victims to be presented and considered, where the victims' personal interests are affected, at stages of the proceedings determined to be appropriate by the Court and in a manner which is not prejudicial to or inconsistent with the rights of the accused and a fair and impartial trial.

Under article 75(2), the Court may order convicted individuals to make reparations to victims, including restitution, compensation and rehabilitation. In accordance with article 79, a Trust Fund has been established by the Assembly of States Parties for the benefit of victims of crimes within the jurisdiction of the Court, and of the families of such victims. The Court can order money and other property collected through fines or forfeiture to be transferred to the Fund. Technically, the Trust Fund is independent of the Court and can act for the benefit of victims of crimes, regardless of whether there is a conviction by the ICC.

§ 4–17   SITUATIONS

As of June 2013, proceedings were under way before the Court with regard to eight separate situations. Five have been initiated by referral from States Parties themselves—Uganda, the Democratic Republic of the Congo, the Central African Republic, Côte d'Ivoire, and Mali. In addition, the UN Security Council has referred two situations— Darfur/Sudan and Libya. The eighth, involving the situation in Kenya, was initiated by the Prosecutor *proprio motu* and subsequently authorized by the Pre-Trial Chamber.

1. *Uganda/LRA*

A rebel movement known as the Lord's Resistance Army (LRA) has been fighting the Ugandan government in northern Uganda for nearly eighteen years. It seeks to overthrow the government. Years of violence have caused tens of thousands of civilian deaths and the displacement of 1.5 million people. Among the LRA's most notorious tactics has been the abduction and enlistment of children under the age of fifteen years. Uganda ratified the Rome Statute in 2002 and the following year referred the LRA situation to the Court.

In late 2005, Pre-Trial Chamber II issued arrest warrants for LRA leader Joseph Kony and a number of his senior commanders. The action reportedly created difficulties in peace negotiations between the government and the LRA, since the rebels are said to have made peace dependent on the ICC charges being dropped. Evidently, a settlement reached in February 2008 involved establishment of a special war crimes division within the Ugandan courts to try LRA leaders for the most serious crimes; lesser crimes would be dealt with using a traditional reconciliation method of the Acholi people ("Mato Oput"). In any event, the named defendants remain at large and the case remains pending.

2. *DRC/Katanga*

The ICC's first investigation, initiated in 2002, concerned crimes allegedly committed in the Democratic Republic of Congo (DRC). The situation was referred by the President of the country and has resulted in the ICC's first conviction. Thomas Lubanga Dyilo founded and led one of the most dangerous militia groups in the conflict in Ituri province between 1999 and 2007. Forces under his command were said to have been responsible for massive human rights violations, including ethnic massacres, murder, torture, rape, mutilation, and forcibly conscripting child soldiers. Arrested and transferred to the Court in 2006, he was found guilty in March 2012 of war crimes for forcibly enlisting and conscripting children under age fifteen into the Patriotic Force for the Liberation of Congo (FPLC) and using them to participate actively in hostilities. He was sentenced to fourteen years imprisonment. *See Prosecutor v. Lubanga*, Judgment, Trial Chamber, ICC–01/04–01/06 (Aug. 7, 2012).

Another FPLC leader, Germain Katanga, was surrendered to the Court in 2006 and charged with crimes against humanity and war crimes arising from mass rape, murder, and sexual enslavement. He was prosecuted along with Mathieu Ngudjolo Chui, a colonel in the DRC military and former senior member of the Front for National Integration. The cases were severed in November 2012; the next month Trial Chamber II acquitted Chui and ordered him released.

3. *Sudan/Darfur*

Since 2003, an on-going conflict has taken place in the Darfur region of western Sudan, mainly between the Sudan Liberation Army (SLA) and the Justice and Equality Movement (JEM) on the one hand, and the so-called "Janjaweed" (a militia group recruited from local Arab tribes and supported by the Sudanese Government) on the other. As many as 400,000 people are thought to have died; perhaps 2.5 million more have been displaced, mostly seeking refuge in camps or in neighboring Chad. The Sudanese government is said to have provided arms and assistance and participated in joint attacks with the group.

By Resolution 1593 (2005), the UN Security Council referred the situation in Darfur to the Court. (Sudan is not party to the Rome Statute.) The Prosecutor opened an investigation and in April 2007, the first arrest warrants were issued, for former Sudanese government minister Ahmad Harun and Janjaweed commander Ali Kushayb. On March 4, 2009, Sudanese President Omar al Bashir became the first sitting president to be indicted by ICC. In 2012, a warrant was issued for the arrest of Sudan's Minister of National Defense, Abdel Raheem Muhammad Hussein. None of the accused has been surrendered to the ICC. War crimes charges have also been brought against two other Sudanese officials, Abdallah Banda Abakaer Nourain and Saleh Mohammed Jerbo Jamus; their trial is scheduled to begin in May 2014.

4. *Central African Republic*

Following a 2004 referral by the Government of the Central African Republic, the Prosecutor opened an investigation into crimes committed in that country since 2002. The allegations include the raping and killing of civilians during an armed conflict between government and rebel forces, including the Movement for the Liberation of Congo (MLC) and its militia. In May 2008, Jean-Pierre Bemba, former Vice-President of the Democratic Republic of the Congo and alleged leader of the MLC, was arrested during a visit to Belgium on charges of war crimes and crimes against humanity. His trial began in November 2010 and is still underway.

5. *Kenya*

The most controversial exercise of the Prosecutor's *proprio motu* authority to date has involved the investigation into the 2007–2008 violence that followed the election in which incumbent President Mwai Kibaki was declared the winner. Supporters of opposition candidate Raila Odinga accused the government of electoral fraud. The ensuing protests and demonstrations— frequently along tribal lines—led to many injuries and deaths. In 2010, the Prosecutor issued summonses for six people: Deputy Prime Minister Uhuru Kenyatta, Ministers Henry Kosgey and William Ruto, Cabinet Secretary Francis Muthaura, radio executive Joshua Arap Sang and former police commissioner Mohammed Hussein Ali, all accused of crimes against humanity (variously including murder, persecution, forced population transfer, rape and sexual violence).

Colloquially referred to as the "Ocampo Six," they were indicted in March 2011 and summoned to appear before the Court. The Government of Kenya challenged the admissibility of the cases on grounds that it was "willing and able" to conduct its own investigation and prosecution. Notwithstanding this opposition, the accused chose to cooperate with the proceedings and attended hearings in The Hague in 2011. In January 2012, the Pre-Trial Chamber confirmed the charges against four of the six, and their trials were scheduled to begin in mid-2013.

6. *Libya*

In February 2011, the UN Security Council decided to refer the situation in Libya (from February 15, 2011 forward) to the ICC Prosecutor. (Libya is not a party to the Rome Statute.) The Prosecutor opened an investigation and in June 2011 Pre-Trial Chamber I issued arrest warrants for Libyan leader Muammar Gaddafi, his son and *de facto* Prime Minister Saif Al-Islam Gaddafi, and the head of Libyan military intelligence, Col. Abdullah Al-Senussi. They were accused *inter alia* of crimes against humanity (including murder and persecution) allegedly committed through the State Security Forces during February 2011. Charges against Muammar Gaddafi were terminated following his death at the hands of Libyan rebel forces.

The new government of Libya declined to transfer the other two accused and challenged the admissibility of the case on the grounds that it is willing and able to conduct its own prosecutions. In May 2013 Pre-Trial Chamber I rejected the challenge in the case against Saif Al Islam Gaddafi and ordered Libya to surrender him. Libya promptly appealed the decision.

7. Côte d'Ivoire

Although Côte d'Ivoire is not a party to the Rome Statute, it had accepted the Court's jurisdiction in 2003. In 2011, the Prosecutor sought and received authorization to open investigations *proprio motu* into crimes committed during the civil war in that country. That authorization initially covered the period after November 2010 but was subsequently expanded to include events going back to September 2002. A year later, Pre-Trial Chamber III issued an arrest warrant for Laurent Gbagbo, the former President of Côte d'Ivoire, who had been detained by the Ivorian Government following a contested election which removed him from office. He was charged with crimes against humanity (including murder, rape and other forms of sexual violence, persecution and "other inhuman acts") allegedly committed following the election. He was arrested by Ivorian authorities and transferred to the Court.

In June 2013, Pre-Trial Chamber I asked the Prosecutor to consider providing further evidence or conducting further investigation with respect to the charges against Laurent Gbagbo. An arrest warrant was also issued for Simone Gbagbo, former First Lady of the country, on grounds that she had played a central role in the post-election violence in Côte d'Ivoire. As of June 2013, Mrs. Gbagbo had not yet been transferred to the custody of the Court.

8. *Mali*

The most recent investigations concern alleged war crimes and crimes against humanity (rape, recruitment of child soldiers, summary executions) committed in northern Mali since January 2012. The situation was referred by the Government of Mali in July 2012. After conducting a preliminary examination of the situation, including an assessment of admissibility of potential cases, the OTP determined that a reasonable basis existed to proceed with an investigation.

§ 4–18   U.S. CONCERNS AND OPPOSITION

From the outset, there has been both substantial support for, and concern about, the ICC in various political circles in the United States. The United States participated actively in the negotiation of the Rome Statute and President Clinton signed it on December 31, 2000, the last day it was open for signature. In May 2002, however, before the Statute entered into force, President George W. Bush "unsigned" by declaring that the United States had no intention of ratifying the treaty, thereby arguably releasing the United States from any obligations thereunder. (The issue concerns the responsibilities of treaty "signatories" under art. 18 of the Vienna Convention on the Law of Treaties.) For its part, the Obama administration has pursued a more positive approach, participating in the

Kampala review conference, abstaining on the referral of Sudan, and co-sponsoring the referral of Libya.

Nonetheless, it seems unlikely that the current administration would submit the Rome Statute to the Senate for advice and consent to ratification in the foreseeable future or that, if it did, the Senate would provide its advice and consent to ratification.

For opponents, the main objections concern possible interference with prerogatives of national sovereignty, a fear of politically motivated prosecutions, and worries that members of the U.S. military engaged in international operations (including peacekeeping and humanitarian missions authorized under Chapter VII of the Charter) would be subject to ICC jurisdiction.

Critics have noted that unlike national prosecutors, the ICC Prosecutor is not accountable to any outside agency and thus can wield considerable authority in exercising his power to initiate investigations. (His *propio motu* investigations do require approval of the Pretrial Chamber.) Indeed, the ICC as a whole is not checked by any elected legislature or by an established tradition of international criminal justice. Under article 12 of the Statute, the ICC may take jurisdiction over nationals of a State not a party to the Statute without that State's consent and in the absence of a Security Council referral, if either the State of the territory where the crime was committed or the State of nationality of the accused consents. In some situations, this will expose individuals of non-party States (like the United States) to prosecution before the Court.

§ 4–19 *"ARTICLE 98" AGREEMENTS*

In an effort to avoid ICC jurisdiction, the United States undertook (for a period of time) to negotiate bilateral non-surrender agreements with various countries. These agreements sought to take advantage of article 98 of the Statute, which provides that the Court may not proceed with a request for surrender of a suspect or fugitive if that request would require the requested State "to act inconsistently with its obligations under international agreements pursuant to which the consent of a sending State" is first required. In other words, State A is not obliged to honor an ICC request to turn over a national of State B if States A and B have previously agreed that their nationals cannot be surrendered to the Court without their prior consent.

Over the course of several years, more than 100 such "article 98" agreements were concluded. They typically provided that a national of one party present in the territory of the other cannot be surrendered or transferred to the Court for any purpose. For several years, the U.S. Congress endeavored to promote the conclusion of such agreements by suspending certain kinds of bilateral foreign assistance to countries which were unwilling to conclude article 98 agreements with the United States. *See* the so-called "Nethercutt Amendment" to the Foreign Operations, Export Financing, and

Related Programs Appropriations Act. That provision lapsed in 2009.

The program of negotiating such agreements gradually came to an end, and no new agreements have been concluded for the past several years.

§ 4–20   AMERICAN SERVICE MEMBERS PROTECTION ACT

In 2002, the U.S. Congress adopted the so-called American Service Members Protection Act, which *inter alia* prohibited U.S. accession to the Rome Statute except by means of the treaty provisions of the U.S. Constitution (which require the Senate's advice and consent). It also limited U.S. cooperation with and support for the Court, precluded the extradition of any person from the United States to the Court, and restricted transfer of classified national security information as well as law enforcement information. It precluded U.S. military assistance to countries which had ratified the Rome Statute, subject to important exceptions for NATO members, other major U.S. allies, and countries which concluded article 98 agreements with the United States. The statute authorized the President to permit military aid when it was in the U.S. national interest.

In addition, the statute allowed the President to authorize military force to free any U.S. military personnel held by the ICC (causing some opponents to describe it as "The Hague Invasion Act"). It was subsequently amended to eliminate restrictions on bilateral military assistance and in 2008 all military sanctions provisions were removed. The current version of the statute may be found at 22 U.S.C.A. §§ 7401–02 and §§ 7421–33.

§ 4–21   FURTHER READING

The ICC's official website is at *www.icc-cpi.int*. The Rome Statute, UN Doc. A/CONF.183/9 (1998), is reprinted in 37 I.L.M. 999 (1998) and is available at *http://www.un.org/law/icc/index.html*. *See also* Margaret deGuzman, "Choosing to Prosecute: Expressive Selection at the International Criminal Court," 33 Mich. J. Int'l L. 265 (2012); William A Schabas, *An Introduction to the International Criminal Court* (Cambridge, 4th ed. 2011); Schabas, *The International Criminal Court: A Commentary on The Rome Statute* (Oxford 2010).

IV. THE MIXED TRIBUNALS OR HYBRIDS

Truly international tribunals (like the *ad hocs* or the ICC) are not the only means of dealing with violations of international criminal law. In the past several decades, other alternatives have emerged in the context of post-conflict accountability. In some cases, the choice has been to create specialized courts or chambers within the relevant domestic legal system; in others, the tribunals are free-standing, essentially independent of the domestic legal system. Under either approach, proceedings can be "internationalized" through provision of assistance from other countries or even the appointment of foreign judges. When that occurs, such tribunals are neither domestic nor international but take on features of both.

The following paragraphs provide brief summary descriptions of the various "hybrid" or "internationalized" courts in summary fashion. There is a growing body of literature about these courts and tribunals, and a growing debate over their structures, legitimacy and utility.

§ 4–22   LOCKERBIE

Perhaps the first such tribunal arose out of the bombing of Pan Am Flight 103 on December 21, 1988. The aircraft, en route from London to New York City, exploded over the village of Lockerbie in Scotland. All 259 passengers and crew (mostly Americans) were killed, as were eleven Scots on the ground.

An extensive investigation pointed to the involvement of two Libyan agents, Abdel Basset Ail Al-Megrahi (the former Director of Security for Libyan Airlines) and Al-Amin Khalifa Fhimah (the Director of the Libyan Airlines office in Malta). They denied the accusations, as did their government, but the United States and the United Kingdom demanded their surrender. When Libya refused, the UN Security Council imposed sanctions on Libya, including a travel ban and an embargo against oil-industry spare parts and technology. *See* UN Sec. Coun. Res. 748 (1992) and 883 (1993). Eventually, in April 1999, agreement was reached on a unique solution: a criminal trial would be held, in The

Hague, before a Scottish court and under Scottish law.

For this solution to work, Scottish law had to be amended to allow its courts to conduct an extraterritorial proceeding. The necessary authority was given to the Scottish High Court by legislation, and a special bilateral agreement was concluded between the United Kingdom and the Netherlands to permit the court to sit in The Hague. Under this agreement, *reprinted* at 38 I.L.M. 926 (1999), the court, prosecution and applicable law were all Scottish; otherwise, Dutch law applied.

Libya surrendered the accused and trial began in May 2000. In January 2001, following an 84-day trial, Al-Megrahi was convicted of conspiracy and sentenced to life imprisonment; Fhimah was acquitted. That verdict was upheld on appeal in March 2002. *See Al Megrahi v. HM Advocate*, (2002) J.C. 38 (Scot.). In August 2009, Al-Megrahi returned home to a hero's welcome in Libya after the Scottish government released him from prison on compassionate grounds. Medical examinations indicated that he would die from prostate cancer within a few months; in fact, he survived the next two years and died only in May 2012.

§ 4–23   SIERRA LEONE

The Special Court for Sierra Leone ("SCSL") presents a very different model. It was established in January 2002 by a treaty between the United Nations and the Government of Sierra Leone to prosecute "persons who bear the greatest responsibility for serious violations of international humanitarian law and Sierra Leonean law committed in the territory of Sierra Leone since November 30, 1996, including those leaders who, in committing such crimes, have threatened the establishment of and implementation of the peace process in Sierra Leone."

The SCSL is separate from the Sierra Leonean justice system but shares "concurrent jurisdiction" with it. It applies Sierra Leonean as well as international humanitarian law and (like the *ad hoc* tribunals) can assert "primacy" over Sierra Leonean courts in specific cases. Jointly administered by the UN and the Sierra Leonean government, it includes a majority of international judges. The Chief Prosecutor was appointed by the UN Secretary General.

The Court is organized into a Trial Chamber and an Appeal Chamber, the Prosecutor's office and the Registry. Under art. 20(3) of its Statute, the Appeals Chamber is "guided" by the decisions of the ICTR's Appeals Chamber except in respect of the interpretation and application of the laws of Sierra Leone, in which case the decisions of the Supreme Court of Sierra Leone apply.

The Court's substantive jurisdiction covers crimes against humanity, violations of common article 3 of the Geneva Conventions and Additional Protocol II, "other serious violations of international humanitarian law," and certain crimes under Sierra Leonean law, including abuse of girls and wanton destruction of property. Uniquely, article 4(c) of the

Statute authorizes the Court to prosecute persons for "conscripting or enlisting children under age 15 into armed forces or groups or using them to participate actively in hostilities." This practice was widespread during the Sierra Leone conflict. The SCSL is the first tribunal to prosecute such crimes.

In May 2004, the SCSL Appeals Chamber ruled that the prohibition against child recruitment had crystallized as a rule of customary international law by 1996, thus eliminating any problem regarding retroactivity. *See Prosecutor v. Noonan*, SCSL–2004–14–AR72(E), Decision on Preliminary Motion Based on Lack of Jurisdiction (Child Recruitment), para. 53 (May 31, 2004).

As of June 2013, the Prosecutor had indicted thirteen persons, of whom eleven were detained. Two died in custody and the remaining nine were tried on such charges as murder, rape, extermination, acts of terror, enslavement, looting and burning, sexual slavery, conscription of children into an armed force, and attacks on UN peacekeepers and humanitarian workers. Their cases were consolidated into four separate trials: the Revolutionary United Front (RUF) trial, the Civil Defense Forces trial, the Armed Forces Revolutionary Council (AFRC) trial, and the trial of Charles Taylor, all of which have now concluded.

The last has been the most visible. Taylor, the former President of Liberia, was accused of backing the civil war in Sierra Leone by providing arms and training to the RUF in exchange for diamonds. He was charged with mass murder, mutilation, rape, sexual slavery, and use of child soldiers. His trial began in June 2007. In 2009, the SCSL rejected his claim of Head of State immunity. In April 2012, the Trial Chamber convicted him on all counts, finding that he had participated in the planning of and aiding and abetting crimes committed by rebel forces in Sierra Leone. Its 2,500 page judgment was issued on May 18, 2012, and shortly thereafter, it sentenced Taylor to a prison term of fifty years. As of June 2013, his appeal remained pending.

The Appeals Chamber broke new ground by deciding that the term "other inhumane acts" in article 2 of the Statute is inclusive and, as a matter of customary international law, covers such acts as forcible transfer of persons, sexual and physical violence perpetrated upon dead human bodies, other serious physical and mental injury, forced undressing of women and marching them in public, forcing women to perform exercises naked, and forced disappearance, beatings, torture, sexual violence, humiliation, harassment, psychological abuse, and confinement in inhumane conditions. In the context of the Sierra Leone conflict, it said, the term "forced marriage" describes "a situation in which the perpetrator through his words or conduct, or those of someone for whose actions he is responsible, compels a person by force, threat of force, or coercion to serve as a conjugal partner resulting in severe suffering, or physical, mental or psychological injury to the victim." Such conduct is criminal and constitutes an "other inhumane act" capable of incurring individual criminal responsibility in international law. *See Prosecutor v.*

Alex Tamba Brima, Brima Bazzy Kamara and Santigie Borbor Kanu, Case No. SCSL–2004–16–A, Judgment, (Feb. 22, 2008), paras. 196, 203.

The official website of the SCSL is at *http://www.sc-sl.org/*. *See generally* Valerie Oosterveld, "Gender and the Charles Taylor Case at the Special Court for Sierra Leone," 19 Wm & Mary J. Women & the Law 7 (2012).

§ 4–24   EAST TIMOR

In May 2002, East Timor (Timor-Leste) gained its independence from Indonesia after decades of violence. By some accounts, as many as 200,000 East Timorese were killed during the Indonesian occupation. Immediately after the 1999 UN-supervised referendum on independence, more died and hundreds of thousands were displaced. Two separate processes were eventually established for the purpose of bringing the responsible persons to justice.

The first initiative came from the United Nations. Acting under Chapter VII of the Charter, the UN Security Council established the UN Transitional Administration in East Timor (UNTAET) to serve, in effect, as an interim government. In 2000, UNTAET created the "Special Panels for Serious Crimes" to prosecute individuals accused of war crimes, crimes against humanity, genocide and other serious crimes committed in East Timor between January 1, 1999 and October 25, 2000. The Special Panels (sometimes referred to as the "East Timor Tribunal") operated as part of the District

Court of Dili (the capital city of East Timor) and were composed of one Timorese and two international judges. To conduct the necessary investigations, a Serious Crimes Unit (SCU) was also created consisting of international police investigators. In addition, a Defense Lawyers Unit (DLU) was established to represent the defendants.

All investigations were concluded in November 2004, and the Special Panels closed in May 2005. All told, some 95 indictments were filed involving nearly 400 persons, and 284 arrest warrants were issued. When the mandate terminated, the Special Panels had completed 55 trials involving 88 persons; four were acquitted and 84 convicted, 24 of whom pleaded guilty. Most of the accused, however, remained outside East Timor and were never prosecuted, including former Indonesian Minister of Defense and Commander of the Indonesian National Military Wiranto, six senior military commanders, and the former Governor of East Timor.

Independently, an *Ad Hoc* Human Rights Court for Timor-Leste in Jakarta was established by the Government of Indonesia to try individuals responsible, *inter alia*, for crimes against humanity committed in April and September of 1999 in Timor-Leste. This court indicted eighteen individuals from the military and the police who were directly in command in East Timor at the material time, as well as two civilian government officials and a militia leader.

§ 4–25   CAMBODIA

The Extraordinary Chambers in the Courts of Cambodia (ECCC) offer yet another model. Created to address crimes committed in that country during the Khmer Rouge regime (1975–79), they form part of the Cambodian legal system, include both Cambodian and foreign judges, and apply a combination of international law and Cambodian criminal law and procedure.

Between 1975 and 1979, nearly two million people are thought to have died in Cambodia (then known as Democratic Kampuchea) as a result of starvation, disease, overwork or atrocities committed during the rule of the Khmer Rouge. Eventually, Pol Pot and his followers were ousted by the Vietnamese army, but little was done to bring the responsible individuals to justice. The scale of the atrocities, and the clearly destructive intent that motivated the violence, led some commentators to classify the acts as genocide. Yet the indiscriminate nature of the violence, and the fact that it was not directed against a particular religious, national, ethnic or cultural group, appeared to exclude it from the definition in the 1948 Genocide Convention.

In 1997, the Cambodian government sought UN assistance in creating a domestic tribunal. In 2001, the Cambodian Parliament adopted a Law on the Establishment of Extraordinary Chambers in the Courts of Cambodia for the Prosecution of Crimes Committed During the Period of Democratic Kampuchea. In 2003, Cambodia and the United

Nations concluded a bilateral agreement providing for UN assistance.

The ECCC's mandate is to prosecute those "most responsible for the crimes and serious violations of Cambodian penal law, international humanitarian law and custom, and international conventions recognized by Cambodia that were committed during the period from 17 April 1975 to 06 January 1979." The offenses include genocide under the 1948 Genocide Convention, crimes against humanity as defined in the ICC Statute, grave breaches of the 1949 Geneva Conventions, and certain other crimes (homicide, torture and religious persecution) under the 1956 Cambodian Penal Code. The agreement with the United Nations included a commitment by the Cambodian Government not to request "an amnesty or pardon for any persons who may be investigated for or convicted of crimes referred to in the present Agreement."

While some former Khmer Rouge leaders have died (including Pol Pot), others are alive and subject to prosecution. Four trials have been initiated. The first case involved charges of crimes against humanity and grave breaches of the Geneva Conventions against Kaing Guek Eav, alias "Duch," the former head of the notorious S–21 prison. On July 26, 2010, Duch was convicted and sentenced to thirty-five years' imprisonment. On appeal, his sentence was increased to life imprisonment. The second case involved charges against former foreign minister Ieng Sary, his wife Ieng Thirith, former Khmer Rouge ideological leader Nuon Chea, and former Head of State of Democratic Kampuchea Khieu Samphan. The case against Ieng Sary was terminated in March 2013 following his death; Ieng Thirith was declared unfit to stand trial in November 2011, owing to dementia. The trial of Nuon Chea and Khieu Samphan continues and has spawned Cases 003 and 004 as new investigations have been initiated against new co-accused.

The ECCC has pioneered efforts to increase victim participation during the proceedings, including establishing a Victims Support Section for that purpose. The Internal Rules allow victims to join as civil parties, receive compensation and make appeals. However, due to its ground-breaking nature and the lack of specificity in the Rules, the civil parties' participation has added considerably to confusion and slow pace of the proceedings. The work of the Chambers has also been hampered by financial shortfalls.

The official website of the Extraordinary Chambers is at *http://www.eccc.gov.kh/en*. The website of the independent Documentation Center of Cambodia, a depository of evidence and documentation regarding the ECCC, is at *http://www.dccam.org*.

§ 4–26   IRAQI SPECIAL TRIBUNAL

An Iraqi Special Tribunal was established by the Iraqi Governing Council (and promulgated by the Coalition Provisional Authority) in December 2003 to prosecute former Iraqi President Saddam Hussein and other Iraqi leaders for war crimes, crimes against humanity, and aggression. The court was later renamed the Iraqi High Tribunal by the Iraqi Transitional National Assembly when, in August 2005, it adopted the legislation approving the Tribunal's Statute and Rules. Initially independent of the Iraqi court system, the Tribunal is now integrated into the domestic judicial system of Iraq. Its membership consists exclusively of Iraqi judges, although they have been assisted by international experts.

The Tribunal's jurisdiction extended from July 1968 (when the Ba'athists seized power) to May 2003 (when U.S. President Bush declared an end to major hostilities in Iraq). Its subject matter jurisdiction includes genocide, crimes against humanity, and war crimes (all defined almost exactly as in the ICC Statute) as well as violations of certain Iraqi laws. The Tribunal's jurisdiction *ratione loci* is not confined to Iraqi territory, permitting prosecution for crimes committed in connection with Iraq's war against Iran and its invasion of Kuwait.

Multiple cases were brought in the Iraqi High Tribunal. The most notorious began in October 2005, in which Saddam Hussein and eleven other former high-ranking officials were prosecuted in connection with the execution of 148 Shiite civilians in Dujail. Saddam was convicted of crimes against humanity in November 2006 and sentenced to death. After his appeal was rejected, he was hanged. For an English translation of the Judgment in the Dujail Case (Nov. 26, 2006), *see http://www.law. case.edu/saddamtrial/dujail/opinion.asp.*

The second trial began in August 2006 and dealt with atrocities committed against Iraqi Kurds during the so-called Anfal campaign, involving the use of chemical warfare against the Kurdish population in northern Iraq. Over 100,000 individuals perished. In June 2007, the Tribunal convicted former Iraqi Defense Minister Ali Hassan al-Majid (known as "Chemical Ali") and five others of international crimes including genocide. A translation of the Judgment is available at http:// www.law.case.edu/grotian-moment-blog/anfal/ opinion.asp.

§ 4–27   LEBANON

On February 14, 2005, former Lebanese Prime Minister Rafiq Hariri and twenty-two others were killed by a massive bomb killed in Beirut. The UN Security Council established a Commission to assist the Lebanese authorities in their investigation into the event. The Commission recommended creation of a Special Tribunal for Lebanon. *See* Report of the Secretary-General on the establishment of a Special Tribunal for Lebanon, U.N. Doc. S/2006/893 (Nov. 15, 2006).

After extended negotiations, an agreement was concluded between the United Nations and the Lebanese Republic on the establishment of such a tribunal. The UN Security Council approved the creation of a tribunal in May 2007. *See* UN Sec.Coun. Res. 1757 (2007), to which is annexed the Agreement between the United Nations and the Lebanese Republic on the establishment of a Special

Tribunal for Lebanon (STL). The Tribunal sits in The Hague but, by arrangement with the Government of the Netherlands, persons convicted will not be detained there.

The Special Tribunal's jurisdiction is unique in several important respects. First, it is charged with prosecuting those responsible for a single event (the assassination of an important political figure) in a particular country. By comparison, other tribunals have been given jurisdiction over situations involving large scale crimes committed in countries over a substantial period of time. Second, the STL has been given explicit authority to expand its temporal jurisdiction. Article 1 of the Agreement provides that, if the Special Tribunal determines that other attacks occurring in Lebanon between October 1, 2004 and December 12, 2005, were "connected in accordance with the principles of criminal justice" and were "of a nature and gravity similar to the attack of 14 February 2005," then it may also prosecute those persons. The relevant period of time may be further expanded by agreement of the Parties and with the consent of the Security Council.

Third, although it is treaty-based and approved by the UN Security Council, the STL is not part of the United Nations or the Lebanese judicial system. It consists of Lebanese and international judges. Its substantive jurisdiction is based on Lebanese law and it has concurrent jurisdiction with the Lebanese courts except that, for matters within its jurisdiction, it will have "primacy over the national courts of Lebanon." *See* art. 4(1) of its Statute. Finally, the STL's jurisdiction is exclusively based on crimes defined under Lebanese domestic law and it does not have jurisdiction over any international crime. Notably, however, the first orders rendered suggest that the STL is "embedding international standards in a domestic jurisdiction."

The Tribunal opened on March 1, 2009, and in January 2011, the Prosecutor submitted the first indictment and supporting materials for review by the pre-trial judge. Although the indictment remains secret, the Tribunal is expected to indict members of Lebanon's Hezbollah. There are currently two cases before the tribunal. Trial proceedings have not started in either case.

Definition of Terrorism. On February 16, 2011, the STL's Appeal Chamber published a ruling setting out the definition of terrorism that would guide the tribunal in its deliberations. The Chamber suggested that there existed a customary international law definition of the crime of terrorism in times of peace, consisting of the following elements: "(i) the intent (dolus) of the underlying crime and (ii) the special intent (dolus specialis) to spread fear or coerce authority; (iii) the commission of a criminal act, and (iv) that the terrorist act be transnational." *See* Interlocutory Decision on the Applicable Law: Terrorism, Conspiracy, Homicide, Perpetration, and Cumulative Charging, available at *http://www.stl-tsl.org/en/the-cases/stl-11-01/ rule-176bis/filings/orders-and-decisions/appeals- chamber/f0010*. The Chamber argued that this customary international law definition was consistent with that under Lebanese law, and that in any case the gravity of the crimes and the fact that they had occupied the attention of the Security Council demanded adoption of a definition of terrorism in accordance with international law.

The Chamber's identification of a customary international definition of terrorism has been treated with skepticism by most publicists and States. *See, e.g.,* Ben Saul, "Legislating from a Radical Hague: The United Nations Special Tribunal for Lebanon Invents an International Crime of Transnational Terrorism," 24 Leiden J. Int'l L. 677 (2011).

The Special Tribunal's website is at *http://www.stl-tsl.org/en.*

§ 4–28   KOSOVO

Yet another approach was adopted by the UN Interim Administration Mission in Kosovo (UNMIK), concerning prosecution of individuals responsible for atrocities committed during the armed conflict in Kosovo in 1999. Neither the ICTY nor the Kosovar domestic justice system could handle the possible caseload. UNMIK responded by creating panels comprising at least two international judges and one Kosovar judge to adjudicate cases where it is "necessary to ensure the independence and impartiality of the judiciary or the proper administration of justice." Known as "Regulation 64 Panels," they were intended to function within the overall context of the existing

Kosovar court system to hear cases under Kosovar law involving serious crimes committed during the conflict including war crimes trials against Kosovo Serbs. The panels conducted over two dozen war crimes trials, including the trials of Milo Jokić and Dragan Nokolić. Additional information can be found at the United Nations Interim Administration Mission in Kosovo (UNMIK) website: *www. unmikonline.org.*

§ 4–29   BOSNIA-HERZEGOVINA

Unlike the Regulation 64 Panels, the War Crimes Chamber of the State Courts of Bosnia and Herzegovina is an entirely domestic court to which the ICTY can refer cases against lower level individuals accused of crimes against Croatian civilians. Created in January 2005, and located in Sarajevo, the Chamber operates under domestic law. Several former soldiers in the Bosnian Serb army have been convicted by the Chamber. Several cases have been referred to the Cantonal Court in Sarajevo. For additional information, *see www. sudbih.gov.ba.*

§ 4–30   SENEGAL/CHAD

Hissène Habrè, the former President of Chad, has been accused of more than 40,000 political killings and more than 20,000 cases of torture during his eight years in office. Deposed in 1990, he has been in Senegal under house arrest since 2005. Senegal has been under pressure from the international community to prosecute Habrè, with criticisms from the African Union, the Committee Against Torture, and the European Parliament.

Habrè was convicted *in absentia* in Chad in 2011 and indicted in Belgium in 2005. In July 2012, at the instance of Belgium, the International Court of Justice ordered Senegal to prosecute Habrè for torture in fulfillment of its obligations under the Convention against Torture. *See Questions Relating to the Obligation to Prosecute or Extradite* (Belg. v. Sen.), Judgment, 2012 I.C.J. Rep. 1, para. 121 (July 20, 2012).

Finally, in cooperation with the African Union, the Extraordinary African Chambers in the Senegalese Courts were established in 2012. A large part of Senegal's reluctance to initiate prosecutions was related to concerns regarding funding and was finally addressed through a November 2010 agreement between international donors regarding funding. The Court's Statute allows it to exercise jurisdiction over genocide (defined as under the Genocide Convention), crimes against humanity (defined as under the Rome Statute), war crimes, (defined as under the Rome Statute) and torture (defined as under the Convention against Torture). The judges of the Court will all be Senegalese. Its jurisdiction is restricted crimes committed on the territory of Chard during Habrè's tenure as President.

The Court initiated investigations in early 2013. In May 2013, Chad and Senegal were reported to have signed an agreement permitting the latter's judges to carry out investigations in Chad.

§ 4–31   BANGLADESH

In 2009, the government of Bangladesh constituted a special International Crimes Tribunal to prosecute those responsible for atrocities committed during the 1971 Bangladeshi war of liberation from Pakistan. In that conflict, thousands of civilians died at the arms of the Pakistani army and its collaborators. However, the Tribunal has been plagued by confusion and conflict. Among other difficulties, the presiding judge resigned in the midst of allegations that he had sought advice from an expatriate Bangladeshi international law expert, undermining the tribunal's independence.

The first convictions (in late 2012 and early 2013) sparked unrest in the Bangladeshi capital Dhaka and provoked criticism that the tribunal is a political device being manipulated by the government. International human rights groups have expressed serious concerns about the Tribunal's independence and impartiality, the extent of governmental interference, and the conditions of detention for those accused and convicted.

§ 4–32   GACACA COURTS

In Rwanda, a very different type of post-conflict mechanism was established, called *gacaca* (literally, "justice from the grass"), as a domestic supplement to the formal processes of the ICTR. These courts were more representative of truth and reconciliation commissions than formal prosecutorial mechanisms. Founded on customary law and practice, and focused at the local or community level, the *gacaca* courts aimed at revealing the truth about what happened and contributing to reconciliation within Rwanda. They were formally closed in 2012.

One useful source for additional information on general developments in this area is *http://law. case.edu/grotian-moment-blog/*. *See also* Paul Kristoph Bornkamm, *Rwanda's Gacaca Courts: Between Retribution and Reparation* (2012).

§ 4–33   RESTORATIVE JUSTICE MECHANISMS

As the examples indicate, international criminal justice mechanisms often find application in situations where entire societies have been torn apart by conflict and large numbers of people are either perpetrators or victims of violent crimes. Formal prosecutions are typically aimed at punishing the leaders and instigators of the worst atrocities. In some situations, however, determining individual criminal responsibility can be impossible and undesirable, both because of the severe logistical and financial challenges involved and because prosecution and punishment of a large section of society (often members of the some community) might cripple the human resources of that society and deepen its pre-existing rifts.

When that is the case, other types of transitional justice mechanisms may be appropriate, including truth and reconciliation commissions, official fact-finding commissions, amnesties, etc. These mechanisms aim primarily to "tell the story" by uncovering the truth, identifying perpetrators, and achieving some measure of reconciliation between victims and perpetrators—without necessarily imposing criminal punishments on all who may bear responsibility.

Depending on the particular circumstances, these alternatives can provide a different and constructive approach to post-conflict justice. In lieu of criminal prosecutions, they may provide non-adversarial mechanisms for conducting investigations, establishing the facts, determining accountability, and promoting social healing and forgiveness. They can furnish an opportunity for victims (and even perpetrators) to come forward with their stories to help establish the factual record of the atrocities, for recommending compensation, and for formulating reforms to prevent a repeat of past violence. They may be empowered to grant amnesties to encourage former perpetrators to come forward. In some cases the option of criminal prosecution may be retained.

However important these goals, some critics nonetheless contend that failure to convict and punish the guilty means the triumph of "impunity," so that alternative mechanisms can never be acceptable substitutes for genuine criminal trials.

The paradigmatic example of a truth and reconciliation commission is the one set up on South Africa following the end of apartheid. However, different types of commissions have also been experimented with in one form or another in Guatemala, Peru, Chile, Haiti, South Korea, Timor-Leste, Liberia, Mauritius, Canada, Morocco, Argentina, El Salvador, Germany, Ghana, Sierra

Leone, Paraguay, Ecuador, Mauritius, the Solomon Islands, Togo, Kenya, Mozambique, Cambodia, Uganda, Bolivia, Uruguay, Zimbabwe, Philippines, Nepal, Chad, Sri Lanka, Nigeria, Panama, Yugoslavia and Congo.

§ 4–34   FURTHER READING

Boas, Schabas and Scharf, eds., *International Criminal Justice: Legitimacy and Cohesion* (Elgar 2012); Scheffer, *All The Missing Souls: A Personal History of the War Crimes Tribunals* (Princeton 2012); Williams, *Hybrid and International Criminal Tribunals: Selected Jurisdictional Issues* (Hart, 2012); Fatou Bensouda, "Reflections from the International Criminal Court Prosecutor," 45 Vand. J. Transn'l L. 955 (2012); Priscilla B. Hayner, *Unspeakable Truths: Transitional Justice and the Challenge of Truth Commissions* (2d ed. 2011); Carla De Ycaza, "Victor's Justice in War Crimes Tribunals: A Study of the International Criminal Tribunal in Rwanda," 23 N.Y. Int'l L. Rev. 53 (2010).

CHAPTER 5
THE CORE CRIMES

This chapter discusses in greater detail the specific components of the four so-called "core crimes" of international criminal law. These are sometimes referred to as the "atrocity crimes." The focus is on the relevant provisions of articles 6 through 8 *bis* of the Rome Statute, since those are now internationally agreed-upon standards, but reference is also made to the decisions of the *ad hoc* tribunals and others where appropriate for a fuller understanding of the issues.

In each case, the objective or material elements of the crime (the *actus reus*) and the mental elements (the *mens rea*) are described. Where appropriate, reference is also made to the articulation of the specific elements of each of these crimes as set forth in the Elements of Crimes adopted by the Assembly of States Parties under article 9 of the Statute.

I. APPLICABLE LAW

Because it is an international court, the ICC requires specific guidance about what law it should apply in judging the cases before it. Article 21(1) of the Rome Statute contains a hierarchy of applicable law. It provides that the Court *shall* apply (1) "in the first place, the Statute, Elements of Crimes and the Rules of Procedure and Evidence;" (2) "in the second place, where appropriate, applicable treaties and the principles and rules of international law, including the established principles of the international law of armed conflict," and (3) "failing that, general principles of law derived by the Court from national laws of legal systems of the world including, as appropriate, the national laws of States that would normally exercise jurisdiction over the crime, provided that those principles are not inconsistent with this Statute and with international law and internationally recognized norms and standards."

In addition, under article 21(2), the Court *may* apply "principles and rules of law as interpreted in its previous decisions." The Statute rejects the strict reliance on decisional precedent (*stare decisis*), which is a hallmark of traditional Anglo-American common law, but adopts a permissive approach which recognizes implicitly that consistency in the application of the law is especially important in the context of criminal liability.

Finally, article 21(3) states that "the application and interpretation of law must be consistent with internationally recognized human rights, and be without any adverse distinction founded on grounds such as gender as defined in article 7, paragraph 3, age, race, colour, language, religion or belief, political or other opinion, national, ethnic or social origin, wealth, birth or other status."

II. THE FOUR CORE CRIMES

Article 5 of the Rome Statute limits the Court's substantive jurisdiction "to the most serious crimes of concern to the international community as a whole." More specifically, the Court's jurisdiction *ratione materiae* covers (1) genocide, (2) crimes against humanity, (3) war crimes and (4) the crime of aggression. They are addressed sequentially in articles 6, 7, 8 and (following the 2010 amendments) article 8 *bis* of the Statute.

§ 5–1   GENOCIDE

The term "genocide" is of relatively recent origin. It was formulated by Raphaël Lemkin, a Polish lawyer, to describe the horrific atrocities taking place in Nazi-dominated Europe before and during World War II. The indictment at Nuremberg actually employed the phrase "deliberate and systematic genocide," but, because the term itself had not been included in the London Charter, it was not a distinct crime within the jurisdiction of the International Military Tribunal.

However, the crime was codified shortly afterwards, in the Convention on the Prevention and Punishment of the Crime of Genocide, adopted by the UN General Assembly in UN G.A. Res. 260 A (III), on December 18, 1948. That Convention entered into force on January 12, 1951, and as of June 2013 had been ratified or adhered to by 142 States.

Interestingly, in the same year as the Genocide Convention entered into force, the International Court of Justice declared that genocide constituted a violation of customary international law. *See Reservations to the Convention on the Prevention and Punishment of the Crime of Genocide*, Advisory

Opinion, (1951) ICJ Rep. 15 at 3. Today, many consider the prohibition against genocide to be the paradigmatic rule of *jus cogens,* binding on all States whether or not they are parties to the Convention. Many States have criminalized genocide under their domestic laws.

Article VI of the Convention provides that persons charged with genocide can be tried either "by a competent tribunal of the State in the territory of which the act was committed, or by such international penal tribunal as may have jurisdiction." It may seem odd to provide that a crime of genocide should, in the first instance, be prosecuted within the domestic judicial system of the country where the genocide occurred, since in many situations that might be the *least likely* place for justice to be rendered. It was, however, entirely consistent with prevailing notions of sovereignty in 1948. By comparison, the second option was distinctly more radical: trial before an international tribunal. No such tribunal was established by the Convention itself, and no international court with jurisdiction over the crime of genocide was created until the two *ad hoc* Tribunals were established by the UN Security Council in 1993 and 1994, respectively.

The first international convictions for genocide were rendered by the ICTR in September 1998 in *Prosecutor v. Akayesu*, ICTR 96–4–T, Judgment, (Sept. 2, 1998), and *Prosecutor v. Kambanda,* ICTR 97–23–S, Judgment and Sentence, (Sept. 4, 1998). The first genocide conviction in the ICTY came in

August 2001 in *Prosecutor v. Krstić*, IT–98–33–A, Judgment, (Aug. 2, 2001). More recently, in June 2010, the ICTY convicted two Bosnian Serb Army officers of genocide in connection with the 1995 Srebrenica massacre in *Prosecutor v. Popović, Beara et al.*, IT–05–88, Judgment, (June 10, 2010).

1. *Elements of the Crime*

Article 6 of the Rome Statute replicates the definition of genocide in the 1948 Convention.

> For the purpose of this Statute, 'genocide' means any of the following acts committed with intent to destroy, in whole or in part, a national, ethnical, racial or religious group, as such:
>
> (i) Killing members of the group;
>
> (ii) Causing serious bodily or mental harm to members of the group;
>
> (iii) Deliberately inflicting on the group conditions of life calculated to bring about its physical destruction in whole or in part;
>
> (iv) Imposing measures intended to prevent births within the group;
>
> (v) Forcibly transferring children of the group to another group.

Note the three essential elements of the crime of genocide: (A) certain acts must have been committed (B) against a particular type of group (C) with a specific intent to destroy that group "as such" and "in whole or in part." Absence of any one of these three elements will constitute a failure to meet the definition.

A. Genocidal Acts

The list of "genocidal acts" includes five specific categories: (i) killing members of the group, (ii) causing serious bodily or mental harm to members of the group, (iii) deliberately subjecting members of the group to adverse conditions of life calculated to bring about its physical destruction in whole or in part, (iv) imposing measures intended to prevent births within the group, and (v) forcibly transferring children of the group to another group.

i.   Murder or Killing

For most people, the term "genocide" implies murder on a massive scale aimed at the extinction of entire human groups, such as occurred during the Holocaust during World War II. Clearly, the Statute's definition would encompass that situation. However, it does not actually specify a quantum or a minimum number of victims, or even require that these constitutive acts have been committed as part of a widespread or systematic attack or as part of a general or organized plan. A single act by a "lone genocidal maniac," however unlikely, would be sufficient to entail criminal liability as long as it otherwise fell within the definition and was committed against a specific group with the requisite intent. In this respect, genocide differs markedly from crimes against humanity.

ii.   Serious Bodily or Mental Harm

In fact, the definition does not require killing at all. It clearly covers such brutal acts as torture, rape, and non-fatal physical violence causing disfigurement or serious injury to the external or internal organs, if the other requirements are also met. It also extends to serious mental harm as well as the infliction of "conditions of life" calculated to bring about a group's physical destruction in whole or in part.

As stated by the ICTR Appeals Chamber in *Prosecutor v. Seromba,* ICTR 2001–66–A, Judgment, (Mar. 12, 2008), para. 46, the "quintessential examples of serious bodily harm" include torture, rape, and "non-fatal physical violence that causes disfigurement or serious injury to the external or internal organs." Serious mental harm includes "more than minor or temporary impairment of mental faculties such as the infliction of strong fear or terror, intimidation or threat" and typically involves rapes or killings. To the same effect, the Trial Chamber in *Prosecutor v. Akayesu,* ICTR 96–4–T, Judgment, (Sept. 2, 1998), para. 731, said that rape and sexual violence can constitute genocide in the same way as any other act and are "one of the worst ways of inflict[ing] harm on the victim as he or she suffers both bodily and mental harm."

iii.   Conditions of Life

Various methods can be used to inflict "conditions of life" calculated to bring about a group's physical destruction in whole or in part, including subjecting people to a subsistence diet, systematically expelling them from their homes and reducing essential services below a minimum level necessary to sustain existence. By itself, however, forced displacement or migration from a traditional homeland is not, in most circumstances, likely to meet the standard.

During the conflict in the former Yugoslavia, a widespread policy of forced removal ("ethnic cleansing") was pursued by Serbs in Bosnia and Herzegovina to require Muslims and Croats to leave areas desired by their enemies in order to create a "Greater Serbia." Where it could be established that this was intended as a "slow death," it could qualify as a form of genocide. In several cases, however, the Chambers declined to find individuals guilty of genocide even where there had been a coherent, consistent strategy of ethnic cleansing against Bosnian Muslims and Bosnian Croats through mass forcible displacement.

iv. Preventing Births

Imposing measures intended to prevent births within the group includes such practices as sexual mutilation, enforced sterilization and birth control, forced separation of males and females, and prohibition of marriage. *See Prosecutor v. Tolimir*, IT–05–88/2–T, Judgment, (Dec. 12, 2012), para. 743. In *Prosecutor v. Akeyesu*, ICTR 96–4–T, Judgment, (Sept. 2, 1998), para. 508, the Trial Chamber noted that rape can also be a means intended to prevent births "when the person raped refuses subsequently to procreate, in the same way that members of a

group can be led, through trauma, not to procreate."
In other words, this provision may apply when the
trauma from rape prevents the victim from wanting
to bear children, or when the victim is raped so that
she will then be considered unworthy of procreation.

v.   Transferring Children

Forcibly transferring children of the group to
another group can constitute an act of genocide
when the intent is to destroy the group's existence.
The assumption underlying this prohibition is that
having been transferred, children lose the cultural
identity of the group to which they originally belong.
Lawfully transferring children for social or economic
reasons, or for their protection, would not fall within
the prohibition. *Cf. Prosecutor v. Tolimir*, IT–05–
88/2–T, Judgment, (Dec. 12, 2012), paras. 793–94.

B. The Targeted Group

To constitute genocide, the genocidal acts must
have been committed against a "national, ethnical,
racial or religious" group. This second key
requirement is an exclusive list, meaning that other
kinds of groups (such as those defined by their
political beliefs or other characteristics) are not
included. Many believe that the narrowness of this
list is one of the definition's major shortcomings.

However, there is no internationally agreed-upon
definition of these various groups, and over time the
ad hoc Tribunals have articulated differing criteria.
The ICTR's Trial Chamber, for example, has defined
the term "national group" as "a collection of people

who are perceived to share a legal bond based on common citizenship, coupled with reciprocity of rights and duties." *Prosecutor v. Akayesu*, 96–4–T, Judgment, (Sept. 2, 1998), para. 512. By comparison, an "ethnic group" is "a group whose members share a common language or culture," while members of a "racial group" share "the hereditary physical traits often identified with a geographical region, irrespective of linguistic, cultural, national or religious factors." *Id.* at paras. 513–514.

A somewhat broader definition was subsequently adopted by the ICTR, giving greater weight to self-identification. "An ethnic group is one whose members share a common language and culture; or, a group which distinguishes itself, as such (self-identification); or, a group identified as such by others, including perpetrators of the crimes (identification by others). A racial group is based on hereditary physical traits often identified with geography. A religious group includes denomination or mode of worship or a group sharing common beliefs." *Prosecutor v. Kayishema and Ruzindana*, ICTR 95–1–T, Trial Judgment, (May 21, 1999), para. 98.

In *Prosecutor v. Semanza*, ICTR 97–20–T, Judgment, (May 15, 2003), para. 317, the ICTR's Trial Chamber stated that whether a group is a protected one should be "assessed on a case-by-case basis by reference to the *objective* particulars of a given social or historical context, and by the *subjective* perceptions of the perpetrators." Thus, a group might be distinguished according to characteristics, which are deemed essential for including people within that group or by identifying characteristics which exclude individuals from the group. In either case, having (or not having) the relevant characteristic can provide the perpetrators of the crime a basis for stigmatizing individuals on the basis of group identity.

C. Specific Intent

The third basic element of the genocide definition is the requirement of specific intent (*dolus specialis*) to eliminate the targeted group *as such*, whether in whole or in part. It is insufficient for a prosecutor simply to prove that the accused intended to commit one or more of the constitutive acts, or that the acts were in fact directed against members of one of the protected groups. What is also required is proof that the accused actually intended those acts for the purpose of destroying *that* group, *as a group*.

It is this requirement of specific intent that, as a legal matter, most clearly distinguishes genocide from "persecution" as a crime against humanity. In the latter, the perpetrator also chooses his victims because they belong to a specific community and is liable for his acts. But, in the former, even if the purpose is discriminatory, he does not commit genocide if he does not seek to destroy the group as such, in whole or substantial part. Moreover, in distinction to crimes against humanity, the existence of a plan or policy is not a legal requirement of genocide.

It is not necessary to aim at the complete annihilation of a group. The intent can be to destroy at least a substantial part of the protected group within the confines of a limited geographical area. In *Prosecutor v. Krstić*, IT–98–33–T, Judgment, (Aug. 2, 2001), the ICTY Trial Chamber convicted General Krstić of genocide for his participation in the extermination of some 8,000 Bosnian Muslim men in Srebrenica in 1995. Krstić's defense lawyers had argued that the Bosnian Muslims of Srebrenica did not constitute a specific national, ethnical, racial or religious group within the meaning of "genocide" and that it was impermissible to create an artificial "group" by limiting its scope to a specific geographical area. However, the Trial Chamber ruled that "[t]he intent to kill all the Bosnian Muslim men of military age in Srebrenica constitutes intent to destroy in part the Bosnian Muslim group within the meaning of article 4 and therefore must be qualified as genocide."

D. Inferred Intent

In some situations, there may actually be direct evidence of genocidal intent in the perpetrator's own oral or written statements. Where such direct evidence is absent, the intent may be inferred from the circumstances of the crime.

As the Trial Chamber stated in *Prosecutor v. Akayesu*, ICTR 96–4–T, Judgment, (Sept. 2, 1998), para. 523, "[i]t is possible to deduce the genocidal intent inherent in a particular act charged from the general context of the perpetration of other culpable acts systematically directed against that same group, whether these acts were committed by the same offender or by others." In the Chamber's view, it also possible to infer the necessary intent from "other factors, such as the scale of atrocities committed, their general nature, in a region or a country, or furthermore, the fact of deliberately and systematically targeting victims on account of their membership of a particular group, while excluding the members of other groups."

Inferring intent from circumstantial evidence needs to be approached with caution. In *Prosecutor v. Mugenzi and Mugiraneza*, ICTR 99–56–A, Judgment, (Feb. 4, 2013), paras. 91–92, the Appeals Chamber overturned a conviction for conspiracy to commit genocide because, in its view, the facts adduced at trial did not demonstrate the requisite *mens rea*, given that there were alternative explanations for the conduct in question. *See also Prosecutor v. Brdanin,* IT–99–36–A, Judgment, (Apr. 3, 2007), para. 228, in which the Appeals Chamber applied the standard that "no reasonable trier of fact could have concluded that the inference drawn was the only reasonable inference that could be drawn from the evidence provided."

2. Note on "Cultural or Political Genocide."

The definition of genocide in the Rome Statute (as well as in the Genocide Convention and under customary international law) only covers acts aimed at the physical or biological destruction of one of the four specified groups (in whole or in part). Some have criticized this limitation and sought to expand the definition to include acts aimed at suppressing or destroying the culture, religion or language of a targeted group, particularly when intended to achieve its forced assimilation rather than physical destruction.

In *Prosecutor v. Krstić*, IT–98–33–T, Judgment, (Aug. 2, 2001), the ICTY noted that the idea of "cultural genocide" had been considered and expressly rejected during the negotiation of the 1948 Convention. Thus, activities calculated to destroy the distinctive *cultural or sociological* character of a group, the elements that distinguish the group from others, do not fall under the definition of genocide. Neither do efforts to eliminate groups defined solely by their political beliefs or affiliation. Nonetheless, some perceive a trend toward broader interpretation including cultural as well as physical destruction. In particular, *see* the Partially Dissenting Opinion of Judge Shabbuddeen, which was followed in *Prosecutor v. Blagojević*, IT–02–60–T, Judgment, (Jan. 17, 2005).

3. *Direct and Public Incitement*

Uniquely, the Statute (like the Convention) criminalizes "direct and public incitement" to genocide. This form of liability does not apply to other core crimes.

The first convictions for direct and public incitement were rendered by the ICTR, and that tribunal has produced a number of seminal decisions in this regard. For example, in *Prosecutor v. Akayesu*, 96–

4–T, Judgment, (Sept. 2, 1998), para. 559, the Trial Chamber defined the crime as "directly provoking the perpetrator(s) to commit genocide, whether through speeches, shouting or threats uttered in public places or at public gatherings, or through the sale or dissemination, offer for sale or display of written material or printed matter in public places or at public gatherings or through the public display of placards or posters, or by any other means of audiovisual communication." *See also Prosecutor v. Nzabonimana*, ICTR 98–44D–T, Judgment, (May 31, 2012), para. 1175, convicting the defendant *inter alia* because he had "directly called for the destruction of the Tutsi ethnic group."

The crime lies in the incitement. The prosecution need not show that anyone acted upon the incitement or that it produced any other result. *See Akayesu*, paras. 561–562. It can be difficult, however, to distinguish clearly between legitimate political speech (or even propaganda) and criminal incitement, especially since incitement need not be explicit but can be subdued or indirect.

4. *Current U.S. Law*

The United States ratified the Genocide Convention in 1988 and has implemented its provisions through federal law. Under 18 U.S.C. § 1091, whoever commits the offense of genocide (defined as in the Convention), whether in time of peace or in time of war, and whoever "directly and publicly incites another" to do so, is subject to prosecution. The statute also covers attempt and conspiracy. However, it only applies when the offense has been committed in whole or in part within the United States, or when the alleged offender is a U.S. national or lawful permanent resident, or a stateless person habitually resident in the United States, or when, after the conduct required for the offense has taken place, the alleged offender is present in the United States, even if that conduct occurred outside the United States. *See* 18 U.S.C. § 1091(e).

The statute also defines the term "ethnic group" to mean "a set of individuals whose identity as such is distinctive in terms of common cultural traditions or heritage." The term "national group" means "a set of individuals whose identity as such is distinctive in terms of nationality or national origins." "Racial group" means "a set of individuals whose identity as such is distinctive in terms of physical characteristics or biological descent." "Religious group" means "a set of individuals whose identity as such is distinctive in terms of common religious creed, beliefs, doctrines, practices, or rituals." The term "incites" is defined to mean "urges another to engage imminently in conduct in circumstances under which there is a substantial likelihood of imminently causing such conduct." *See* 18 U.S.C. § 1093.

See generally Schabas, *Genocide in International Law: The Crime of Crimes* (Cambridge, 2nd ed. 2009).

§ 5–2   CRIMES AGAINST HUMANITY

The concept of "crimes against humanity" was first articulated as an international offense in the London Charter. Article 6(c) of that Charter defined the offense to encompass "murder, extermination, enslavement, deportation, and other inhuman acts committed against any civilian population, before or during the war, or persecutions on political, racial, or religious grounds in execution of or in connection with any crime within the jurisdiction of the Tribunal, whether or not in violation of the domestic law of the country where perpetrated." A majority of the defendants at Nuremberg were in fact convicted under this heading.

Similar definitions were contained in article 5(c) of the Tokyo Charter of the IMTFE as well as in article 2(11) of the 1954 Draft Code of Offences, although the latter included persecution on "social" grounds and limited the offense to acts "by the authorities of a State or by private individuals acting at the instigation or with the toleration of such authorities."

In article 5 of the ICTY Statute, the UN Security Council limited the definition to "crimes when committed in armed conflict, whether international or internal in character" and added imprisonment, torture and rape to the list. By comparison, the ICTR Statute, in article 3, replaced this "armed conflict" nexus with a more general requirement that the specific crimes have to have been "committed as part of a widespread or systematic attack against any civilian population on national, political, ethnic, racial or religious grounds."

Article 7 of the Rome Statute broadened the concept even further, eliminating the ICTY's discriminatory test. Under that article, the term "crime against humanity" means any one of eleven enumerated acts "when committed as part of a widespread or systematic attack directed against any civilian population, with knowledge of the attack."

1. *Elements of the Crime*

As defined in the Rome Statute, the key elements of the crime against humanity are (A) commission of one or more specific acts (B) as part of a "widespread or systematic attack" (C) which is directed against "any civilian population" (D) and the perpetrator must know that his or her acts constitute part of the attack.

A. *Specific Acts*

The list of enumerated acts constituting crimes against humanity in article 7(1) is long and detailed. It includes murder, extermination (killing as well as other measures calculated to end life, such as deprivation of food), enslavement (including trafficking in persons), deportation or forcible transfer of population (which would encompass "ethnic cleansing"), imprisonment or other severe deprivation of physical liberty in violation of fundamental rules of international law, torture, rape, sexual slavery, enforced prostitution, forced pregnancy, enforced sterilization, or any other form of sexual violence of comparable gravity, enforced disappearance of persons, the crime of apartheid, and "other inhumane acts of a similar character intentionally causing great suffering, or serious injury to body or to mental or physical health." Art. 7(1)(a)–(k).

i. Extermination as Crime Against Humanity

Article 7(2) defines "extermination" to mean "the intentional infliction of conditions of life, *inter alia* the deprivation of access to food and medicine, calculated to bring about the destruction of part of a population." In *Prosecutor v. Tolimir*, IT–05–88/2–T, Judgment, (Dec. 12, 2012), para. 723, the Chamber described this crime as involving "the crime of killing on a large scale together with the intention to kill on a large scale or to systematically subject a large number of people to conditions of living that would lead to their death." *See also Prosecutor v. Semanza*, ICTR 97–20–T, Judgment, (May 15, 2003), para. 340, which differentiated extermination from murder because it is directed against a population rather than individuals. "The material element of extermination is killing that constitutes or is part of a mass killing of members of a civilian population. The scale of the killing required for extermination must be substantial. Responsibility for a single or a limited number of killings is insufficient." *Id.* Obviously, this crime is closely analogous to genocide.

ii. Persecution as a Crime Against Humanity

By contrast, the "persecution" crime against humanity involves discriminatory acts "against any identifiable group or collectivity on political, racial, national, ethnic, cultural, religious, gender . . . or other grounds that are universally recognized as impermissible under international law, in connection with any act referred to in this paragraph or any crime within the jurisdiction of the Court." Rome Statute, art. 7(1)(h). Under art. 7(2)(g), this means "the intentional and severe deprivation of fundamental rights contrary to international law by reason of the identity of the group or collectivity."

As the Appeals Chamber noted in *Prosecutor v. Tolimir*, IT–05–88/2–T, Judgment, (Dec. 12, 2012), para. 846, this crime is based on an "act or omission that discriminates in fact, which denies or infringes upon a fundamental right laid down in international customary or treaty law, and which was carried out deliberately with the intention to discriminate on grounds of race, religion or political opinion." Not every infringement of rights constitutes persecution. To qualify, it must "constitute a gross or blatant denial of a fundamental right" reaching a particular level of gravity. *Id.* at para. 848.

Clearly, there is some overlap between this provision and the crime of genocide, and in specific circumstances a prosecutor may have the option of charging either.

iii. Gender-Based Acts

Article 7(1)(g) specifies several gender-based crimes, in particular those involving sexual violence ("rape, sexual slavery, enforced prostitution, forced pregnancy, enforced sterilization, or any other form of sexual violence of comparable gravity"). The term "forced pregnancy" is defined as "the unlawful confinement of a woman forcibly made pregnant, with the intent of affecting the ethnic composition of any population or carrying out other grave violations of international law." Art. 7(2)(f). Additional criteria are supplied in the Elements of Crimes, which for example describes "enforced sterilization" as applying to situations where the perpetrator has deprived one or more persons of biological reproductive capacity and when such conduct was neither justified by the medical or hospital treatment of the persons concerned nor carried out with their consent. *See* Elements of Crimes, art. 7(1)(g)–5.

iv. Enforced Disappearance

Article 7(2)(i) defines the term "enforced disappearance of persons" to mean the arrest, detention or abduction of persons by, or with the authorization, support or acquiescence of, a State or a political organization, followed by a refusal to acknowledge that deprivation of freedom or to give information on the fate or whereabouts of those persons, with the intention of removing them from the protection of the law for a prolonged period of time. This crime may be committed by arresting, detaining or abducting a person with knowledge that a refusal to acknowledge or give information would be likely to follow in the ordinary course of events, or by refusing to acknowledge the deprivation of freedom or to provide information on the fate or whereabouts of the person with knowledge that such deprivation may well have occurred.

B. Widespread or Systematic Attack

To constitute a crime against humanity, the specific acts described above must have been committed "as part of a widespread or systematic attack" directed against any civilian population. Art. 7(1). In other words, the attack must be characterized by significant size and gravity, for example involving a multiplicity of victims, with measures being carried out collectively, with some degree of organization and following a regular pattern, on the basis of a common policy and involving substantial public or private resources. In *Prosecutor v. Tolimir*, IT–05–88/2–T, Judgment, (Dec. 12, 2012), para. 698, the Trial Chamber said that the term "widespread" refers to the large-scale nature of the attack and the number of victims, while the word "systematic" ' refers to the organized nature of the acts associated with the attack and the improbability of their random occurrence. However, "a single act or limited number of acts can qualify as a crime against humanity provided the act or acts are not isolated or random and that all other elements [of the crime] are met." *Id*. The attack need not be military in nature.

i. State Action

Some controversy exists over whether the requirement necessarily implies a State-sponsored plan or policy. Article 7(2)(a) of the Rome Statute defines the term "attack directed against any civilian population" to mean "a course of conduct involving the multiple commission of acts . . . against any civilian population, pursuant to or in furtherance of *a State or organizational policy* to commit such attack" (emphasis added).

One reading is that actions by non-State entities would qualify. In this regard, *Prosecutor v. Akayesu*, ICTR 96–4–T, Judgment, (Sept. 2, 1998), para. 580, reached much the same conclusion interpreting the ICTR Statute: "The concept of 'widespread' may be defined as massive, frequent, large scale action, carried out collectively with considerable seriousness and directed against a multiplicity of victims. The concept of 'systematic' may be defined as thoroughly organized and following a regular pattern on the basis of a common policy involving substantial public or private resources. There is no requirement that this policy must be adopted formally as the policy of a State. There must however be some kind of preconceived plan or policy." *See also Prosecutor v. Blašić*, IT–95–14–T, Judgment, (Mar. 3, 2000), para. 204.

The ICC's Pre-Trial Chamber adopted this view in its decision to approve the Prosecutor's investigation of post-election violence in Kenya. *See Situation in the Republic of Kenya*, ICC–01/09, Decision of March 31, 2010, para. 92 ("organizations not linked to a

State may, for purposes of the Statute, elaborate and carry out a policy to commit an attack against a civilian population").

In dissenting from that decision, ICC Judge Hans-Peter Kaul rejected the Chamber's broad view, arguing that article 7(2)(a) should be read only to encompass "organizational policies" of State-like entities and not non-State actors such as "groups of organized crime, a mob, groups of (armed) civilians or criminal gangs groups . . . [or] violence-prone groups of persons formed on an *ad hoc* basis." Dissenting Opinion, para. 52. This more restrictive interpretation, he said, focuses the attention of the Court on circumstances where the State adopts or promotes a policy of attacking the civilian population, which is in his view when the greatest atrocities have occurred.

ii. *Armed Conflict*

As defined in the Rome Statute, crimes against humanity do not require a connection to an armed conflict (whether internal or international). This was not always true.

In article 6(c) of the London Charter, a distinction was made between one class of crimes against humanity committed "before or during the war" and a second group (persecutions on political, racial, or religious grounds) that had been committee "in execution of or in connection with any crime within the jurisdiction of the Tribunal"—meaning war crimes or an unlawful war of aggression. This bifurcation reflected a reluctance to hold individuals internationally responsible for acts taken by a government within its own territory with regard to its own citizens, since under then-prevailing notions of sovereignty such matters were considered "internal" and not appropriately regulated by international law unless they occurred during an armed conflict or military occupation.

The "armed conflict" nexus requirement did not long survive. It was eliminated from Allied Control Council Law No. 10 (1945). It was also omitted from the ILC Draft Code of Offences against the Peace and Security of Mankind (1954). It was included, however, in article 5 of the ICTY Statute, which limited the Tribunal's jurisdiction over crimes against humanity to those "committed in armed conflict, whether international or internal in character, and directed against any civilian population." No such requirement was included in the case of the ICTR, and none was incorporated into the Rome Statute.

C. Civilian Population

Crimes against humanity are considered "collective crimes" in the sense that they must be directed against a civilian population rather than only against individual victims. In this context, "civilian" means non-combatants. The phrase "directed against" means that the civilian population must be the primary object of the attack. It is not necessary for the entire population of the relevant geographical entity to have been targeted. As the ICTY Appeals Chamber has said, "it is sufficient to show that enough individuals were targeted in the course of the attack, or that they were targeted in such a way as to satisfy the Chamber that the attack was in fact directed against a civilian 'population,' rather than against a limited and randomly selected number of individuals." *Prosecutor v. Kunarac*, IT–96–23 and 96–23/1–A, Judgment, (June 12, 2002), para. 90.

2. *Mens Rea and Knowledge*

Unlike genocide, specific intent is not required for a crime against humanity. However, in addition to the ordinary intent (*mens rea*) to commit the specific acts in question, the perpetrator must also have "knowledge" of the "widespread or systematic" attack of which those acts are a part. An individual who is not aware that his or her acts are part of a widespread or systematic attack on a civilian population may be guilty of a serious crime, such as murder, perhaps even of war crimes, but cannot be convicted of crimes against humanity.

It is not necessary for the perpetrator to share in the purpose or goals of the larger attack. The ICTY Appeals Chamber has said that the accused's motives are irrelevant, and it does not matter whether the accused intended his acts to be directed against the targeted population or merely against his particular victim. Rather, it is the attack, and not the acts of the accused, which must be directed against the targeted population. The perpetrator only needs to have knowledge of the wider context in which his acts occur. *Prosecutor v. Kunarac,* IT–

96–23 and 96–23/1–A, Judgment, (June 21, 2002), para.103.

In *Prosecutor v. Tolimir,* IT–05–88/2–T, Judgment, (Dec. 12, 2012), para. 700, the ICTY Trial Chamber said that "the motives of the accused are irrelevant. A crime against humanity can be committed for purely personal reasons and it is not necessary for the accused to share in the purpose or goal behind the attack." However, in *Prosecutor v. Kayishema and Ruzindana*, lCTR 95–1–T, Judgment, (May 21, 1999), paras. 133–34, the ICTR Trial Chamber said: "The perpetrator must knowingly commit crimes against humanity in the sense that he must understand the overall context of his act. Part of what transforms an individual's act(s) into a crime against humanity is the inclusion of the act within a greater dimension of criminal conduct; therefore an accused should be aware of this greater dimension in order to be culpable thereof."

Note, however, that "persecution" as a crime against humanity under art. 7(1)(h) of the Statute *does* require a discriminatory intent (in addition to the "knowledge" element). *See also Prosecutor v. Lukić*, IT–98–32/1–A, Judgment, (Dec. 12, 2012), para. 458–59 (calling persecution as a crime against humanity a "specific intent" crime).

3. *Crimes Against Humanity Distinguished From Genocide*

Like genocide, crimes against humanity may be prosecuted whether committed in peace time or during an armed conflict. Genocide can be committed by State or non-State actors; the same is true for crimes against humanity, although the "widespread and systematic attack" must be "pursuant to or in furtherance of a State or organizational policy." For ICC purposes, it remains disputed whether policies of non-State actors will qualify.

Where genocide must be targeted against "a particular social, ethnical, racial or religious group," crimes against humanity need only affect a "civilian population." The term "civilian" excludes armed forces and certain kinds of militias, but the population need not be exclusively civilian; it will qualify if it is predominantly civilian. *See Prosecutor v. Tolimir*, IT–05–88/2–T, Judgment, (Dec. 12, 2012), paras. 695–96.

While genocide must aim at the destruction of the group in whole or in part, a crime against humanity need only be part of a "widespread or systematic attack." Unlike genocide, crimes against humanity do not require "specific intent," only an intent to commit the particular act in question and "knowledge" of the broader context in which it takes place.

See generally Leila Sadat, *Forging a Convention for Crimes Against Humanity* (Cambridge 2013); Leila Sadat, "Crimes Against Humanity in the Modern Age," 107 Am. J. Int'l L. 334 (2013); David Luban, "A Theory of Crimes Against Humanity," 29 Yale J. Int'l. L. 85 (2004).

§ 5–3   WAR CRIMES

Broadly conceived, "war crimes" are violations of the specialized laws and customs of war applicable in armed conflict. Article 8 of the Rome Statute contains a lengthy and detailed list of "war crimes" that can be prosecuted before the International Criminal Court. In order to understand these provisions properly, some background is necessary.

1. *Law of Armed Conflict*

For centuries, international lawyers have used the term "law of war" to cover two distinct areas: (i) the law relating to the decision to use force (*jus ad bellum*, or when it was lawful or unlawful to go to war) and (ii) the law governing the actual conduct of hostilities (*jus in bello*, or the specific rules relating how armed conflict had to be conducted).

Following World War II, the UN Charter prohibited the use of force in international relations *unless* authorized by the UN Security Council or in self-defense against an armed attack. These new provisions replaced the older ideas of just and unjust war.

The idea that some legal rules regulate the means and methods by which armed force is used during hostilities and that violations of those rules can be punished remains important. Over time, this second area came to be referred to as "Hague Law," because its main principles were contained in conventions concluded in The Hague in 1899 and 1907. Additional treaties were concluded over the following decades regulating, for example, the use of such weapons as poisonous gases and bacteriological methods of warfare. More recent international agreements have covered such means and methods of warfare as chemical weapons and landmines.

Following World War II, new protections were adopted in the four Geneva Conventions of 1949: (I) for the Amelioration of the Condition of the Wounded and Sick In Armed Forces in the Field, (II) for the Amelioration of the Condition of Wounded, Sick and Shipwrecked Members of the Armed Forces at Sea, (III) Relative to the Treatment of Prisoners of War, and (IV) Relative to the Protection of Civilians in Time of War. These treaties apply primarily in "international armed conflicts." In 1977, two additional Protocols to these Conventions were adopted: (I) Relating to the Protection of Victims of International Armed Conflicts and (II) Relating to the Protection of Victims of Non-International Armed Conflict. The primary focus of these protocols was the protection of civilians and those out of the fight (*hors de combat*). Together, these conventions and protocols came to be called the "Geneva Law."

2. *International Humanitarian Law*

Because "Hague Law" focused primarily on the actual use of force, it was sometimes described as the law of armed conflict (or LOAC). "Geneva Law" focused on protecting those no longer in the fight and was sometimes referred to as "international humanitarian law" (or IHL). Today, the distinctions are mostly of historical relevance, and the two terms are used interchangeably. Other distinctions are more important.

3. *Armed Conflict*

A key feature of international humanitarian law is that it applies only in connection with armed conflicts. The Geneva Conventions do not contain a definition of "armed conflict" but one has been crafted by the ICTY (in part, because its jurisdiction depends on it). In *Prosecutor v. Boškoski and Tarčulovski*, IT–04–82–A, Judgment, (May 19, 2010), para. 21, the Appellate Chamber said that armed conflict exists "whenever there is a resort to armed force between States or protracted armed violence between governmental authorities and organized armed groups or between such groups within a State."

4. *International vs. Non-International Armed Conflict*

The Geneva Conventions did introduce an important distinction between "international armed conflicts" and "armed conflicts not of an international character." While it is not always easy to tell one from the other, in general an international armed conflict is one in which two or more States are formally engaged in combat with each other, while a non-international armed conflict is typically "internal," that is, one occurring in the territory of one State. In recent years, however, armed conflicts with international terrorist groups have been characterized as non-international even though hostilities may be conducted in more than one country, because the conflict is not between States.

The difference is important, since the four 1949 Geneva Conventions and the first additional Protocol apply primarily to situations of "declared war or of any other armed conflict which may arise between two or more of the High Contracting Parties, even if a state of war is not recognized by one of them." By contrast, more limited protections apply in the case "armed conflict not of an international character occurring in the territory of one of the High Contracting Parties."

5. *Common Article 3*

Common Article 3 of the Geneva Conventions (called "common" because it appears in all four Conventions) obligates States Parties to provide at least a minimum of humanitarian protection to victims of armed conflicts, including in particular "persons taking no active part in hostilities, including members of armed forces who have laid down their arms and those placed *hors de combat* by sickness, wounds, detention or any other cause." Textually, the protection afforded by Common Article 3 is limited in two particular respects. First, it only applies to a certain category of internal hostilities (those occurring on the territory of one of the High Contracting Parties). Second, it only protects certain categories of victims of war (civilians or individuals who are taking no active part in the hostilities, because for example they are wounded or held prisoner).

In *Prosecutor v. Tolimir*, IT–05–88/2–T, Judgment, (Dec. 12, 2012), para. 683, the Appeals Chamber held that Common Article 3 applies in all armed conflicts, international and non-international alike, but there must be a "nexus" between the armed conflict and the crime in question. That connection need not have been causal but has to have played a "substantial part in the perpetrator's ability to commit the crime."

6. *War Crimes vs. Grave Breaches*

Not every violation of the 1949 Geneva Conventions amounts to a war crime. Among those that do, certain violations of these Conventions constitute more serious offenses and are termed "grave breaches." The four Conventions each define the term "grave breach" by reference to specific offenses, including among others willful killing, torture or inhumane treatment, willfully causing great suffering or serious injury, and taking of hostages. Grave breaches only arise when committed in international armed conflicts, and the victims of grave breaches must be persons specifically protected by a Geneva Convention such as a prisoner of war or a soldier who, due to wounds, is no longer capable of fighting. A State Party is obligated to bring those who commit grave breaches before its national courts or to hand them over to another State Party.

7. *Laws and Customs of War*

Finally, not all the rules relevant to armed combat were contained in the Hague, Geneva or other conventions. Over time, a body of principles developed, known as the "laws and customs of war," which were held to apply to all States and all combatants, no matter whether the conflict was internal or international. The heart of this body of rules is found in four fundamental principles.

A. *Distinction*

In order to ensure respect for and the protection of the civilian population and civilian objects, the parties to an armed conflict must distinguish between the civilian population and combatants, and between civilian objects and military objectives. They must direct their operations only against military objectives. Combatants can be uniformed military personnel, members of a government-organized militia or a non-State armed group, or a civilian directly participating in hostilities. Military objectives can include military bases, equipment or supplies, as well as any object that, by virtue of its nature, location, purpose or use, makes an effective contribution to military action and whose destruction, capture or neutralization offers a definite military advantage. Within these broad categories, any intended target must be a combatant or military objective.

B. Proportionality

When attacking military objectives, combatants must take measures to avoid or minimize collateral civilian damage and refrain from attacks that would cause incidental loss of civilian life, injury to civilians or damage to civilian objects that would be excessive in relation to the anticipated concrete and direct military advantage of the attack.

C. Military Necessity

This principle limits the measures not forbidden by international law to legitimate military objectives whose engagement offers a definite military advantage. The use of military force must not exceed the level necessary to achieve the military goal.

D. Unnecessary Suffering

The use of armed force must avoid subjecting an opponent to superfluous injury or unnecessary suffering beyond that necessary to bring about the opponent's prompt submission. It should include precautions to spare the civilian population before and during an attack.

From the perspective of international criminal law, it is important to recognize that an individual's criminal responsibility depends of the legality of his or her particular acts, not on the overall lawfulness of the broader conflict or whether the State was entitled to use force under international law. Put differently, a war crime remains a war crime, whether committed during an armed conflict resulting from a lawful use of force or one that violates international law. *See, e.g., Prosecutor v. Boškoski and Tarčulovski*, IT–04–82–A, Judgment, (May 19, 2010), para. 51.

8. *The Court's Jurisdiction*

Article 8(1) of the Rome Statute states that the Court has jurisdiction "in respect of war crimes in particular when committed as a part of a plan or policy or as part of a large-scale commission of such crimes." This provision reflects a compromise between those who wanted the Court to have jurisdiction "only" when war crimes are part of a broad plan or large-scale commission of offenses, and those who wanted no jurisdictional threshold at all. The "in particular" language presumptively limits the Court's jurisdiction but gives the Court leeway to act if circumstances mandate, even without evidence of either a plan or the large scale commission of war crimes.

Article 8(2) provides an extensive list of offenses (including nearly sixty separate provisions) divided between those occurring in international armed conflicts and those taking place in armed conflicts not of an international character.

9. *International Armed Conflicts*

With respect to international armed conflicts, article 8(2)(a) covers "grave breaches" of the Geneva Conventions such as willful killing, torture and hostage taking, and 8(2)(b) lists some 26 "other serious violations of the laws and customs applicable in international armed conflict," including (among many others) "intentionally launching an attack in the knowledge that such attack will cause incidental loss of life or injury to civilians or damage to civilian objects or widespread, long-term and severe damage to the overall environment."

10. *Non-International Armed Conflicts*

With respect to non-international armed conflicts, article 8(c) covers violations of Common Article 3 including acts of violence to life and person, outrages upon personal dignity, taking of hostages, and "the passing of sentences and the carrying out of executions without previous judgment [sic] pronounced by a regularly constituted court, affording all judicial guarantees which as generally recognized as indispensable." Under article 8(2)(d), however, this provision does *not* apply to "situations of internal disturbances and tensions, such as riots, isolated and sporadic acts of violence or other acts of a similar nature."

Article 8(2)(e) details a list of 12 other "serious violations of the laws and customs applicable in armed conflicts not of an international character," including "intentionally directing attacks against the civilian population as such or against individual civilians not taking part in hostilities." Here again, the Rome Statute provides that this provision does *not* apply to situations of internal disturbances and tensions, such as riots, isolated and sporadic acts of violence or other acts of a similar nature.

11. *The Belgian Amendment*

At the 2010 Review Conference in Kampala, a proposal by Belgium was accepted to add to article 8(2)(e) the following three crimes in the context of non-international armed conflicts (they are already included in the crimes in article 8(1) applicable to international armed conflicts): (i) employing poison or poisoned weapons; (ii) employing asphyxiating, poisonous or other gases, and all analogous liquids, materials or devices; and (iii) employing bullets which expand or flatten easily in the human body, such as bullets with a hard envelope which does not entirely cover the core or is pierced with incisions.

12. *Distinction Between War Crimes, Crimes Against Humanity and Genocide*

Clearly, there can be some overlap between war crimes, genocide and crimes against humanity. For example, the mass killing of civilians during an armed conflict might constitute a war crime, an act of genocide, or a crime against humanity, depending on the specific circumstances.

Unlike genocide, however, war crimes are not limited to specific groups and do not require specific intent. Unlike crimes against humanity, war crimes need not be part of a widespread or systematic attack on a civilian population nor do they require a governmental element or common plan; a single isolated incident can constitute a war crime. Unlike either of the others, however, war crimes can only be committed during (or be connected to) an armed conflict. Like the others, they can be committed by combatants and civilians alike. Finally, the term "war crime" has different meanings in different contexts (consider the variations, for example, between the Statutes of the ICTY, the ICTR and the ICC).

13. *U.S. Law*

Enacted in 1996 and codified at 18 U.S.C. § 2441, the War Crimes Act imposes criminal penalties on U.S. nationals and members of the U.S. armed forces who commit (among other offenses) grave breaches of the Geneva Conventions (or grave breaches of Common Article 3 during non-international armed conflicts).

See generally Detter, *The Law of War* (Ashgate, 3rd ed. 2013); Solis, *The Law of Armed Conflict: International Humanitarian Law in War* (Cambridge 2010).

§ 5–4   THE CRIME OF AGGRESSION

What has come to be called the crime of aggression was formerly covered under the term "crime against the peace." That is how article 6(a) of the London Charter, for example, characterized the "planning, preparation, initiation or waging of a war of aggression, or a war in violation of international treaties, agreements or assurances, or participation in a common plan or conspiracy for the accomplishment of any of the foregoing."

At Nuremberg, the IMT emphasized that "[t]o initiate a war of aggression ... is not only an international crime; it is the supreme international crime differing only from other war crimes in that it contains within itself the accumulated evil of the whole crime of aggression." Opinion and Judgment of the International Military Tribunal at Nuremberg (1946). The "common plan or conspiracy" charged in the indictment covered twenty-six years from the formation of the Nazi Party in 1919 to the war's end in 1945. In fact, the IMT disregarded the conspiracy allegations and considered only the "common plan to prepare, initiate, and wage aggressive war."

In 1974, the UN General Assembly adopted (by consensus) a resolution defining an act of aggression as "the use of armed force by a State against the sovereignty, territorial integrity or political independence of another State, or in any other manner inconsistent with the Charter of the United Nations." UN G.A. Res. 3314 (XXIX), Dec. 14, 1974, art. 1. Article 3 of the resolution listed a number of specific examples of acts of aggression, including *inter alia* the invasion or attack by the armed forces of a State of the territory of another State; any military occupation, however temporary, resulting from such invasion or attack; bombardment or blockade of another State; and the action of a State in allowing its territory, which it has placed at the disposal of another State, to be used by that other State for perpetrating an act of aggression against a third State.

Article 2 of the resolution stated that "the first use of armed force by a State in contravention of the Charter shall constitute prima facie evidence of an act of aggression." However, it also acknowledged that the Security Council could conclude that a determination that an act of aggression has been committed "would not be justified in the light of other relevant circumstances, including the fact that the acts concerned or their consequences are not of sufficient gravity."

With this resolution as background, there was broad agreement during the negotiation of the Rome Statute that aggression should be included within the core crimes. No consensus could be reached, however, on how exactly to define that crime or what role the Security Council should have in determining when it had taken place. As a consequence, the Statute left the issue open, providing only in article 5(2) that the crime could be prosecuted once a definition had been adopted and the Statute amended accordingly.

That goal was accomplished at the Review Conference held in Kampala in July 2010, and the crime is now defined in a new article 8 *bis*. The actual implementation of this provision was deferred for an additional seven years, to 2017, and even then, a two-thirds majority of States Parties to the Statute must approve. The amendments adopted in Kampala provide that the Court may only exercise jurisdiction (i) after a decision has been taken by a majority of States Parties following January 1, 2017 and (ii) only "with respect to crimes of aggression committed one year after the ratification or acceptance of the amendments by thirty States Parties," whichever is later. *See* art. 15 *bis* and Resolution RC/Res. 6 of June 11, 2010, in Official Records of the Review Conference, UN doc. RC/9/11 of June 11, 2010, available at *http://www.icc-cpi.int/iccdocs/asp_docs/ASP9/ OR/RC-11-ENG.pdf.*

In consequence, no investigations or prosecutions for aggression will take place for some time. Still, adoption of this amendment to the Statute marks a significant development in the field of international criminal law. As of June 2013, six States had ratified the Kampala Amendment; thirty ratifications are required.

1. *Elements of the Crime*

The term "crime of aggression" is defined in article 8 *bis* (1) as "the planning, preparation, initiation or execution, by a person in a position effectively to exercise control over or to direct the political or military action of a State, of an act aggression which, by its character, gravity and scale, constitutes a manifest violation of the Charter of the United Nations."

A. *Act of Aggression*

The "crime of aggression" must be predicated on an "act of aggression." That term is defined in article 8 *bis* (2): "the use of armed force by a State against the sovereignty, territorial integrity or political independence of another State, or in any other manner inconsistent with the Charter of the United Nations." Note, however, that not everything that qualifies as an "act of aggression" will constitute a prosecutable crime of aggression.

The following acts will qualify as "an act of aggression:"

(a) The invasion or attack by the armed forces of a State of the territory of another State, or any military occupation, however temporary, resulting from such invasion or attack, or any annexation by the use of force of the territory of another State or part thereof;

(b) Bombardment by the armed forces of a State against the territory of another State or the use of any weapons by a State against the territory of another State;

(c) The blockade of the ports or coasts of a State by the armed forces of another State;

(d) An attack by the armed forces of a State on the land, sea or air forces, or marine and air fleets of another State;

(e) The use of armed forces of one State which are within the territory of another State with the agreement of the receiving State, in contravention of the conditions provided for in the agreement or any extension of their presence in such territory beyond the termination of the agreement;

(f) The action of a State in allowing its territory, which it has placed at the disposal of another State, to be used by that other State for perpetrating an act of aggression against a third State;

(g) The sending by or on behalf of a State of armed bands, groups, irregulars or mercenaries, which carry out acts of armed force against another State of such gravity as to amount to the acts listed above, or its substantial involved therein.

B. State Action

These acts must have been committed by a State (most of them by the armed forces of a State) and directed against another State. It appears, therefore, that the definition would not apply to non-State actors such as insurgents or terrorists, or to actions by State authorities against their own citizens.

C. Leadership and Control

The accused must have (i) planned, prepared, initiated or executed the relevant act of aggression and (ii) must have been in a position effectively to exercise control over or to direct the political or military action of the State which committed the act of aggression.

Thus, lower-level officials or members of the military would presumably not be covered by article 8 *bis*. The scope of application of the "crime of aggression" was additionally qualified by an amendment to article 25 of the Statute, adding a new paragraph 3 *bis* providing that "[i]n respect of the crime of aggression, the provisions of this article shall apply only to persons in a position effectively to exercise control over or to direct the political or military action of a State." *See* RC/9/11 of June 11, 2010, Annex I, para. 5 (*bis*).

D. Character, Gravity and Scale

The act of aggression, by its character, gravity, and scale, must have constituted a manifest violation of the Charter of the United Nations. At Kampala, the Assembly of States Parties adopted a resolution stating that "aggression is the most serious and dangerous form of the illegal use of force" and accordingly that "a determination whether an act of aggression has been committee requires consideration of all the circumstances of each particular case, including the gravity of the acts concerned and their consequences, in accordance with the Charter of the United Nations. *See* RC/9/11 of June 11, 2010, Annex III, para. 6. In a second resolution, the ASP agreed that "in establishing whether an act of aggression constitutes a manifest violation of the Charter of the United Nations, the three components of character, gravity and scale must be sufficient to justify a 'manifest' determination. No one component can be significant enough to satisfy the manifest standard by itself." *See* RC/9/11 of June 11, 2010, Annex III, para 7.

E. Mens Rea

The perpetrator of the crime of aggression must have been aware of the factual circumstances that established the manifest violation of the Charter of the United Nation and that established that such a use of armed force was inconsistent with the UN Charter. Under article 30(3), "knowledge" means awareness that a circumstance exists or a consequence will occur in the ordinary course of events.

2. *Conditions of Jurisdiction*

In addition, the Court's jurisdiction over the crime of aggression is subject to several significant limitations. It will not be able to exercise jurisdiction over (i) acts committed on the territory or by the nationals of a non-State Party or (ii) crimes of aggression committed by nationals of one State Party if that State has "opted out" in advance under article 15 *bis* (4). There is no expiration date on the right to "opt out," although States are required to reconsider such declarations within three years of lodging them.

Moreover, different provisions were adopted with respect to how the Court's jurisdiction could be "triggered" in cases of (A) Security Council referral, (B), investigations initiated by the Prosecutor *proprio motu* and (C) referral by States Parties. Security Council referrals and investigations initiated *proprio motu* are discussed below.

A. Security Council Referrals

A major issue at Kampala concerned the role to be played by the UN Security Council in determining when aggression has taken place. Under the UN Charter the Security Council has primary responsibility for the maintenance of international peace and security. Article 39 of the Charter gives the Council the power to determine when a threat to or breach of the peace or act of aggression has occurred.

The amendments to the Rome Statute acknowledge the Security Council's role in this regard. They provide that the Security Council may refer a case to the Court under its Chapter VII authority and the Court will have jurisdiction under article 13(b), but they also specify that the Court will not necessarily be bound by the Security Council's determination that an act of aggression has taken place. Under art. 15 *ter* (4), "a determination of an act of aggression by an organ outside the Court shall be without prejudice to the Court's own findings under this Statute." Under art. 13(b), the ICC is empowered to exercise jurisdiction over situations referred by the Security Council without regard to whether the specific State concerned has accepted the Court's jurisdiction in this regard.

B. Investigations Proprio Motu

In the absence of a referral by a State Party, the Prosecutor can initiate an investigation into crimes of aggression but only if, six months after having been notified, the Security Council has taken no action and if the Pretrial Chamber authorizes the investigation. *See* art. 15 *bis* (6) and (7). The Security Council can, of course, act under article 16 to defer the investigation for a year (and that decision is renewable).

Under these amendments, the Court will not be able to consider alleged crimes of aggression by nationals of a State Party against a non-State Party except in cases referred by the UN Security Council, even though paradoxically it does have jurisdiction over war crimes and crimes against humanity in the same situation. Neither will it be able to adjudicate acts of aggression by nationals of a non-State Party against a State Party, although it would have jurisdiction over war crimes, crimes against humanity and genocide occurring on the latter's territory. In RC/9/11 of June 11, 2010, Annex III, para. 2, the Kampala Conference adopted an "understanding" that the Court shall have jurisdiction over Security Council referrals of the crime of aggression "irrespective of whether the State concerned has accepted the Court's jurisdiction in this regard."

3. *Complementarity*

To date, only a few States have criminalized the act of aggression in their domestic law, and adoption of the amendments does not impose any obligation on States Parties to the Statute to do so. As a practical matter, however, failure to harmonize their domestic laws with the Statute might deprive States Parties of the ability to invoke the principles of complementarity and admissibility by contending that they are "willing and able" to conduct such prosecutions.

See generally Carrie McDougall, *The Crime of Aggression Under the Rome Statute* (Cambridge 2013); Michael Scharf, "Universal Jurisdiction and the Crime of Aggression," 53 Harv. Int'l L.J. 357 (2012); Jennifer Trahan, "A Meaningful Definition of the Crime of Aggression: A Response to Michael Glennon," 33 U. Pa. Int'l L. J. 907 (2012).

CHAPTER 6

MODES OF PARTICIPATION AND RECOGNIZED DEFENSES

I. INTRODUCTION

Chapter 3 discussed the basic principles of international criminal law, including the concept of individual personal responsibility. That principle is reflected in article 25(2) of the Rome Statute, which states: "A person who commits a crime within the jurisdiction of the Court shall be individually responsible and liable for punishment in accordance with this Statute."

In specific cases, however, a more precise analysis is necessary in order to determine who can be held individually responsible for which acts, or put differently, exactly what must be proven in order to hold an individual criminally liable for a given crime. Different domestic legal systems approach this question in different ways. In general, however, the analysis focuses on two aspects: (i) what conduct is required, and (ii) what motive or intent is required. The first is sometimes referred to as the "objective" aspect of the conduct or omission (or *actus reus*) and the second as the "subjective" state of mind (*mens rea*). The latter can be critical: in U.S. law for example, it is the difference between murder and manslaughter.

This chapter focuses on the approach taken by the Rome Statute, which established the International

Criminal Court. Technically, its provisions apply only with respect to proceedings before that Court. As a recently negotiated multilateral treaty, however, the Rome Statute represents an internationally agreed set of common principles on principles of criminal liability, including questions of intent, motive and purpose.

II. KNOWLEDGE AND INTENT

Article 30(1) states that "[u]nless otherwise provided, a person shall be criminally responsible and liable for punishment for a crime within the jurisdiction of the Court only if the material elements are committed with intent and knowledge." These are the fundamental elements of criminal liability. As the ICTY Appeals Chamber said in *Prosecutor v. Natelić and Martinović*, IT–98–34A, Judgment, (May 3, 2006), para. 114, "[t]he principle of individual guilt requires that the accused can only be convicted for a crime if his *mens rea* comprises the *actus reus* of the crime. To convict him without proving that he knew of the facts that were necessary to make his conduct a crime is to deny his entitlement to the presumption of innocence."

For this purpose, article 30(2) states that a person has "intent" where (a) in relation to conduct, that person means to engage in the conduct and (b) in relation to a consequence, that person means to cause that consequence or is aware that it will occur in the ordinary course of events. Article 30(3) defines "knowledge" to mean "awareness that a circumstance exists or a consequence will occur in the ordinary course of events."

With respect to intent, international criminal lawyers tend to use some technical terms not familiar to most U.S. lawyers or students, to make some basic distinctions: (1) the actual intent to carry out the guilty act in question is often called *dolus directus*; (2) the intent to carry out a particular act with a more general awareness that there could be certain consequences to that act is called *dolus eventualis*; and (3) the precise or "specific" intent to carry out a particularly heinous act is called *dolus specialis*. This last is relevant only to cases of genocide, persecution as a crime against humanity, aggression and some forms of terrorism.

III. MODES OF PARTICIPATION

In addition to requiring both a "guilty act" and a "guilty mind," most legal systems draw distinctions between the ways an individual may commit, or be involved in committing, a crime. For example, the person who commits murder during a bank robbery may be held to a different standard than the other members of his or her gang who served as lookouts, or drove the get-away car, or provided the necessary "inside" information about the combination of the safe, etc.

It is common to distinguish "direct" from "indirect" participation and to acknowledge that persons acting together with a common objective may share liability for the overall crime. A line is often drawn between those who actually commit the crime (the "principals" or "perpetrators") and those who are otherwise involved or complicit (the "accessories" or "accomplices"). In most instances, the liability of the accessories or accomplices is "derivative" because it depends on the commission of a crime by the principal(s). Thus, if the principal is not guilty, then by definition neither is the accomplice.

However, U.S. law students should appreciate that foreign legal systems frequently define these categories differently than U.S. law does. In consequence, the developing international criminal law system often uses the terms differently. This can create some confusion. For example, U.S. law minimizes accessorial liability; "aiding and abetting" is typically treated as a form of "principal" liability. Internationally the opposite is true; aiding and abetting normally results only in liability as an accessory. For another example, U.S. criminal law relies heavily on the concept of a criminal "conspiracy;" most foreign legal systems do not have the concept and it is therefore rarely used in international practice (genocide is the main exception).

For ICC purposes, article 25(3) defines the "modes of participation" which will entail criminal responsibility under the Rome Statute. In general, article 25(3)(a) provides for liability as a principal when an individual is a *perpetrator* (i.e., physically carries out all elements of the offense) as well as when that individual is a *co-perpetrator* (commits the crime jointly with others) or is an *indirect perpetrator* (by exercising control over those who commit the offense) or is an indirect co-perpetrator (for example, contributes to the joint scheme through some form of organization).

Article 25(3) lists six specific modes of participation. Article 25(3)(a) addresses direct participation in "committing" a crime; articles 25(3)(b)–(e) discuss various modes of accessorial liability. Some are clearer than others, and the ICC itself has not yet had an opportunity to clarify all the issues they raise.

§ 6–1   COMMITS

First, article 25(3)(a) provides that a person can be held criminally liable when he or she commits a crime, whether as an individual, jointly with another, or through another person, regardless of whether that other person is criminally responsible.

The first part of this formulation is unremarkable, since it covers the familiar situation of the individual as direct perpetrator. If the crime in question is killing someone, then the person who did the killing is the one who "committed" the crime. If the crime is "planning" or "preparing" to kill someone, then everyone involved in the planning and preparation can be charged as a direct perpetrator of that crime. Recall that at Nuremberg, one of the main charges against the individual defendants was planning and preparing a war of aggression.

Article 25(3)(a) also covers co-perpetrators. Persons who act "jointly" or "through another person" can be charged with the crime(s) in question. This is true "regardless of whether that other person is criminally liable."

For specific crimes, what actually constitutes "commission" may require special consideration. For example, in *Prosecutor v. Seromba*, ICTR 2001–66–A, Judgment, (Mar. 12, 2008), para. 161, the ICTR Appeals Chamber noted that in the context of genocide, "direct and physical perpetration" does not necessarily mean physical killing but can include other acts as well. The Trial Chamber, it said, had erred by holding that "committing" requires direct and physical perpetration of the crime by the offender. The correct test was whether Seromba's actions were "as much an integral part of the genocide as were the killings which [they] enabled" and whether he "became a principal perpetrator of the crime itself by approving and embracing as his own the decision to commit the crime."

With regard to aggression under the Rome Statute, only persons "in a position effectively to exercise control over or to direct the political or military action of a State" can commit the crime.

§ 6–2   ORDERS, SOLICITS, INDUCES

Under article 25(3)(b), a person can be held criminally liable who "orders, solicits or induces the commission of such a crime which in fact occurs or is attempted." In contrast to the direct commission of a crime, these modes of participation are accessorial and thus can lead to criminal liability only if the crime "*in fact occurs or is attempted.*"

The concept of "ordering" rests on a hierarchical relationship and the notion of one person's authority to compel compliance by another. The relevant intent is that of the person issuing the order, not the one who obeys it, and that person must be aware of the substantial likelihood that the crime will in fact be committed pursuant to the order. As the ICTY has said, "[T]he actus reus of ordering requires that a person in a position of authority instruct another to commit an offence. There is no requirement that the order be given in any particular form. . . . [I]t is sufficient to demonstrate that the order substantially contributed to the physical perpetrator's criminal conduct." *See Prosecutor v. Boškoski and Tarčulovski,* IT–04–82–A, Judgment, (May 19, 2010), para. 160.

"Ordering" liability under article 25(3)(b) may seem similar to command or superior responsibility in article 28, but the former contemplates liability for an *affirmative* wrongful act while the latter depends on an *omission*—the failure to prevent or punish a crime committed by subordinates. To put it another way, a superior may liable for ordering a war crime only if her subordinate attempts it or succeeds in carrying it out. If the subordinate takes no steps to carry out that order, the superior cannot be held liable for having ordered the crime. On the other hand, if the soldier commits the crime on her own, the superior might be held liable (even if no orders were given) on the basis of command responsibility for having failed to prevent the crime.

By comparison, "soliciting" or "inducing" do not rest on a hierarchical relationship but instead focus on the ability of one person to convince another to commit an offense. These modes probably cover "instigation" as well. Here, the issue is whether the actions of an individual prompt, provoke or "bring about" the conduct of another which constitute a covered crime. It appears those actions can be express or implied but must include a "causal result." *See Prosecutor v. Blašić*, IT–95–14–5T, Judgment, (Mar. 3, 2000), para. 280.

§ 6–3   AIDS, ABETS, ASSISTS

Article 25(3)(c) recognizes a form of "accomplice" liability for an individual who, for the purpose of facilitating the commission of a covered crime, aids, abets or otherwise assists in its commission or its attempted commission, including providing the means for its commission.

This mode of participation is broad enough to cover all acts specifically directed to assist, encourage or lend moral support to the perpetration of covered crimes. It is an "inchoate" offense, meaning that the preparatory acts are punishable even if the core crimes they are intended to facilitate are not actually carried out.

It would seem to cover situations in which an individual gives practical assistance, encouragement, and moral support to the principal perpetrator(s), with knowledge that these actions will assistant the perpetrator(s) in the commission of the crime. It may also cover planning. The aider and abettor need not share the precise intent of the principals but must know that his conduct would assist the principals in their commission of the crime, and the support he or she provided must have had a substantial effect on the perpetration of that crime. *See, e.g., Prosecutor v. Lukić*, IT–9–32/1–A, Judgment, (Dec. 12, 2012) para. 450 (the aider and abettor must know that his acts would assist in the commission of the crime by the principal perpetrators and must be aware of the 'essential elements' of the crime committed by the principal perpetrators but need not share the *mens rea* for such crime).

In *Prosecutor v. Perišić*, IT–04–81–A, Judgment, (Feb. 28, 2013) para. 36, the Appeals Chamber reversed the conviction of the former chief of staff of the Yugoslav Army on the grounds that that specific direction is a required element of aiding and abetting, at least in the context of the liability of a superior for actions of his subordinates. In that case, the prosecutor had not proved Gen. Perišić had effective control over his soldiers at the time of the Zagreb shelling. "[N]o conviction for aiding and abetting may be entered if the element of specific direction is not established beyond reasonable doubt, either explicitly or implicitly."

§ 6–4   CONTRIBUTES WITH A COMMON PURPOSE

Article 25(3)(d) permits the imposition of criminal liability on a person who "[i]n any other way contributes to the commission or attempted commission" of one of the crimes "by a group of persons acting with a common purpose." It provides that "[s]uch contribution must be intentional" and made either (i) "with the aim of furthering the criminal activity or criminal purpose of the group" or (ii) "in the knowledge of the intention of the group to commit the crime."

The exact reach of this mode remains unclear. Based on the text, the prosecutor must show that a group of persons acting with a common purpose attempted to commit or committed a crime within the ICC's jurisdiction. The actions of the accused must have "contributed" to the commission or attempted commission of the crime in some way "other than" those set out in subparagraphs (a) to (c) (commits, orders, aids and abets). The contribution must have been intentional and made either with the aim of furthering the criminal activity or criminal purpose of the group or in the knowledge of the intention of the group to commit the crime.

By imposing liability for complicity in group crimes, this mode raises some difficult (and as yet unresolved) questions. It seems clearly distinct from what a U.S. lawyer would call conspiracy, since it does not appear to require any agreement among the participants and can only result in liability if the core crime is actually committed or attempted. It differs from "joint criminal enterprise" because it requires a contribution to the crime itself.

§ 6–5   DIRECT AND PUBLIC INCITEMENT

Article 25(3)(e) provides that, *only* in respect of the crime of genocide, criminal responsibility can be imposed on an individual who directly and publicly incites others to commit genocide. It thus incorporates the relevant provisions of Article III of the 1948 Genocide Convention, which includes "direct and public incitement" as one form of responsibility along with conspiracy, complicity and attempt.

The term "incitement" in this context involves convincing, encouraging, or persuading another to commit a crime. The ICTR Trial Chamber has noted that the "public" element of incitement involves an inquiry into two factors: (i) the place where the incitement occurred and (ii) whether or not assistance was collective or limited. "According to the International Law Commission, public incitement is characterized by a call for criminal action to a number of individuals in a public place or to members of the general public at large by such means as the mass media, for example, radio or television." *See Prosecutor v. Akayesu*, ICTR 96–4–T, Judgment, (Sept. 22, 1988) para. 556.

§ 6–6   ATTEMPTS

Under article 25(3)(f), liability may be imposed on someone who attempts to commit a covered crime by "taking action that commences its execution by means of a substantial step, but the crime does not occur because of circumstances independent of the person's intentions." It also provides that "a person who abandons the effort to commit the crime or otherwise prevents the completion of the crime shall not be liable for punishment under this Statute for the attempt to commit that crime if that person completely and voluntarily gave up the criminal purpose."

An attempt is an inchoate crime because, by definition, it rests entirely on preliminary actions which do not produce the intended consequences. The crime of attempt is complete when "substantial" steps have been taken, even though those steps have been frustrated (and the intended crime remains "incomplete") because of "independent" or external factors. As an example, if an individual seeks to kill another person by actually shooting at him but fails because the shot is deflected by a passing truck (or because a policeman arrives just before the accused can pull the trigger), he or she could be prosecute for an attempt—but not if the accused has a last-minute change of heart and lays down the loaded gun without firing it.

IV. CONSPIRACY AND JOINT CRIMINAL ENTERPRISE

Several of the modes discussed above would apply to different types of joint commission (co-perpetration) in a given crime. An individual may be held criminally responsible, for example, when he or she acts jointly with another or through another person to "commit" the crime, solicits or induces or aids and abets others to do so, or "contributes" to the commission of the crime. For those trained in U.S.

law, however, the description of modes seems odd, even deficient, because the Rome Statute does *not* deal separately with joint commission and in particular does *not* include the concept of conspiracy.

§ 6–7   CONSPIRACY

Conspiracy is generally punished in common law systems but it is unknown or severely limited in civil law systems. In U.S. law, the crime of conspiracy generally requires an agreement between two or more persons with the intention of committing a particular crime. The core of the charge of conspiracy is the agreement among those charged. All participants in the agreement can be held equally liable, including for the foreseeable acts of any of them. Typically, conspiracy stands on its own as a separate crime and is said to be an "inchoate" crime because the object of the conspiracy need not be consummated. To prove a charge of conspiracy, it is enough to show that the participants had agreed carry out the crime in question and (at least in U.S. law) had committed at least one substantive act in furtherance of the conspiracy.

Because many foreign criminal systems do not recognize the concept of conspiracy, it has been controversial at the international level. Both the London Charter and Allied Control Council Law No. 10 did include the concept but only in respect of crimes against peace. By contrast, they offered an alternative but related concept providing that those who participated in a "common plan" to commit any of the crimes covered in those instruments could be held responsible for acts performed in execution of such a plan.

The Nuremberg Indictment and CCL No. 10 also included the notion of "criminal organizations" and charged a number of groups and entities (including the Leadership Corps of the Nazi Party, the Gestapo, the Reich Cabinet, etc.) on this ground. Doing so was in a sense analogous to charging a criminal conspiracy, since those groups had been formed and organized for a common criminal purpose, but declaring the group itself to be unlawful did not mean that every member of the group was therefore liable for the group's actions. A member might be found liable on another basis (such as complicity) but not simply by virtue of membership in the group.

§ 6–8   JOINT CRIMINAL ENTERPRISE

Neither conspiracy nor the idea of a "criminal organization" were included in the Statutes of the two *ad hoc* tribunals, and as a result the ICTY and the ICTR struggled with the need to attribute criminal liability in situations involving massive crimes committed by large groups of individuals sharing a common criminal plan or purpose. The solution was the doctrine of "joint criminal enterprise" (or "JCE").

The ICTY Appeals Chamber has held that article 7(1) of that tribunal's Statute did not exclude imposing responsibility where several persons have a common purpose act together. "Whoever contributes to the commission of crimes by the group of persons or some members of the group, in execution of a common criminal purpose, may be held to be criminally liable." In this formulation, "common purpose" liability can be imposed only where (i) the participants share an intention to take part in a joint criminal enterprise and to contribute—individually and jointly—to the criminal purposes of that enterprise and (ii) actually "contribute" to those purposes. *See Prosecutor v. Tadić*, IT–94–1–A, Judgment, (July 15, 1999) para. 190.

The *Tadić* Chamber actually created three separate "categories" of JCE. All three require the existence of a group of individuals, a common criminal purpose which involves the commission of a covered crime, and the participation of the accused therein.

1. *The Basic Form: Common Intent and Purpose*

Here, the co-participants in the common plan or design possess the same criminal intent to commit a crime and one or more of them actually perpetrates the crime according to the common design. The accused individual must have knowingly participated in at least one aspect of the common design. All the participants can be held liable for the crime if they have made a significant contribution to the achievement of the common design. They can have played various roles. It is not necessary for each perpetrator to be seeking to carry out the plan for the same reason.

2. *The Systemic Form: Common Institutional Context*

This form contemplates the situation of a "concentration camp" or other "system of ill-treatment," in which the accused knowingly participates in some fashion, helping to implement or achieve the common design through some kind of institutional framework. There is no need to prove an express or implied agreement; the organizational context supplies the evidence of common plan and purpose. But the accused must know about the systematic nature of ill-treatment, must share the intent to contribute to it, and must have made a significant contribution. Typically, the accused will have held a position of some sort within the organizational hierarchy of the relevant entity (camp guard, for example).

3. *The Extended Form: Foresight and Assumption*

The third form addresses the situation where one of the perpetrators has committed a crime outside the common plan that was nevertheless a natural and foreseeable consequence of the plan. Here, all members of the plan can be held liable when that crime was a natural and foreseeable consequence of the realization of the common plan. The accused need not have known of or intended that act, only to have intended to participate in and to contribute to its execution. He or she is nonetheless responsible for "extraneous crimes" occurring as a reasonably foreseeable or predictable consequence of the underlying the common design. It is not necessary that the accused have been either reckless or indifferent to that risk.

Note the differences in the *mens rea* requirements. In the first JCE category, the accused must intend both to commit the crime and to participate in a common plan aimed at its commission. In the second, the accused must have personal knowledge of an organized criminal system and intend to further the criminal purpose of the system. For the third, the accused must also share in the common purpose but can be held responsible for a crime outside that common purpose if it was foreseeable that such a crime might be perpetrated by one or other members of the group and the accused willingly took that risk (*dolus eventualis*).

In *Prosecutor v. Brdanin*, IT–99–36–A, Judgment, (Apr. 3, 2007), paras. 410–419, the ICTY Appeals Chamber stressed that what matters in a first category JCE is not whether the person who carried out the *actus reus* of a particular crime is a member of the common plan but whether the crime in question forms part of the common purpose. Where the principal perpetrator of a particular crime is not a member of the JCE, this essential requirement may be inferred from the particular circumstances. It is not necessary to prove that an agreement or understanding existed between the actual perpetrator and the accused to commit that particular crime. For the third category, in order to hold a member of the JCE responsible for crimes committed by non-members of the enterprise, it has to be shown that the crime can be imputed to one member of the joint criminal enterprise, and that this member—when using a principal perpetrator—acted in accordance with the common plan. The existence of this link must be assessed case-by-case.

The ICTY continues to apply the JCE concept rigorously. In *Prosecutor v. Gotovina*, IT–06–90–A, Judgment, (Nov. 16, 2012) para. 96, the Appeals Chamber reversed the JCE conviction of two high-level Croatian leaders for crimes against humanity and violations of the laws and customs of war. "No reasonable trial chamber," it said, "could conclude that the only reasonable interpretation of the circumstantial evidence on the record was the existence of a JCE with the common purpose of permanently removing the Serb civilian population from the Krajina by force or threat of force." In *Prosecutor v. Stanišić and Simatović*, IT–03–69–T, Judgment, (May 30, 2013), the ICTY acquitted two former high-level officials in the Serbian State Security organization *inter alia* of JCE-based charges because it could not be established that they shared the necessary common criminal purpose.

Most recently, in *Prosecutor v. Prlić*, IT–04–74T, Judgment, (May 29, 2013), the Trial Chamber found that six high-level members of the Croatian Defense Council (HVO) had participated in a Joint Criminal Enterprise between November 1991 and April 1994 designed to remove Muslims and other non-Croats living in parts of Bosnia and Herzegovina claimed by the Croatian community in order to create a Croatian territory with the borders of the Croatian Banovina. This JCE, it said, was aimed at the establishment of a Croatian territorial entity to enable a reunification of the Croatian people. The participants implemented a system to expel the Muslim population from those areas by displacement and confinement of civilians, murder and destruction of property, ill-treatment and harsh conditions in detention, wide-spread use of detainees to work on the frontline and even to serve as human shields at times. The six were convicted of various crimes against humanity, grave breaches of the Geneva Conventions, and violations of the "laws and customs of war."

The JCE concept remains contentious. The main criticism of JCE category 3 has been that the accused is convicted for crimes that he neither committed nor intended to be committed. However, that can also be true of other modes of liability. The real problem would seem to arise when the doctrine is applied to large-scale, well-planned atrocities which involve large numbers of perpetrators, where it can be truly difficult to say that any one individual could reasonably foresee all the possible actions of all the others. This might make sense with regard to the overall high-level political or military leaders, the ones who initiate and in some way direct the common plan, but it seems more problematic for the low-level participants.

The "guilt by mere association" argument was raised and rejected in *Brdanin*, where the Appeals Chamber said (at para. 424) that because JCE responsibility does require the accused's participation (which can consist of assistance in, or contribution to, the execution of the common purpose), there is no risk that attaching JCE liability to an individual who is "structurally remote" from the crimes in question.

The concept of "joint criminal enterprise" is not explicitly included in the listing of modes in the Rome Statute. Whether the *ad hoc* tribunals' JCE jurisprudence will be relied on in the ICC, for example in assessing liability under article 25(3)(a) or (d), remains unclear. For a recent analysis, *see* the Defence Observations on Article 25(3)(d) in *Situation in the Democratic Republic of the Congo (Prosecutor v. Katanga)*, ICC–01/04–01/07, April 15, 2013.

§ 6–9   DIFFERENCE BETWEEN JCE AND CONSPIRACY

In U.S. law, conspiracy requires an agreement among the participants to commit a crime. It is punished as a crime itself, whether or not the underlying intended crime (the object of the conspiracy) was actually carried out. Generally, the accused must have committed at least some act in furtherance of the conspiracy. Under so-called *Pinkerton* liability, co-conspirators can be held substantively liable for foreseeable crimes committed in furtherance of the conspiracy.

By comparison, JCE is not a crime in itself but a "mode" of assessing criminal liability for other crimes. It does not require an agreement, only a common plan or design. It does require that some member of the group have committed a covered crime and that the accused made a significant contribution to the achievement of the common plan. The extended form of JCE is not unlike *Pinkerton* liability.

§ 6–10 DIFFERENCE BETWEEN JCE AND AIDING AND ABETTING

Aiding and abetting requires the accused to have made a substantial contribution to another's crime. The accused must know (and have intended) that his assistance will help the perpetrator commit the crime in question. As an "inchoate" offense, it is punishable even if the underlying crime is not actually carried out.

By comparison, JCE is based on the existence of a common plan or design. The accused must be aware that his participation in some way supports the overall objective shared by the group. He or she may be held liable for the crimes committed in furtherance of that common purpose as a whole and not simply the crimes which he committed or assisted.

§ 6–11 CONSPIRACY TO COMMIT GENOCIDE

The 1948 Genocide Convention, in article 3(b), criminalized conspiracy as a particular inchoate crime related to genocide, but the proposal was controversial and had been debated intensely during the conference that preceded its adoption. It was included within their Statutes (ICTY article 4(3)(a) and ICTR article 2(3)(b)). It was *not* included in the Rome Statute and accordingly is not discussed in the Elements of Crimes.

The ICTR has rendered a few informative decisions on the subject. In *Prosecutor v Karemera and Ngirumpatse*, ICTR 98–44–T, Judgment, (Feb. 2, 2012) para. 1578, the Trial Chamber said that conspiracy can be inferred from circumstantial evidence "as long as the existence of conspiracy to commit genocide is the only reasonable inference." The decision in *Prosecutor v. Musema,* ICTR 96–13–T, Judgment, (Jan. 27, 2000) paras. 189–203, discussed the differing origins and concepts of common law "conspiracy" and civil law "complot," concluding that "the crime of conspiracy to commit genocide is punishable even if it fails to produce a result, that is to say, even if the substantive offence, in this case genocide, has not actually been perpetrated." It also concluded that an accused could not be convicted of both genocide and conspiracy to commit genocide on the basis of the same acts.

V. COMMAND OR SUPERIOR RESPONSIBILITY

The notion that military commanders should be held responsible for crimes committed by their subordinates has long been an accepted principle of the law of war. Most famously, it was applied in the case of Japanese General Tomoyuki Yamashita, the military governor of the Philippines near the end of World War II, for his failure to prevent widespread atrocities committed by troops under his authority. As stated by the U.S. Military Commission, sitting in Manila in 1945, "where murder and rape and vicious, revengeful actions are widespread offences, and there is no effective attempt by a commander to discover and control the criminal acts, such a commander may be held responsible, even criminal liable, for the lawless acts of his troops." *See* IV Law Reports of Trials of War Criminals 335 (l948). The conviction imposed by the IMTFE was upheld by the U.S. Supreme Court in *In re Yamashita*, 327 U.S. 1 (1946).

The principle can also apply to civilian (non-military) individuals in a superior-subordinate relationship. For example, the IMTFE also found Japanese Prime Minister Hideki Tojo and Foreign Minister Mamoru Sigemitsu criminally liable for their failure to prevent or punish the criminal acts of the members of the Japanese military. The doctrine was also applied by the Nuremberg Tribunal and incorporated into the Statutes of the ICTY and the ICTR. In the former, most decisions concerned military leaders; in the ICTR, the doctrine was applied to civilian leaders in a number of circumstances.

Article 28 of the Rome Statute explicitly recognizes both types of responsibility, one for military commanders and the relationships other for others in "superior and subordinate" relationship.

As to the first, article 28(a) provides that "a military commander or person effectively acting as a military commander shall be criminally responsible for crimes within the jurisdiction of the Court committed by forces under his or her effective command and control, or effective authority and control as the case may be, as a result of his or her failure to exercise control properly over such forces" in two circumstances:

(i) That military commander or person either knew or, owing to the circumstances at the time, should have known that the forces were committing or about to commit such crimes; and

(ii) That military commander or person failed to take all necessary and reasonable measures within his or her power to prevent or repress their commission or to submit the matter to the competent authorities for investigation and prosecution.

As to the second, concerning non-military situations (for example, those involving civilian governments), article 28(b) states that a superior shall be criminally responsible for crimes committed by "subordinates under his or her effective authority and control, as a result of his or her failure to exercise control properly over such subordinates," where:

(i) The superior either knew, or consciously disregarded information which clearly indicated, that the subordinates were committing or about to commit such crimes;

(ii) The crimes concerned activities that were within the effective responsibility and control of the superior; and

(iii) The superior failed to take all necessary and reasonable measures within his or her power to prevent or repress their commission or to submit the matter to the competent authorities for investigation and prosecution.

Note the difference in the "knowledge" requirement. Military commanders must have had actual knowledge or a duty to have known; non-military superiors can only be held liable if they knew or "consciously disregarded" relevant information. This distinction is new. In the ICTY, a more general standard has been applied. In *Prosecutor v. Blašić*, IT–95–14–A, Judgment, (July 29, 2004) para. 62, the Appeals Chamber stressed that "a superior will be criminally responsible through the principles of superior responsibility only if information was available to him which would have put him on notice of offences committed by subordinates." This knowledge cannot simply be presumed but must be proved by direct or circumstantial evidence. On the other hand, conscious avoidance (sometimes called "willful blindness") cannot justify failure to act.

The central fact in both circumstances is the existence of the superior-subordinate relationship. This relationship does not depend on formal status alone; the important thing is the superior's ability to prevent and punish the commission of the crimes in question. The power or authority to prevent or to punish does not solely arise from *de jure* authority conferred through official appointment. In many contemporary conflicts, there may be only *de facto*, self-proclaimed governments and therefore *de facto* armies and paramilitary groups subject to their authority. *See Prosecutor v. Delalić*, IT–96–21–A, Judgment, (Feb. 20, 2001) para. 193. What is essential, in the view of the ICTY Appeals Chamber, is "effective control," which it has recently defined as the power to prevent or punish the offenses of the subordinates. *See Prosecutor v. Perišić*, IT–04–81–A, Judgment, (Feb. 28, 2013) para. 119 ("absent a finding of effective control over subordinates, superior responsibility cannot be established").

It is also necessary in both circumstances for the superior not to have taken all "necessary and reasonable measures" to prevent the crime or to punish the perpetrator or perpetrators. What is necessary and reasonable must be determined case-by-case. Some decisions apply a "due diligence" standards. *See, e.g., Prosecutor v. Blaškić*, IT–95–14–T, Judgment, (Mar. 3, 2000) para. 332. This may be characterized as a failure to exercise proper control over subordinates.

It is important to note that article 28 does not impose either vicarious liability or automatic or "strict" criminal liability. Liability arises when the superior culpably violates the duties of control assigned to him or her. What is central is the commander's own acts or omissions in failing to prevent or punish the acts of his subordinates whom he knew or had reason to know were about to commit serious crimes or had already done so.

In this sense, command responsibility is responsibility for a "culpable omission"—the failure to carry out his legal duty to control his subordinates. In *Prosecutor v. Bemba*, ICC–01/05–01/08–424, Decision Confirming Charges, para. 405–07 (June 15, 2009), the ICC's Pre-Trial Chamber said that a superior may be held responsible for the prohibited conduct of his subordinates for failing to fulfill his duty to prevent or repress their unlawful conduct or submit the matter to the competent authorities. *See also Prosecutor v. Ntagerura*, ICTR 96–10A, Judgment, (Sept. 1, 2009) para. 659 (holding that command responsibility requires a duty to act, the ability to act, the failure to act, intending the consequences or at least awareness and consent that consequences would occur, and that the failure results in commission of the crime).

VI. DEFENSES AND MITIGATION

The defenses to liability, as well as factors which can be pleaded in mitigation, are set forth in article 31 of the Rome Statute. The list is not exhaustive: article 31(3) states clearly that "[a]t trial, the Court may consider a ground for excluding criminal responsibility *other than* those referred to in paragraph 1 where such a ground is derived from applicable law as set forth in article 21."

§ 6–12   MENTAL DISEASE OR DIMINISHED CAPACITY

Because crimes within the scope of the Court's jurisdiction rest on the concept of purpose and intent, an individual cannot be convicted if he or she is unable to understand that the conduct in question would violate the law or to control his or her behavior. Thus, under article 31(1)(a), criminal responsibility cannot be imposed if the accused "suffers from a mental disease or defect that destroys that person's capacity to appreciate the unlawfulness or nature of his or her conduct" or the capacity "to control his or her conduct to conform to the requirements of law." Incapacity must affect the perpetrator at the time the act was committed, not afterwards. This defense does not apply to temporary states of exhaustion or excitement.

§ 6–13   INTOXICATION

Article 31(1)(b) excludes liability if the accused was at the time of the crime "in a state of intoxication that destroy[ed] that person's capacity to appreciate the unlawfulness or nature of his or her conduct, or capacity to control his or her conduct to conform to the requirements of law." This defense does not apply, however, when the person had become "voluntarily intoxicated under such circumstances that the person knew, or disregarded the risk, that, as a result of the intoxication, he or she was likely to engage in conduct constituting a crime within the jurisdiction of the Court."

The term "intoxication" presumably applies whether the condition results from alcohol, drugs or narcotics or other mind-altering psychotropic substances. However, it does not exclude responsibility in all situations—only when the result was a loss of capacity to appreciate the unlawfulness of one's acts or to control one's own conduct. Voluntary intoxication only works to free the perpetrator from responsibility if he or she is not aware of the risk of committing a crime while intoxicated.

§ 6–14   SELF-DEFENSE

Acts in self-defense may also be excluded. Article 31(1) (c) permits such a defense when the person accused "acts reasonably to defend himself or herself or another person or, in the case of war crimes, property which is essential for the survival of the person or another person or property which is essential for accomplishing a military mission, against an imminent and unlawful use of force in a manner proportionate to the degree of danger to the person or the other person or property protected." The article also states that "[t]he fact that the person was involved in a defensive operation conducted by forces shall not in itself constitute a ground for excluding criminal responsibility under this subparagraph."

The provision is thus available in two circumstances: (a) defense of oneself or another and (b) defense of property "essential for the survival" of the person or another person or "essential for accomplishing a military mission." However, the fact that the accused was "involved in a defensive operation conducted by forces shall not *in itself* constitute a ground for excluding criminal responsibility under this subparagraph."

The criterion of "reasonableness" applies to both situations. This must be judged in the particular circumstances of the event. Inherent in this defense are the concepts of imminence and proportionality. Acts of self-defense are only permissible in response to force directed against the life, limb or freedom of movement of the defender or a third party. The object of the defense must be an "imminent and unlawful use of force" and the response must be proportionate and reasonable.

§ 6–15   DURESS AND NECESSITY

Under article 31(1)(d), it may be a defense that the conduct alleged to constitute a crime "has been caused by duress resulting from a threat of imminent death or of continuing or imminent serious bodily harm against that person or another person, and the person acts necessarily and reasonably to avoid this threat, provided that the person does not intend to cause a greater harm than the one sought to be avoided." Such a threat may either be made by other persons or "constituted by other circumstances beyond that person's control."

The defense of duress has long been controversial. The reasons are illustrated by the now-famous case of Drazen Erdemović, a soldier in the Bosnian Serb Army who was involved in the massacre of unarmed Bosnian Serb men near Srebrenica in July 1995. He admitted to shooting some 70 individuals but claimed that he had been compelled to do so. At first, he had refused to participate but was told by his superiors, "if you don't wish to do it, stand in the line with the rest of them and give others your rifle so that they can shoot you." Before the ICTY he pled guilty but later appealed his sentence and succeeded in obtaining a reduction.

In *Prosecutor v. Erdemović*. IT–96–22–A, Judgment, (Oct. 7, 1997), para. 19, the Appeals Chamber said categorically that "duress does not afford a complete defence to a soldier charged with a crime against humanity and/or a war crime involving the killing of innocent human beings."

In their Joint Separate Opinion, Judges McDonald and Vohrah explained their position as follows (at para. 80): "There must be legal limits as to the conduct of combatants and their commanders in armed conflict. In accordance with the spirit of international humanitarian law, we deny the availability of duress as a complete defence to combatants who have killed innocent persons. In so doing, we give notice in no uncertain terms that those who kill innocent persons will not be able to take advantage of duress as a defence and thus get away with impunity for their criminal acts in the taking of innocent lives."

In his Separate and Dissenting Opinion, Judge Antonio Cassese provided a thoughtful review of prior decisions relating to the defense, and concluded (at para. 44) that "the customary rule of international law on duress, as evolved on the basis of case-law and the military regulations of some States, does not exclude the applicability of duress to war crimes and crimes against humanity whose underlying offence is murder or unlawful killing. However, as the right to life is the most fundamental human right, the rule demands that the general requirements for duress be applied particularly strictly in the case of killing of innocent persons."

The Rome Statute reflects much of Judge Cassese's nuanced approach. It conditions the availability of the defense on the existence of a threat of imminent death or of continuing or imminent serious bodily harm and requires both that the accused have acted "necessarily and reasonably to avoid this threat" and that he or she not have intended to cause "a greater harm than the one sought to be avoided." It combines the concepts of necessity and duress into a single ground for excluding criminal responsibility.

§ 6–16   MISTAKE OF FACT OR LAW

According to article 32(1), a mistake of *fact* can operate to exclude criminal responsibility "only if it negates the mental element required by the crime." By contrast, under article 32(2), a mistake of *law* as to whether a particular type of conduct is a crime within the jurisdiction of the Court does not exclude criminal responsibility, although it may do so "if it negates the mental element required by such a crime, or as provided for in article 33" (which relates to superior orders). Thus, it would not be a defense if a perpetrator's mistaken perception concerned the material elements of the crime (the individual thought that rape was not a crime, for example) but it might be if the defendant lacked the necessary *mens rea.*

§ 6–17   SUPERIOR ORDERS

Under article 33(1), "the fact that a crime within the jurisdiction of the Court has been committed by a person pursuant to an order of a Government or of a superior, whether military or civilian, shall not relieve that person of criminal responsibility unless: (a) [t]he person was under a legal obligation to obey orders of the Government or the superior in question; (b) [t]he person did not know that the order was unlawful; and (c) [t]he order was not manifestly unlawful."

These three conditions are cumulative. In other words, the defense only applies when the accused had a legal obligation to obey, and even then, if the accused knew it was an unlawful order, he or she could not claim the "superior orders" defense. In any event, the defense is not available with respect to "manifestly unlawful" orders, which are defined in article 33(2) to include "orders to commit genocide or crimes against humanity." This provision reflects long-standing principles, embodied in the Nuremberg and Tokyo Charters, Control Council Law No. 10, and the Statutes of the two *ad hoc* tribunals.

Propriety Under Domestic Law. While the Rome Statute does not specifically address the issue, it seems clear that article 33 would apply to the situation in which the compulsion results not from a specific command from a superior but by the general operation of domestic law. This rule was stated at Nuremberg, where a number of defendants sought to justify their actions as having been not merely compliant with, but required by, applicable domestic law. As expressed by the International Law Commission, the response is straightforward: the fact that internal law does not impose a penalty for an act which constitutes a crime under international law does not relieve the person who committed the act from responsibility under international law. *See Formulation of the Nürnberg Principles*, 1950 Y.B. Int'l Law Comm'n, vol. II, p. 374.

§ 6–18   OTHER ISSUES

1. *Juveniles*

Under Article 26, the ICC has no jurisdiction "over any person who was under the age of 18 at the time of the alleged commission of a crime."

2. *Statute of Limitations*

There is none in the ICC. As stated in article 29, "[t]he crimes within the jurisdiction of the Court shall not be subject to any statute of limitations."

3. *Official Status or Immunity*

The official position of a defendant (for example, as Head of State or Government, as a diplomat or some other governmental official) cannot protect him or her individual in the International Criminal Court.

Article 27(1) states that the Rome Statute applies "equally to all persons without any distinction based on official capacity. In particular, official capacity as a Head of State or Government, a member of a Government or parliament, an elected representative or a government official shall in no case exempt a person from criminal responsibility under this Statute, nor shall it, in and of itself, constitute a ground for reduction of sentence.

Article 27(2) provides that "[i]mmunities or special procedural rules which may attach to the official capacity of a person, whether under national or international law, shall not bar the Court from exercising its jurisdiction over such a person."

The "no immunity" rule is common to international tribunals. A different approach typically governs in domestic courts, which give effect to the international recognized principles of immunity for foreign officials, diplomats, Heads of State, etc. But with rare exceptions, foreign officials are not subjected to criminal prosecution in foreign courts. A State is of course able to subject its officials to prosecution in its own; it can also waive the immunity of its own officials from prosecution in foreign courts.

Consider this example. The King of Bellehaven has ordered and directed a campaign of persecution and ethnic cleansing against his own citizens in his own country. As King, he would likely be immune from prosecution in Bellehaven's own courts; under customary international law he would be entitled to "Head of State" immunity in foreign courts. However, he would have no immunity from prosecution for genocide or crimes against humanity in the International Criminal Court. Following his overthrow, the Bellehaven legislature could remove any domestic immunity he might have had to permit his prosecution in Bellehaven. If, by some chance, the King were to flee to the neighboring country of Justicia, he would still have "Head of State" immunity from prosecution in Justicia's courts unless and until Bellehaven's new government formally waived that immunity. (Justicia might have an obligation to surrender him to the ICC.)

4. *Tu Quoque*

Another general principle recognized in international tribunals is the non-applicability of the so-called *tu quoque* ("you too") defense. It was raised as a defense in post-World War II trials and universally rejected. As a general matter, an accused may not avoid liability by demonstrating that others committed the same act but were not punished. *See Prosecutor v. Zoran Kuprešić*, IT–96–12–T, Judgment, (Jan. 14, 2000) para. 516.

5. *Double Jeopardy*

International law does not generally apply the concept of double jeopardy (*non bis in idem*) to prosecutions by different sovereigns. For example, it is technically possible for an individual of State A who kills a citizen of State B while they are both in State C, to be subjected to sequential prosecutions in C, B and A. For practical reasons, it seldom happens.

The rule would not, in theory, prohibit prosecution by an international court with jurisdiction. As reflected in article 20 of the Rome Statute, the rule is somewhat more protective of the individual. The concept of double jeopardy is applied with respect to multiple proceedings in the ICC itself and to subsequent proceedings in other courts with respect to crimes for which the accused has already been tried (convicted or acquitted) in the ICC. Where the accused has previously been tried by another court, however, the ICC can also prosecute him or her "with respect to the same conduct" only where the prior proceedings were "for the purpose of shielding the person concerned from criminal responsibility for crimes within the jurisdiction" of the ICC or "[o]therwise were not conducted independently or impartially in accordance with the norms of due process recognized by international law and were conducted in a manner which, in the circumstances, was inconsistent with an intent to bring the person concerned to justice."

CHAPTER 7
TRANSNATIONAL CRIMES

I. INTRODUCTION

This chapter addresses crimes which have been identified by the international community as violations of international law but which, unlike the "core crimes" within the jurisdiction of international tribunals, are left to individual States to prosecute under their domestic law. Most international crimes fall into this "transnational" category. Most are the subject of international treaties.

Serious transnational crime is increasing. Not only does criminal activity cross national borders more frequently, but so do criminal organizations. Trafficking in people, drugs, arms, and other commodities is big business today, and money laundering is a major support base for terrorist organizations. Organized Russian criminal networks have been associated with the proliferation of stolen Soviet nuclear materials and weapons, and drug cartels in Latin America have been associated with insurgent movements and terrorist organizations.

At the same time, it has become harder for individual States to deal with the challenges presented by these criminal activities. By definition, transnational crime requires coordinated action by all States affected. Yet some States serve as sanctuaries for criminal organizations because of corruption, resource constraints or ineffective laws, or political orientation. Sharing information between national law enforcement agencies is critical to controlling cross-border crime. Interpol (the International Criminal Police Organization) was created in 1914 for this purpose, to "enable police around the world to work together to make the world a safer place" and relying on "high-tech infrastructure of technical and operational support" to "meet the growing challenges of fighting crime in the 21st century."

It is obviously not possible for international courts to exercise jurisdiction over all types of cases of transnational criminal activity. Instead, the international community has chosen to address the most significant types of transnational crime through a series of international agreements aimed at harmonizing the law and facilitating the response of law enforcement.

§ 7–1   COMMON CHARACTERISTICS

Most of the instruments addressing transnational crimes share a few broad characteristics. First, they describe the conduct in question as an "international crime" or a crime "of international concern." Second, they define the crime, usually through a description of the specific conduct which constitutes that crime. Third, they require States Parties to prosecute that crime whenever it occurs in specified jurisdictional circumstances. Fourth, they impose an "extradite or prosecute" obligation with respect to alleged offenders discovered in the territory of States Parties in certain circumstances. Fifth, they require States Parties to cooperate with each other with respect to the investigation, prosecution or prevention of the specified crimes; the more recent treaties contain novel provisions related to transfer of prisoners or criminal proceeding, assets forfeiture and other forms of mutual legal assistance. Finally, many of the treaties impose specific duties of cooperation on States Parties such as sharing information and providing training and technical assistance.

Not all treaties contain all these provisions, and there is considerable variation among them. As a general matter, the more recent treaties have stronger provisions. Still, the effectiveness of these agreements depends entirely on domestic implementation. It is not uncommon for a given transnational crime to be prosecuted more vigorously in some countries than in others. In fact, there is no real agreement on what constitutes the body of "transnational crimes" or which crimes should be covered. The following discussion describes a number of the most significant crimes that have been addressed internationally.

II. TRADITIONAL CRIMES

§ 7–2   PIRACY

Piracy is the classic international or transnational crime. It has existed as long as maritime routes have been used for commerce and navigation. The vast expanses of the high seas have made shipping an easy target for pirates. Those who commit piracy threaten the interests of all trading States and have been considered enemies of all mankind (*hostis humani generis*). For that reason, States have long been empowered to capture and prosecute pirates on a "universal" basis, without regard to territoriality or nationality.

In recent years, piracy has become endemic in certain areas, including the Strait of Malacca between the Malay Peninsula and Sumatra, off the west coast of Africa, and especially in Gulf of Aden and the Indian Ocean off the coast of Somalia. In the latter case, the UN Security Council has adopted several Chapter VII resolutions authorizing States to use "all necessary means" to counter the threat posed by piracy. An international task force called the Combined Maritime Forces has been created to protect shipping in the area.

1. *Definition*

The current definition of piracy is contained in the 1982 UN Convention on the Law of the Sea, 1833 U.N.T.S. 3. As of June 2013, the Convention had been ratified by 165 States. Article 101 defines "piracy" to include the following offenses:

(a) any illegal acts of violence or detention, or any act of depredation, committed for private ends by the crew or the passengers of a private ship or a private aircraft, and directed:

(i) on the high seas, against another ship or aircraft, or against persons or property on board such ship or aircraft;

(ii) against a ship, aircraft, persons or property in a place outside the jurisdiction of any State;

(b) any act of voluntary participation in the operation of a ship or of an aircraft with knowledge of facts making it a pirate ship or aircraft;

(c) any act of inciting or of intentionally facilitating an act described in subparagraph (a) or (b).

Under this definition, the crime of piracy includes (i) acts of violence or depredation (ii) committed for private ends (iii) by crew or passengers of one private ship against another (iv) on the high seas or other place "outside the jurisdiction of any State." Private aircraft are also covered. Governmental ships or aircraft are generally excluded.

2. *U.S. Statute*

The principal U.S. statute criminalizing piracy (18 U.S.C. § 1651) was recently interpreted to include "attempted piracy" and to apply to violent conduct on the high seas. *United States v. Dire*, 680 F.3d 446 (4th Cir. 2012), *cert. denied*, 133 S.Ct. 982 (2013). In *United States v. Ali*, 718 F.3d 929 (D.C. Cir. 2013), the statute was interpreted to cover a charge of "aiding and abetting" even though the relevant conduct did not occur on the high seas. In

Institute of Crustacean Research v. Sea Shepherd Conservation Society, 708 F.3d 1099 (9th Cir. 2013), the court interpreted the term "private ends" broadly, to include personal or political goals as well as monetary benefit.

The 1985 hijacking of an Italian cruise ship, *MS Achille Lauro*, by members of the Palestine Liberation Army, illustrated the narrowness of the traditional definition. The PLA's goal was to pressure the Israeli government to release "political" prisoners. Because that situation would not qualify as "piracy," the international community undertook to negotiate a new instrument covering acts of maritime terrorism. The result was the 1988 Convention for the Suppression of Unlawful Acts against the Safety of Maritime Navigation, 1678 U.N.T.S. 221. *See* **§ 8–11**.

§ 7–3 SLAVERY

Slavery and slave trading have long been proscribed by the international community. For example, international agreements for the suppression of the African slave trade date from the early 19th century. The first major multilateral instrument on the subject was the Slavery Convention of 1926, which mandated the imposition of sanctions on slavery and slave trading.

The first international criminal provisions against slavery were included in the 1956 UN Supplementary Convention on the Abolition of Slavery, the Slave Trade, and Institutions and Practices Similar to Slavery, 226 U.N.T.S. 3. That treaty remains the primary applicable international treaty proscribing slavery and currently has 123 ratifications. It requires States Parties to criminalize the "conveying of slaves," "enslavement," and "inducing" individuals to place themselves or their dependents into "servile status" (including attempts, aiding and abetting, and conspiring). A separate provision prohibits mutilation, branding or otherwise marking slaves or persons of servile status as indication of status, punishment or for any other reason (including attempts, aiding and abetting thereof, and conspiring thereto).

However, the Convention did not create extraterritorial jurisdiction, nor did it impose an extradite-or-prosecute (*aut dedere aut judicare*) obligation common in more modern international treaties on transnational crimes. Its ambit was limited to obligations requiring States Parties to make internal, individual efforts to restrict and abolish slavery within their jurisdictions.

Today, the proscription of slavery and the slave trade is more clearly addressed in the non-criminal context of contemporary international human rights law. *See, e.g,* art. 4 of the Universal Declaration of Human Rights, and art. 8 of the International Covenant on Civil and Political Rights. Officially, slavery and the slave trade are prohibited everywhere.

§ 7–4   APARTHEID

The crime of apartheid can be characterized as an exaggerated, more deeply entrenched version of racial discrimination. The term originally referred to the institutionalized, State-sanctioned and widely-condemned system of racial discrimination prevalent in South Africa until 1990. International law today prohibits such conduct in any State by any government.

The 1966 Convention on the Suppression and Punishment of the Crime of Apartheid, 1015 U.N.T.S. 243, entered into force in 1976 and as of June 2013 had been ratified by 108 States. It declares apartheid to be a crime against humanity and, more generally, that "inhuman acts resulting from the policies and practices of apartheid and similar policies and practices of racial segregation and discrimination . . . are crimes violating the principles of international law, in particular the purposes and principles of the Charter of the United Nations, and constituting a serious threat to international peace and security."

The Convention defines the crime of apartheid broadly, to include a number of "inhuman acts committed for the purpose of establishing and maintaining domination by one racial group of persons over any other racial group of persons and systematically oppressing them." It also prohibits legislative measures and other measures calculated to prevent racial group from participating in the political, social, economic and cultural life of the country, as well as measures "designed to divide the population along racial lines by the creation of separate reserves and ghettos for the members of a racial group or groups, the prohibition of mixed marriages among members of various racial groups, the expropriation of landed property belonging to a racial group or groups or to members thereof."

Article III applies international criminal responsibility to "individuals, members of organizations and institutions and representatives of the State, whether residing in the territory of the State in which the acts are perpetrated or in some other State," irrespective of motive, for the committing, participating in or inciting apartheid, and for inchoate offenses (aiding, abetting, conspiring) relating to the commission of apartheid. States Parties must prosecute and punish individuals charged with covered crimes whether or not they reside in the State where the acts are committed or are nationals of that State.

It does not appear that anyone has ever been prosecuted for the international crime of apartheid under this convention. However, article 7(1)(j) of the 1998 Rome Statute of the International Criminal Court (ICC) includes apartheid within the definition of a crime against humanity when committed as part of a widespread systematic attack directed against any civilian population.

See   http://untreaty.un.org/cod/avl/ha/cspca/cspca. html for information concerning the 1966 Apartheid Convention.

III. HUMAN RIGHTS CRIMES

§ 7–5   TORTURE

The prohibition against torture is well established today in international law. It has been criminalized by international agreement, and many people contend that it is prohibited as a peremptory norm (*jus cogens*).

The Convention against Torture and Other Cruel, Inhuman or Degrading Treatment or Punishment, 1465 U.N.T.S. 85, was adopted by the UN General Assembly in 1984 and today has 153 States Parties. Article 1(1) defines torture to include:

> any act by which severe pain or suffering, whether physical or mental, is intentionally inflicted on a person for such purposes as obtaining from him or a third person information or a confession, punishing him for an act he or a third person has committed or is suspected of having committed, or intimidating or coercing him or a third person, or for any reason based on discrimination of any kind, when such pain or suffering is inflicted by or at the instigation of or with the consent or acquiescence of a public official or other person acting in an official capacity. It does not include pain or suffering arising only from, inherent in or incidental to lawful sanctions.

Article 4 requires each State Party to ensure that "all acts of torture are offences under its criminal law" (including attempts, complicity, and "participation in torture") and that they are "punishable by appropriate penalties which take into account their grave nature."

Each State Party must establish domestic jurisdiction to prosecute such offenses when committed in any territory under its jurisdiction or on board a ship or aircraft registered in that State, when the alleged offender is a national of that State, and when the victim was a national of that State if that State considers it appropriate. Each State Party must have jurisdiction to prosecute "where the alleged offender is present in any territory under its jurisdiction and it does not extradite him" to another State with one of the jurisdiction grounds mentioned above. Art. 5.

Torture crimes must be included as extraditable offenses in any extradition treaty existing between States Parties. Art. 8. States Parties must afford each other "the greatest measure of assistance in connection with criminal proceedings brought in respect of any of the offences referred to in article 4, including the supply of all evidence at their disposal necessary for the proceedings." Art. 9. The Convention also specifies various undertakings with respect to arrest, interrogation and detention, civil redress for victims of torture, the use of evidence obtained through torture, applications for asylum and refugee status, and the prevention of "acts of cruel, inhuman or degrading treatment or punishment which do not amount to torture."

The United States ratified the Convention in 1984. Acts meeting the Convention's definition of torture are criminal everywhere in the United States under state or federal law. In accordance with the Convention, acts committed outside the United States have been criminalized in 28 U.S.C. § 2340A.

The ICTY, the ICTR, and the ICC are all empowered to consider charges of torture both as "grave breaches" of the Geneva Conventions and as "crimes against humanity." It can also be prosecuted as a component of other recognized international crime, for example as an act "causing serious bodily or mental harm" within the definition of genocide.

For the text of the Convention Against Torture, *see* *http://www.hrweb.org/legal/cat.html. See generally* Nowak and McArthur, *The United Nations Convention against Torture: A Commentary* (2008).

§ 7–6 DISAPPEARANCES

Enforced disappearances are a tool all too often used by military dictatorships and other authoritarian regimes to silence their opponents. Persons deemed undesirable by the governing regime are spirited away in the dead of night, possibly never to be heard of again. They are detained secretly, often indefinitely, tortured, killed, their bodies rarely returned to their families. Because the governing authorities ordinarily relied on to protect people are the ones responsible for the abductions, disappeared individuals are effectively outside the protective framework of the law and at the mercy of the State.

Enforced disappearances are included in the definition of "crimes against humanity" in article 7 of the 1998 Rome Statute. The term is defined to include: "the arrest, detention or abduction of persons by, or with the authorization, support or acquiescence of, a State or a political organization, followed by a refusal to acknowledge that deprivation of freedom or to give information on the fate or whereabouts of those persons, with the intention of removing them from the protection of the law for a prolonged period of time."

A more comprehensive approach is contained in the International Convention for the Protection of All Persons from Enforced Disappearance, G.A. Res. 61/177, U.N. Doc. A/RES/61/177 (Dec. 20, 2006). As of June 2013 that treaty had been signed by 91 States and ratified or acceded to by 38 (including most of Central and South America). Art. 2 defines enforced disappearances to mean:

> the arrest, detention, abduction or any other form of deprivation of liberty by agents of the State or by persons or groups of persons acting with the authorization, support or acquiescence of the State, followed by a refusal to acknowledge the deprivation of liberty or by concealment of the fate or whereabouts of the disappeared person, which place such a person outside the protection of the law.

The Convention describes enforced disappearances as a crime against humanity and requires States Parties to make such acts an offense punishable by appropriate penalties. States Parties must hold criminally responsible anyone who commits, orders, solicits or induces the commission of, attempts to commit, is an accomplice to, or participates in an enforced disappearance. They must also be in a position to prosecute any superior who (i) knew, or consciously disregarded information which clearly indicated, that subordinates under his or her effective authority and control were committing or about to commit a crime of enforced disappearance, or who (ii) exercised effective responsibility for and control over activities which were concerned with the crime of enforced disappearance; and who (iii) failed to take all necessary and reasonable measures within his or her power to prevent or repress the commission of an enforced disappearance or to submit the matter to the competent authorities for investigation and prosecution. No order or instruction from any public authority, civilian, military or other, may be invoked to justify an offense of enforced disappearance.

States Parties must establish jurisdiction over the offense when it is committed in any territory under its jurisdiction or on board a ship or aircraft registered in that State, when the alleged offender is one of its nationals, and when the disappeared person is one of its nationals (if the State Party considers it appropriate). They must also establish "extradite or prosecute" jurisdiction. For purposes of extradition, the offense of enforced disappearance may not be regarded as a political offense or as an offense connected with a political offense or as an offense inspired by political motives. The Convention also sets out obligations of mutual legal assistance and other duties of inter-State cooperation.

A regional criminal law convention on the topic also exists. In 1994, the Organization of American States adopted the Inter-American Convention on Forced Disappearance of Persons (OAS A–60), sometimes referred to as the "Convention of Belem do Para." It defines forced disappearance as "the act of depriving a person or persons of his or their freedom, in whatever way, perpetrated by agents of the State or by persons or groups of persons acting with the authorization, support, or acquiescence of the State, followed by an absence of information or a refusal to acknowledge that deprivation of freedom or to give information on the whereabouts of that person, thereby impeding his or her recourse to the applicable legal remedies and procedural guarantees." States Parties must criminalize that act when committed in their territory or by their nationals, and may do so when committed against their nationals. To date, fourteen OAS Member States have ratified this treaty.

See   http://www.ohchr.org/EN/HRBodies/CED/ Pages/ConventionCED.aspx for the text of the UN Convention, and *http://www.oas.org/juridico/ english/treaties/a-60.html* or the text of the OAS Convention. *See generally* Marthe Lot Vermeulen, *Enforced Disappearance: Determining State Responsibility under the International Convention for the Protection of all Persons from Enforced Disappearance* (2012).

IV. WHITE COLLAR AND FINANCIAL CRIMES

§ 7–7   ORGANIZED CRIME

In an increasingly "globalized" world with fewer trade restrictions or border controls, people, money and goods flow quickly across international boundaries. Transnational organized criminal networks have learned to take advantage of these developments and today engage in a broad range of transborder activities from human and drug trafficking to corruption and money laundering. Their defining features are a well-developed organizational structure, the ability to create and operate in multiple jurisdictions, and skill in exploiting weaknesses in governmental supervision through deceit or corruption.

The 2000 UN Convention Against Transnational Organised Crime, 2237 U.N.T.S. 319, was specifically aimed to combat this phenomenon. Sometimes referred to as the "Palermo Convention" or "UNTOC," it entered into force in 2003 and has been widely ratified; as of June 2013, there were 176 States Parties. It is also one of the most detailed and complicated criminal law treaties and contains several unique provisions. One reason is that it was intended to provide a textual basis for helping States to modernize their domestic laws, especially where no prior legislation had addressed the issues related to organized criminal activities.

Core Offenses. The Convention addresses four main categories of offenses: (1) participation in organized criminal groups, (2) money laundering, (3) corruption, and (4) obstruction of justice. Its provisions also apply to certain other "serious crimes" when they are "transnational" and involve an "organized criminal group."

Offenses are "transnational" under article 3(2) if (i) the acts of commission, preparation, planning, direction or control of the offense are spread across more than one State, or (ii) if they involve an organized criminal group engaged criminal activities in more than one State, or (iii) if they have substantial effects in a State different from the State(s) of commission. The term "organized criminal group" is defined in article 2(a) to mean "a structured group of three or more persons, existing for a period of time and acting in concert with the aim of committing one or more serious crimes or offenses established in accordance with this Convention, in order to obtain, directly or indirectly, a financial or other material benefit."

1. *Participation in Organized Crime*

The heart of the Convention is its specification of the "modes" by which individuals can participate in organized criminal groups. Under article 5(1)(a), States Parties must criminalize one or both of two forms of intentional participation—conspiracy or direct participation. The first is by agreement with others persons to commit a serious crime for a purpose relating directly or indirectly to the obtaining of a financial or other material benefit and, where required by domestic law, involving an act undertaken by one of the participants in furtherance of the agreement. The second involves conduct by a person who takes an active part the criminal activities of the organized criminal group or other activities of the organized criminal group in the knowledge that his or her participation will contribute to the achievement of the above-described criminal aim. Article 5(1)(b) covers secondary forms of participation such as organizing, directing, aiding, abetting, facilitating or counseling the commission of serious crime involving an organized criminal group.

2. *Money Laundering*

This term includes several intentional acts: (i) the conversion or transfer of property "knowing that such property is the proceeds of crime, for the purpose of concealing or disguising the illicit origin of the property or of helping any person who is involved in the commission of the predicate offence to evade the legal consequences of his or her action," and (ii) the concealment or disguise of the true nature, source, location, disposition, movement or ownership of or rights with respect to property, knowing that such property is the proceeds of crime. It can also include (subject to the basic concepts of the legal system in question) (i) the acquisition, possession or use of property, knowing, at the time of receipt, that such property is the proceeds of crime, and (ii) participation in, association with or conspiracy to commit, attempts to commit and aiding, abetting, facilitating and counseling the commission of any of the offenses established in accordance with this article.

3. *Corruption*

Under article 8, each State Party is required to criminalize (a) promising, offering or giving to a public official "an undue advantage" (i.e., a bribe) to cause that official to act or refrain from acting in the exercise of his or her official duties, as well as (b) the solicitation or acceptance of any such "undue advantage" by a public official. Additionally, States Parties must "consider" criminalizing such conduct when it involves a foreign public official or international civil servant as well as "other forms of corruption." The term "public official" means a person who provides a public service as defined in the domestic law and as applied in the criminal law of the State Party in which the person in question performs that function.

4. *Obstruction*

Under article 23, States Parties must also criminalize the intentional use of physical force, threats or intimidation or the promise, offering or giving of an undue advantage to induce false testimony or to interfere in the giving of testimony or the production of evidence in a proceeding in relation to a covered offenses or to interfere with the exercise of official duties by a justice or law enforcement official in relation to the commission of a covered offense.

Jurisdiction. States Parties to the UNTOC are required to exercise jurisdiction over covered crimes only when they occur within their territory or on board their vessels. Subject to the need to respect the sovereignty of other countries, States Parties may establish jurisdiction to prosecute those offenses when committed against their nationals or by their nationals or stateless persons with habitual residence in their territory. Extraterritorial jurisdiction is permitted only with respect to certain instances of "participation" or "money laundering." But each State Party must be able to prosecute "when the alleged offender is present in its territory and it does not extradite such person solely on the ground that he or she is one of its nationals." Article 15(3).

Extradition. Under article 16, covered offenses shall be deemed "extraditable offenses" in any existing extradition treaty between States Parties, States Parties may not refuse a request for extradition "on the sole ground that the offence is also considered to involve fiscal matters," and before refusing extradition, States Parties must "where appropriate" consult with the requesting State Party to allow it to provide additional information.

Mutual Legal Assistance. The treaty obligates States Parties to afford each other "the widest measure of mutual legal assistance in investigations, prosecutions and judicial proceedings." Mutual legal assistance must be afforded to the fullest extent possible under relevant laws, treaties, agreements and arrangements of the

requested   State   Party   with   respect   to
investigations, prosecutions and judicial proceedings
in relation to covered offenses. States Parties may
not refuse a request for mutual legal assistance on
the sole ground that the offense involve "fiscal"
matters.

Seizure, Confiscation and Forfeiture. The treaty
contains important provisions regarding domestic
confiscation of the proceeds of crime derived from
covered offenses (or property the value of which
corresponds to such proceeds) as well as the
property, equipment or other instrumentalities used
in or destined for use in covered offenses. States
Parties must, upon request of another State Party,
take measures to identify, trace and freeze or seize
the proceeds of crime, property, equipment or other
instrumentalities for the purpose of eventual
confiscation.

Transfer of Convicted Persons. States Parties
may consider entering into bilateral or multilateral
agreements on "the transfer to their territory of
persons sentenced to imprisonment or other forms of
deprivation of liberty for offences covered by this
Convention, in order that they may complete their
sentences there."

Joint Investigations. States Parties must consider
concluding bilateral or multilateral agreements or
arrangements for the creation of "joint investigative
bodies" for matters subject to investigation,
prosecution or judicial proceeding in one or more
States. Joint investigations can also be undertaken
on a case-by-case basis.

Special Investigative Techniques. States Parties are encouraged to conclude appropriate bilateral or multilateral agreements or arrangements regarding the use of "controlled deliveries" and other techniques such as electronic surveillance and undercover operations.

Transfer of Criminal Proceedings. The treaty contemplated the possibility of transferring criminal proceedings ("prosecutions") from one State Party to another "where such transfer is considered to be in the interests of the proper administration of justice, in particular in cases where several jurisdictions are involved, with a view to concentrating the prosecution."

The Convention has three optional protocols dealing with human trafficking, human smuggling and the trafficking of firearms. These are dealt with in greater detail in the sections on trafficking offenses.

See http://www.unodc.org/unodc/en/treaties/CTOC/ index.html for the text of the UNTOC. *See generally* McClean, *Transnational Organised Crime: a Commentary on the UN Convention and its Protocols* (2007).

§ 7–8   CORRUPTION

Corruption refers to the payment of illicit bribes or the "greasing of palms" to secure preferential treatment, for instance, by making private payments to public officials to win contracts. In some places, the practice is so deeply ingrained in everyday practice that even essential services are conditioned on the payment of bribes.

International or transnational corruption has only recently attracted the attention of the international community. A significant development was the 1977 enactment of the Foreign Corrupt Practices Act in the United States. Since then many other States, including the United Kingdom and South Africa, have adopted similar statutes providing for extraterritorial jurisdiction over the foreign corrupt practices of locally domiciled entities.

The first major international attempt at regulation was the 1997 OECD Convention on Combating Bribery of Foreign Public Officials in International Business Transactions, reprinted at 37 I.L.M. 1 (1998). Around the same time, the Organization of American States adopted an Inter-American Convention against Corruption (1996) and the EU adopted a Convention on the Fight against Corruption involving Officials of the European Communities or Officials of Member States of the European Union (1997).

The major international instrument in this area is the UN Convention Against Corruption, 2349 U.N.T.S. 1. It is sometimes referred to as "UNCAC." Adopted in 2003, it had been ratified by 167 States as of June 2013. The Convention adopts an interesting approach in that it prioritizes both the prevention of corruption and the criminalization of corruption.

Offenses. The UNCAC does not attempt a single definition of the term "corruption" but instead articulates a range of conduct which States Parties must criminalize under their domestic laws. The two main types are: "(1) the bribery of national public officials (article 15), and (2) the bribery of foreign public officials and officials of public international organizations" (article 16).

In both instances, active and passive bribery is covered. Thus, bribery *of national officials* is prohibited, including the promise, offering or giving, to a public official, directly or indirectly, of an undue advantage, for the official himself or herself or another person or entity, in order that the official act or refrain from acting in the exercise of his or her official duties. The convention also prohibits the direct or indirect solicitation or acceptance *by a public official* of an undue advantage to get that official to act or to refrain from acting in the exercise of official duties.

Other covered forms of public sector corruption include embezzlement, misappropriation or other diversion of property by a public official, trading in influence, intentional abuse of functions, and illicit enrichment, defined as a significant increase in the assets of a public official that he or she cannot reasonably explain in relation to his or her lawful income (arts. 17–20).

Articles 21–27 address bribery in the private sector, embezzlement of property in the private sector, laundering of proceeds of crime, concealment, and obstruction of justice.

Freezing, Seizing, Confiscating. Each State Party must take, "to the greatest extent possible within its domestic legal system, such measures as may be necessary to enable confiscation" of the proceeds of crime derived from covered offenses as well as property, equipment or other instrumentalities used in or destined for use in covered offenses.

Bank Secrecy. Each State Party must also ensure that, in the case of domestic criminal investigations of covered offenses, appropriate mechanisms are available within its domestic legal system to overcome obstacles that may arise out of the application of bank secrecy laws.

Jurisdiction. States must establish criminal jurisdiction over covered offenses committed in their territory or on board a vessel flying their flag or an aircraft registered under their laws. Subject to sovereignty considerations, they may also establish jurisdiction over offenses committed against their nationals or by their nationals or a Stateless person habitually resident in their territory. Extraterritorial jurisdiction over money laundering offenses is permitted in some circumstances. Each State Party must establish "extradite or prosecute jurisdiction" for those instances "when the alleged offender is present in its territory and it does not extradite such person solely on the ground that he or she is one of its nationals."

Extradition. Covered offenses are deemed extraditable under existing extradition treaties between States Parties and must be included in any future extradition treaty between them. Extradition requests cannot be refused on the sole ground that the offense is considered to involve fiscal matters. In effect, the article is a self-contained extradition treaty since it can be relied upon in cases where States Parties need (but do not have) a bilateral arrangement.

Mutual Legal Assistance. In the same way, the Convention can serve as a stand-alone mutual legal assistance treaty between States Parties, since they must afford each other "the widest measure of mutual legal assistance in investigations, prosecutions and judicial proceedings in relation to the offences covered by this Convention." Mutual legal assistance must be afforded "to the fullest extent possible under relevant laws, treaties, agreements and arrangements of the requested State Party with respect to investigations, prosecutions and judicial proceedings" relating to covered offenses. States Parties may not refuse a request for mutual legal assistance on the sole ground that the offense is also considered to involve fiscal matters.

Transfer of Sentenced Persons. States Parties are encouraged to consider entering into bilateral or multilateral agreements or arrangements on the transfer to their territory of persons sentenced to imprisonment or other forms of deprivation of liberty for offenses established in accordance with this Convention in order that they may complete their sentences there.

Transfer of Criminal Proceedings. States Parties must also consider the possibility of transferring proceedings for the prosecution of covered offenses cases where such transfer is in the interests of the proper administration of justice, in particular where several jurisdictions are involved, with a view to concentrating the prosecution.

Law Enforcement Cooperation. States Parties are encouraged to enhance the effectiveness of their respective law enforcement actions to combat covered offenses, in particular by taking measures to establish and enhance channels of communication between their competent authorities, agencies and services in respect of covered offenses. This could include bilateral or multilateral agreements for the establishment of joint investigative bodies for matters that are the subject of investigations, prosecutions or judicial proceedings in one or more States Parties. The Convention also promotes the use of "controlled deliveries" and other special investigative techniques such as electronic or other forms of surveillance and undercover operations, and encourages States Parties to allow for the admissibility in court of evidence derived there from.

Assets Recovery. Uniquely, the Convention declares that "the return of assets pursuant to this chapter is a fundamental principle of this Convention, and States Parties shall afford one another the widest measure of cooperation and assistance in this regard." Accordingly, States Parties have specific obligations to detect and prevent transfers of the proceeds of crime. They must also allow other States Parties to bring civil actions in their courts to establish title to or ownership of property acquired through the commission of covered offenses and permit their courts to enforce orders of confiscation issued by a court of another State Party and to order payment of pay compensation or damages to another State Party that has been harmed by such offenses.

The Convention provides for the disposal and return of confiscated property to "its prior legitimate owners." States Parties must also consider establishing "a financial intelligence unit to be responsible for receiving, analysing and disseminating to the competent authorities reports of suspicious financial transactions."

See   http://www.unodc.org/documents/treaties/ UNCAC/Publications/Convention/08-50026_E.pdf for the text of the UN Corruption Convention.

§ 7–9   MONEY LAUNDERING

Because the financial proceeds of illegal activity often cannot be used without arousing law enforcement suspicions, criminals put a lot of energy into the task of disguising the fruits of their endeavours. Broadly speaking, the term "money laundering" refers to the act of converting illicitly obtained funds into legitimate resources. Efforts to regulate these efforts on an international scale are a relatively recent phenomenon.

To date, the focus has been on money laundering as an ancillary offense. In other words, money laundering in and of itself has not been denominated as an international crime but has been addressed as part of the regimes for dealing with other crimes, such as drug trafficking, corruption, organized crime and terrorism. Note that U.S. law takes a different approach; the 1986 Money Laundering Control Act, codified at 18 U.S.C. § 1956, includes a number of substantive money laundering offenses.

Drug Trafficking Convention. The link between money laundering and drug trafficking was specifically addressed in the 1988, discussed below. The preamble of that Convention notes that "illicit traffic generates large financial profits and wealth enabling transnational criminal organizations to penetrate, contaminate and corrupt the structures of government, legitimate commercial and financial business, and society at all its levels." One of express goals of the Convention was to "deprive persons engaged in illicit traffic of the proceeds of their criminal activities and thereby eliminate their main incentive for so doing."

As addressed in this Convention, the offense of money laundering has three basic components: conversion, concealment and use of laundered assets.

Article 3(b)(i) addresses "the conversion or transfer of property, knowing that such property is derived from [any covered offence] . . . or from an act of participation in such offence or offences, for the purpose of concealing or disguising the illicit origin of the property or of assisting any person who is involved in the commission of such an offence or offences to evade the legal consequences of his actions."

Art. 3(b)(ii) refers to "the concealment or disguise of the true nature, source, location, disposition, movement, rights with respect to, or ownership of property, knowing that such property is derived from an offence or offences established in accordance with subparagraph a) of this paragraph or from an act of participation in such an offence or offences."

Art. 3(c)(i) focuses on "the acquisition, possession or use of property, knowing, at the time of receipt, that such property was derived from an offence or offences established in accordance with subparagraph a) of this paragraph or from an act of participation in such offence or offences."

Each State Party must criminalize the intentional commission of these acts when committed in its territory, or on board a vessel flying its flag or an aircraft which is registered under its laws at the time the offense is committed, and may extend jurisdiction over them when committed by one of its nationals or by a person who has his habitual residence in its territory, or "on board a vessel concerning which that Party has been authorized to take appropriate action" by the flag State, or (in some circumstances) committed outside its territory with a view to the commission of an offense within its territory. Art. 4.

Corruption Convention. The 2003 United Nations Convention Against Corruption also deals with money laundering. States Parties must take a number of steps to prevent money-laundering, "including *inter alia* instituting a comprehensive domestic regulatory and supervisory regime" for banks and non-bank financial institutions to deter and detect all forms of money-laundering, ensuring that law enforcement and other authorities are able to cooperate and exchange information at the national and international levels, and considering "feasible measures to detect and monitor the movement of cash and appropriate negotiable instruments across their borders." States Parties to the UNCAC are encouraged to "develop and promote global, regional, sub-regional and bilateral cooperation among judicial, law enforcement and financial regulatory authorities in order to combat money-laundering."

UNCAC requires States Parties to criminalize the conversion or transfer of the proceeds of crime for the purpose of concealing or disguising its illicit origin or helping anyone involved in the commission of the predicate offense to evade the legal consequences of his or her action, as well as concealing or disguising the true nature, source, location, disposition, movement or ownership of or rights with respect to property, knowing that such property is the proceeds of crime. They must also criminalize "the acquisition, possession or use of property, knowing, at the time of receipt, that such property is the proceeds of crime," and "participation in, association with or conspiracy to commit, attempts to commit and aiding, abetting, facilitating and counseling the commission" of covered offenses.

Organized Crime Convention. The UN Convention on Transnational Organized Crime requires criminalization of "laundering the proceeds of crime" in terms almost identical to those in the Corruption Convention.

Terrorism. The 1999 International Convention for the Suppression of the Financing of Terrorism targets the knowing use of laundered funds for the financing of terrorist activities. More particularly, article 2(1) criminalizes the "direct or indirect" provision and collection of "funds with the intention that they should be used or in the knowledge that they are to be used, in full or in part" to carry out an act of terrorism.

COE Convention. In 1990 the Council of Europe adopted a Convention on Laundering, Search, Seizure and Confiscation of the Proceeds from Crime (ETS No. 141). It requires, among other things, that each State Party must adopt legislative and other measures to permit it to confiscate instrumentalities and proceeds (or property equal in value to such proceeds) and co-operate with other States Parties in investigations and proceedings aiming at the confiscation of instrumentalities and proceeds. It has been ratified by 45 Member States of the Council of Europe.

See generally Mark Simpson et al, eds., *International Guide to Money Laundering Law and Practice* (2010).

V. TRAFFICKING

§ 7–10   DRUGS

The global effort to control drug trafficking extends back to the mid-19th century, when European countries tried to regulate the opium trade with China. Today three multilateral instruments address the issues.

Single Convention. The 1961 Single Convention on Narcotic Drugs focuses on manufacture, trade and distribution and possession. Called the "single convention" because it unified provisions of several earlier agreements dealing with different drugs, it creates categories of "controlled substances" which States must regulate. It established an international oversight mechanism (including the UN Commission on Narcotic Drugs and the International Narcotics Control Board). Article 36(1) requires States Parties to criminalize the intentional "cultivation, production, manufacture, extraction, preparation, possession, offering, offering for sale, distribution, purchase, sale, delivery on any terms whatsoever, brokerage, dispatch, dispatch in transit, transport, importation and exportation of drugs . . . and any other action which in the opinion of such Party may be contrary to the provisions of this Convention." The Convention specifies the jurisdictional basis for these offenses, mandates that convention offenses be included in existing extradition treaties, and requires States Parties to establish "extradite or prosecute" provisions.

Psychotropic Substances Convention. The 1971 UN Convention on Psychotropic Substances, 1019 U.N.T.S. 175, adopts a tiered classification of psychotropic substances. It vests responsibility for administering this regime in the World Health Organization. It also addresses the use of various drugs for medical and scientific purposes and makes provision for licenses, prescriptions, packaging warnings, records, international and national trade and transfer, measures against abuse, and illicit traffic. Article 22 requires States to criminalize violations of the Convention and mirrors the 1961 Convention with regard to jurisdiction and extradition.

Illicit Trafficking Convention. The 1988 UN Convention against Illicit Traffic in Narcotic Drugs and Psychotropic Substances, 1582 U.N.T.S. 95, entered into force in 1990 and as of June 2013 had 188 ratifications. As the title suggests, it focuses on trafficking rather than on cultivation, manufacture, regulation or transportation of licit (lawful) drugs. Article 3 contains an extensive list of offenses and sanctions, including contravention of the 1961 and 1971 conventions, as well as inchoate and related offenses.

Article 4 sets out territorial, nationality and protective bases of jurisdiction. Article 6 requires States Parties to include Convention offenses in existing extradition treaties and allow the Convention to serve as the basis for extradition in the absence of a treaty. Article 7 provides for mutual legal assistance.

The Convention imposes a number of other substantive provisions including confiscation of controlled substances and proceeds there from (art. 5) as well as regulation of substances, materials and equipment used in the illicit manufacture of controlled substances, eradication of cultivation, and regulation of trade to prevent trafficking (arts. 12–19). Articles 21–13 invoke the international control organs created under the 1961 convention to supervise the implementation of this instrument.

Finally, the 1988 Convention creates cooperative obligations including transfer of proceedings, information sharing and training, and special assistance for developing nations (arts. 8–10). Article 11 specifically refers to the use of "controlled deliveries" to facilitate incrimination, capture and successful prosecution of broader parts of supply chains.

For the 1961 Single Convention, *see http://www. unodc.org/unodc/en/treaties/single-convention. html*. The 1971 Psychotropic Substances Convention is available at *http://www.unodc.org/unodc/en/ treaties/psychotropics.html*. For information on the 1988 Illicit Trafficking Convention, *see http:// www.unodc.org/pdf/convention_1988_en.p*.

§ 7–11   PEOPLE

The contemporary practice of human trafficking is motivated by the desire to profit from the subjugation of human beings. It differs from slavery in that it does not necessarily involve the reduction of human beings to the status of chattel. In today's parlance, two related crimes are subsumed under this heading: trafficking and smuggling. Each is the subject of a separate protocol to the UN Organized Crime Convention.

Trafficking in Persons Protocol. The 2000 Protocol to Prevent, Suppress and Punish Trafficking in Persons, Especially Women and Children, 2225 U.N.T.S. 209, 40 I.L.M. 377 (2001), entered into force in 2003 and as of June 2013 had been ratified by 155 States. Article 3(a) defines trafficking broadly to mean "the recruitment, transportation, transfer, harbouring or receipt of persons, by means of the threat or use of force or other forms of coercion, of abduction, of fraud, of deception, of the abuse of power or of a position of vulnerability or of the giving or receiving of payments or benefits to achieve the consent of a person having control over another person, for the purpose of exploitation."

For this purpose, "exploitation" includes "the exploitation of the prostitution of others or other forms of sexual exploitation, forced labour or services, slavery or practices similar to slavery, servitude or the removal of organs." The term "exploitation" includes the recruitment, transportation, transfer, harboring or receipt of a child for the purpose of exploitation, and consent of a trafficking victim to the intended exploitation is irrelevant where any of the specified means have been used.

States Parties are required to criminalize trafficking, as defined above, as well as attempts, participation as an accomplice and "organizing or directing other persons to commit" trafficking.

Other provisions impose obligations with respect to prevention (including border measures and travel documents), assistance to and protection of trafficking victims, return and repatriation, prevention policies and programs, cooperation and other measures." Because this is a protocol, issues concerning jurisdiction, extradition, mutual legal assistance, etc., are addressed by reference to the Organized Crime Convention itself.

Smuggling of Migrants Protocol. Unlike trafficking, smuggling often involves the complicity of the person being trafficked, who willingly seeks illegal entry to gain better standards of living and greater economic opportunities. The 2000 Protocol against the Smuggling of Migrants by Land, Sea and Air, 2225 U.N.T.S. 209, 40 I.L.M. 384 (2001), entered into force in 2003 and by June 2013 had been ratified by 136 States.

The Protocol requires States Parties to criminalize smuggling (defined as the procurement of the illegal entry of an individual into a State of which he or she is not a national or permanent resident) as well producing or procuring a fraudulent travel or identity document for that purpose. Enabling a person who is not a national or a permanent resident to remain in the concerned State without complying with the necessary requirements can also be a crime under the Protocol, as can attempts, participation as an accomplice or "organizing or directing other persons to commit" such an offense.

Interestingly, article 5 exempts the migrants themselves from criminal liability under the protocol, although the provision must be read in light of article 6(4), which allows for the application of municipal criminal laws.

Other parts of the Protocol address issues of smuggling of migrants by sea and measures of international cooperation to stem that practice, including stopping and searching foreign-flagged vessels. Later articles discuss information sharing, border measures, security and control of travel documents, training and technical cooperation, education and awareness, return of smuggled migrants, etc.

There was no need to include specific provisions relating to jurisdiction, extradition, mutual legal assistance, etc., because these are covered by the UNTOC convention.

The Trafficking and Smuggling Protocols to the Organized Crime Convention are available at *http://www.unodc.org/unodc/en/treaties/CTOC/ index.html.*

Generally, *see* Hepburn and Simon, *Human Trafficking Around the World: Hidden in Plain*

Sight (Columbia Univ. Press 2013; Wyler and Siskin, *Trafficking in Persons: U.S. Policy and Issues for Congress*, CRS RL 34317, Feb. 19, 2013); *UN Global Report on Trafficking in Persons 2012* (February 2013).

§ 7–12   FIREARMS

Firearms Protocol. The main international agreement regulating trafficking in firearms is the Protocol Against the Illicit Manufacturing of and Trafficking in Firearms, Their Parts and Components and Ammunition, supplementing the United Nations Convention against Transnational Organized Crime, 2326 U.N.T.S. 208. The protocol was adopted in 2001 and entered into force in 2005; as of June 2013, it had been ratified by 101 States.

The protocol addresses the illegal trade in small arms. It defines the term "firearm" as "any portable barreled weapon that expels, is designed to expel or may be readily converted to expel a shot, bullet or projectile by the action of an explosive, excluding antique firearms or their replicas."

Article 5 establishes the criminal offenses. It requires States Parties to criminalize the illicit manufacture of firearms, their parts and components and ammunition, the illicit trafficking in firearms, their parts and components and ammunition, and falsely or illicitly obliterating, removing or altering certain required markings on firearms. They must also criminalize attempts, participation as an accomplice, and organizing, directing, aiding, abetting, facilitating or counseling the commission of covered offenses.

The protocol does not explicitly address questions of jurisdiction, extradition and mutual legal assistance, because (like the trafficking in persons and smuggling of migrants protocols) it incorporates by reference the provisions of the main convention on those fronts.

Beyond establishing criminal offenses, the Protocol sets out a comprehensive regulatory regime, including measures regarding confiscation, seizure and disposal of illicitly manufactured or trafficked firearms, prevention of trafficking, marking and tracing firearms, import-export-transit licensing, deactivation of firearms, regulation of arms brokers, and transnational information sharing, cooperation, training and technical assistance.

Regional Efforts. At the regional level various instruments have been concluded in the same area. These include the 1997 Inter-American Convention against the Illicit Manufacturing of and Trafficking in Firearms, Ammunition, Explosives and other Related Materials, as well as the 2006 ECOWAS Convention on Small Arms and Light Weapons and other Related Materials. The ECOWAS Convention carries the unique distinction of prohibiting trade in firearms, requiring states to seek case-specific exemptions for importing such weapons.

Arms Trade Treaty. The recently-concluded 2013 UN Arms Trade Treaty establishes internationally agreed standards for regulating the international trade in conventional arms (including such items as battle tanks, heavy artillery, combat aircraft and attack but also covering "small arms and light weapons"). It does not, however, include criminal provisions.

For information on the Firearms Protocol to the Organized Crime Convention, *see http:// www.unodc.org/documents/treaties/UNTOC/ Publications/TOC%20Convention/TOCebook-e.pdf.* The 1997 Inter-American Firearms Convention is available at *http://www.oas.org/juridico/english/ treaties/a-63.html.* Information on the new UN Arms Trade Treaty can be found at *http:// www.un.org/disarmament/ATT.*

§ 7–13   ART AND CULTURAL PROPERTY

Several international instruments regulate trafficking in stolen art works. They may be divided into two categories depending on whether they address looting (i) during armed conflict or (ii) in times of peace.

1954 Hague Convention. The widespread looting of art works during the Nazi occupation of Europe led to the adoption of the 1954 Hague Convention for the Protection of Cultural Property in the Event of Armed Conflict, 249 U.N.T.S. 216. It entered into force in 1956 and currently has 126 ratifications. The Convention sets out obligations for the protection of cultural property during armed conflict including obligations of occupying armies, distinctive marking of cultural property, special protection during armed conflict, transportation.

Article 1 defines cultural property as "movable or immovable property of great importance to the cultural heritage of every people, such as monuments of architecture, art or history, whether religious or secular; archaeological sites; groups of buildings which, as a whole, are of historical or artistic interest; works of art; manuscripts, books and other objects of artistic, historical or archaeological interest; as well as scientific collections and important collections of books or archives or of reproductions of the property defined above" and also "buildings whose main and effective purpose is to preserve or exhibit the movable cultural property."

The Convention has two protocols. The first imposes obligations relating to the prevention of expropriation of cultural property from occupied territories and the return of cultural property placed in the hands of occupying powers for safe keeping. The second protocol emphasizes the need for occupying powers to apply the principle of necessity in armed conflict with regard to cultural property.

The rules set out in the Convention and its two protocols are part of the laws of war, and violations are therefore to criminal prosecution under that body of law. Importantly, certain cultural property can be placed under "enhanced protection" and it is an offense to attack such property, to cause its "extensive destruction or appropriation of cultural property, to engage in "theft, pillage or misappropriation of, or acts of vandalism directed against" such property. A State Party must criminalize such offenses under its domestic law. Jurisdiction must be established when such an offense is committed in the territory of that State, by a national of that State, or (in certain instances) when the offender is actually present in that State's territory.

UNESCO Convention. With regard to the trafficking of cultural property in peacetime, the 1970 UNESCO Convention on the Means of Prohibiting and Preventing the Illicit Import, Export and Transfer of Ownership of Cultural Property, 823 U.N.T.S. 231, entered into force in 1972 and to date has been ratified by 123 States. Article 1 defines cultural property to mean property "which, on religious or secular grounds, is specifically designated by each State as being of importance for archaeology, prehistory, history, literature, art or science" and which belongs to one of 11 specified categories. Under article 3, "the import, export or transfer of ownership of cultural property effected contrary to the provisions adopted under this Convention by the States Parties thereto, shall be illicit."

The Convention imposes a range of requirements on States Parties with respect to the import and export of stolen property, maintaining a register of transactions, enforcing the return of stolen property, etc. Article 13(c) requires States Parties to "admit actions for recovery of lost or stolen items of cultural property brought by or on behalf of the rightful owners." However, it makes no reference to questions of extradition, exercise of jurisdiction or mutual assistance.

UNIDROIT Convention*.* The 1995 UNIDROIT Convention on Stolen or Illegally Exported Cultural Objects, 34 I.L.M. 1322, came into force in 1998 and currently has 33 ratifications. This instrument concentrates on obligations regarding the return of stolen or illegally exported cultural objects and does not provide for criminal sanction or deal with the appropriation or theft of cultural property.

The International Committee of the Red Cross is a good source of information on the 1954 Cultural Property Convention. *See http://www.icrc.org/eng/ war-and-law/conduct-hostilities/cultural-property/ index.jsp.* For the 1970 UNESCO Illicit Traffic Convention, see *http://www.unesco.org/new/en/ culture/themes/illicit-traffic-of-cultural-property.*

The 1995 UNIDROIT Convention on Stolen or Illegally Exported Cultural Objects is available at *http://www.unidroit.org/english/conventions/ 1995culturalproperty/main.htm.*

See generally Chamberlain, *War and Cultural Heritage: An Analysis of the 1954 Convention for the Protection of Cultural Property in the Event of Armed Conflict* (Institute of Art and Law 2013); O'Keefe*, Protection of Cultural Property in the Event of Armed Conflict* (Cambridge, 2007).

§ 7–14   NATURAL RESOURCES

The illicit trafficking of natural resources including wild flora and fauna is an emergent focus of international criminal law. The criminalization of trade in such objects is based on the need to preserve and conserve these natural resources. Animal parts, plants, tree bark, etc., find various uses in traditional medicines, objects of aesthetics appeal, charms and amulets, etc. However, reckless exploitation of these resources had led to their endangerment. To stave off extinction of valuable plant and animal species, efforts have been undertaken to control the exploitation of endangered resources and restrict trade in them (*inter alia* from fear of invasive species).

Where the trafficking activities are conducted by organized crime, the UNTOC Convention offers one basis for combating the activity criminally. Another possibility is the 1992 Convention on Biological Diversity, 1760 U.N.T.S. 79. While it does not explicitly criminalize the trade in or exploitation of endangered natural resources, it does direct States to develop or maintain legislation and other regulatory provisions for the protection of threatened species and populations. It also provides extensive prescriptions for policies and legislations to conserve and sustainably use biodiversity and for international cooperation in this regard.

The 1973 Convention on International Trade in Endangered Species ("CITES"), 993 U.N.T.S. 243, aims at ensuring that the international trade in specimens of wild animals and plants does not threaten their survival. As of June 2013, 178 States had ratified or acceded. It covers species currently threatened, those which may become threatened unless trade is regulated, and those in which trade is regulated to prevent exploitation. While much of the Convention deals with trade issues, article VIII requires States Parties to take appropriate measures *inter alia* to penalize trade in, or possession of, "specimens" in violation of the Convention and to provide for the confiscation or return of such specimens to the State of export. It does not provide much detail with regard to other aspects of the international criminal law process, such as jurisdiction, extradition, mutual legal assistance, etc.

For addition information, *see* the website of the UN Office on Drugs and Crime, *http://www.unodc.org/ unodc/en/wildlife-and-forest-crime/index.html.*

VI. CYBERCRIME

Despite the increasing use of the internet for criminal purposes, the international community has yet to formulate a unified approach to the problem. Several reasons for this lack of response are plausible. On the one hand, the issues (like the internet itself) are comparatively new and the technology continues to evolve rapidly. Many, perhaps most States still lack adequate domestic legal frameworks for regulating and controlling the use of the internet for criminal purposes. On the other hand, sharp differences divide States on such issues as access to information, free speech and censorship. As a result, current prospects for early international agreement on how to regulate the internet from a criminal perspective seem dim.

The only existing international instrument on this subject is the Council of Europe's 2001 Convention on Cybercrime (CETS No. 185). Sometimes called the "Budapest Convention," it entered into force in 2004 and currently has thirty-nine States Parties, including the United States.

The Convention is aimed at harmonizing the domestic law of States Parties with respect to cyber-crime, ensuring that sufficient authority exists for the investigation and prosecution of covered offenses, and establishing an effective regime for international co-operation. The substantive provisions in articles 2–10 define nine separate cybercrime offenses: illegal access, illegal interception, data interference, system interference, misuse of devices, computer-related forgery, computer-related fraud, offenses related to child pornography and offenses related to copyright and related rights. Separate provisions address attempts, aiding and abetting, and corporate liability. Other articles deal with procedural matters including, for instance, conditions and safeguards for human rights, preservation of stored computer data, production orders, searches and seizures of stored data, etc.

Under article 22, States must provide jurisdiction over the substantive offenses when committed in their territory, on board their flagged vessels or registered aircraft, or by their national ("if the offence is punishable under the criminal law where it was committed or if the offence is committed outside the territorial jurisdiction of any State"). So-called "extradite or prosecute" jurisdiction is also addressed in that article, and extradition requirements are set forth in article 24. Obligations of mutual legal assistance are addressed extensively in articles 25–34.

See http://conventions.coe.int/Treaty/en/Treaties/ Html/185.htm for the text of the COE Cybercrime Convention. Generally, *see* Ralph D. Clifford, ed., *Cybercrime: the Investigation, Prosecution and Defence of Computer-Related Crime* (2011).

§ 7–15   FURTHER READING

Neil Boister, *An Introduction to Transnational Criminal Law* (Oxford 2012).

CHAPTER 8
INTERNATIONAL TERRORISM

I. INTRODUCTION

Terrorism today clearly ranks at the top of the list of international criminal concerns and presents one of the most serious challenges to the international community. It poses a pervasive and growing threat in every region of the world. More international instruments address terrorism than any other form of criminal activity. At the same time it remains the most contentious issue in the field. No single agreed definition of terrorism exists, no comprehensive treaty has yet been agreed, and terrorism as a matter of international law has not been included as a distinct "core crime" in any international court or tribunal.

II. THE CONCEPT OF TERRORISM

Terrorism itself is hardly a new phenomenon. The assassination of Archduke Francis Ferdinand ignited the First World War. Today, terrorist attacks, including indiscriminate attacks on civilians as well as targeted attacks on government officials and other political leaders, are an increasingly common tactic, used by religious as well as revolutionary movements and other dissident groups to secure their political objectives.

The growth in the use of terrorist tactics may be attributed, among other factors, to technological advances in weapons, their ready availability to non-governmental actors, greater ease of movement of people and material across borders, and growth of global communications. It is easier than ever for aspiring terrorists to obtain small weapons of great destructive power and for terrorist networks to communicate with their members. The almost instantaneous dissemination of news around the world magnifies the impact of any given terrorist act.

§ 8–1   A CONTEXTUAL CRIME?

Most acts of terrorism constitute domestic criminal offenses wherever they occur. The main challenge lies in achieving international agreement to punish those crimes without regard to their political context. By definition, the violence that forms the core of a "terrorist act" is committed for political purposes or objectives. Can such acts ever be legitimate, and if so, when? This question is well reflected in the hoary adage "one man's terrorist is another's freedom fighter."

How do you determine, for example, whether violent efforts to overthrow a government or regime are valid acts of self-determination or crimes? Can some otherwise criminal acts (murder, bank robbery, use of nerve gas, blowing up an aircraft in flight) be legitimized by the perpetrator's purpose? Are some acts simply so heinous that they can never be accepted, no matter what the intent behind them? How do you tell the difference? As long as the use of violence in some circumstances is accepted, consensus on these issues will remain elusive.

§ 8–2   EFFORTS TO DEFINE TERRORISM

Many competing definitions of terrorism exist at the international level. The first serious attempt took place within the League of Nations. In 1937 the Member States adopted a Convention for the Prevention and Punishment of Terrorism, which defined the term as including "criminal acts directed against a State and intended or calculated to create a state of terror in the minds of particular persons, or a group of persons or the general public." An annexed protocol would have established a special international criminal court to prosecute such crimes. However, only one State—India—ratified the Convention, and it never entered into force.

Adopted in 1977, article 51(2) of Protocol I and article 13(2) of Protocol II to the 1949 Geneva Conventions require States Parties to protect civilian populations from "acts or threats of violence the primary purpose of which is to spread terror among the civilian population."

In 1995, the UN General Assembly adopted a resolution calling on all States to adopt measures to eliminate international terrorism. The first paragraph of that resolution stated that all UN Member States "solemnly reaffirm their unequivocal condemnation of all acts, methods and practices of terrorism, as criminal and unjustifiable, wherever and by whomever committed, including those which jeopardize the friendly relations among States and peoples and threaten the territorial integrity and security of States." The resolution continued:

> Criminal acts intended or calculated to provoke a state of terror in the general public, a group of persons or particular persons for political purposes are in any circumstance unjustifiable, whatever the considerations of a political, philosophical, ideological, racial, ethnic, religious or any other nature that may be invoked to justify them . . . .

U.N. G.A. Res. 49/60, para. 3 (February 19, 1995). This has become standard language for the United Nations and is frequently repeated, most recently for example, in paragraph 4 of UN G.A. Res. 67/99 (January 14, 2013).

By comparison, no definition of terrorism was included in the UN's Global Counter-Terrorism Strategy and Plan of Action adopted by the General Assembly (UN G.A. Res. 60/288, Sept. 20, 2006). Instead, that resolution did repeat a formulation which the General Assembly had previously adopted calling on Member States to protect human rights and fundamental freedoms while countering terrorism. That prior resolution had said that:

> acts, methods and practices of terrorism in all its forms and manifestations are activities aimed at the destruction of human rights, fundamental freedoms and democracy, threatening territorial integrity, security of States and destabilizing legitimately constituted Governments, and that the

international community should take the necessary steps to enhance cooperation to prevent and combat terrorism.

UN G.A. Res. 60/158, preambular para. 12 (Feb. 28, 2006).

By comparison, the International Convention for the Suppression of the Financing of Terrorism (art. 2(1)(b)) defines the term to include acts:

> intended to cause death or serious bodily injury to a civilian, or to any other person not taking an active part in the hostilities in a situation of armed conflict, when the purpose of such act, by its nature or context, is to intimidate a population, or to compel a government or an international organization to do or to abstain from doing any act.

A 2011 decision of the Special Tribunal for Lebanon, presided over by the late Judge Antonio Cassese, suggested the existence of a definition of terrorism in customary international law. (Uniquely, the STL has jurisdiction over the crime of terrorism as defined in Lebanese law). The Appeals Chamber addressed the issue more broadly, in the context of Lebanon's international obligations, and identified an emergent definition including three key elements:

> (i) the perpetration of a criminal act (such as murder, kidnapping, hostage-taking, arson, and so on), or threatening such an act; (ii) the intent to spread fear among the population (which would generally entail the creation of public

danger) or directly or indirectly coerce a national or international authority to take some action, or to refrain from taking it; (iii) when the act involves a transnational element.

Para. 85, Interlocutory Decision on the Applicable Law: Terrorism, Conspiracy, Homicide, Perpetration, Cumulative Charging, STL–11–01/I (Feb. 16, 2011), which can be retrieved at *http:// www.stl-tsl.org/*.

For its part, the UN Security Council has been involved in responding to terrorist acts for a number of years, *inter alia* in the context of sanctions regimes imposed under Chapter VII of the UN Charter. In Resolution 1989 (June 17, 2011), for instance, it stated that:

> terrorism in all its forms and manifestations constitutes one of the most serious threats to peace and security and that any acts of terrorism are criminal and unjustifiable regardless of their motivations, whenever and by whomsoever committed, and reiterating its unequivocal condemnation of Al-Qaida and other individuals, groups, undertakings and entities associated with it, for ongoing and multiple criminal terrorist acts aimed at causing the deaths of innocent civilians and other victims, destruction of property and greatly undermining stability.

In U.N. Sec. Coun. Res. 1566, para. 3 (Oct. 4, 2004), the Security Council stated that:

criminal acts, including against civilians, committed with the intent to cause death or serious bodily injury, or taking of hostages, with the purpose to provoke a state of terror in the general public or in a group of persons or particular persons, intimidate a population or compel a government or an international organization to do or to abstain from doing any act, which constitute offences within the scope of and as defined in the international conventions and protocols relating to terrorism, are under no circumstances justifiable by considerations of a political, philosophical, ideological, racial, ethnic, religious or other similar nature . . . .

Accordingly, the Security Council called upon all UN Member States to prevent such acts and, if not prevented, to ensure that such acts are punished by penalties consistent with their grave nature.

§ 8–3   DRAFT COMPREHENSIVE CONVENTION

Potentially the most far-reaching UN effort was undertaken in 1996, when the UN General Assembly established an *Ad Hoc* Committee to prepare a draft comprehensive convention on international terrorism. Progress, however, has been predictably slow. At its most recent meeting in April 2013, the *Ad Hoc* Committee continued to debate how to distinguish terrorism from the legitimate struggle of peoples under colonial or alien domination and foreign occupation in the exercise of their right to self-determination. It also considered how to maintain the integrity of international humanitarian law and how to ensure that governmental military force are not absolved of responsibility for terrorist acts. The full Report of the meeting is available at *http://www.un.org/law/terrorism*.

With respect to the crime of terrorism, the current version of draft article 2(1) provides:

> Any person commits an offence within the meaning of the present Convention if that person, by any means, unlawfully and intentionally, causes:
>
> (a) Death or serious bodily injury to any person; or
>
> (b) Serious damage to public or private property, including a place of public use, a State or government facility, a public transportation system, an infrastructure facility or to the environment; or
>
> (c) Damage to property, places, facilities or systems referred to in paragraph 1 (b) of the present article resulting or likely to result in major economic loss, when the purpose of the conduct, by its nature or context, is to intimidate a population, or to compel a Government or an international organization to do or to abstain from doing any act.

The draft would also criminalize making a "credible and serious threat to commit" such an offense as well as attempts, participating as an accomplice, organizing or directing others to commit the offense, and contributing to the commission of one or more offenses by a group of persons acting with a common purpose.

§ 8–4   NOTE ON STATE-SPONSORED TERRORISM

From the foregoing, it is possible to extract some common elements of a possible definition of terrorism. It might cover (i) one or more acts of violence causing death or injury, or acts such as hostage-taking or kidnapping, or which cause damage to property or governmental facilities or systems, (ii) intended to create fear or "terror" among the public or civilian population, (iii) for the purpose of intimidation or to compel a government to do or abstain from an act. Such acts might also violate internationally recognized human rights and fundamental freedoms, or principles of friendly relations between States or the political independence or territorial integrity of particular States or destabilizing legitimate governments. Such acts cannot be justified on the basis of political, philosophical, ideological, racial, ethnic, religious or other considerations.

But who are the actors? Must the offender be an individual or group of individuals? Can a State or its officials or military personnel commit terrorism? How can a State be held criminally responsible? If it makes no sense to hold a State responsible as an entity, what about the individuals who are just following its policies and direction? What about those it supports, directly or indirectly?

III. TERRORISM CONVENTIONS

Since 1963 the international community has adopted a number of international agreements dealing with terrorism. All of them, however, are addressed to specific acts carried out by terrorists, such as hijacking, hostage taking, sabotage, bombings, etc. This thematic approach results from the fact that the impetus for reaching an agreement was largely generated by a specific incident or threat, which galvanized the international community to action. Some therefore deal with terrorist threats to civil aviation and shipping, some with certain kinds of attacks on individuals, some with concerns about the use of explosives, others with nuclear concerns, etc.

Besides condemning certain acts and making a political statement that States should cooperate to combat them, these conventions share some common characteristics or elements. Not all of the treaties contain all of these elements, nor do they use entirely consistent language in addressing them.

(1) They typically begin by describing the conduct that caused the incident in question.

(2) They state that the proscribed conduct is an international crime, or a crime of international concern, which all States must make an offense under their domestic laws.

(3) They set out the primary jurisdictional basis on which States Parties must be able to prosecute offenders (such as territoriality, nationality, passive personality, etc.).

(4) They create obligations to extradite or prosecute (*aut dedere aut judicare*) so that even where a State lacks one of the primary jurisdictional grounds, it must establish jurisdiction to prosecute the offense when the offender is found in its territory and it does not extradite that offender to another State Party.

(5) They make the offense an extraditable offense in all existing extradition treaties between States Parties; many also provide that for extradition purposes it cannot be considered a "political offense."

(6) They set out obligations of mutual legal assistance and cooperation between States Parties in respect of the covered offense. In a few instances, these obligations extend to training and even prevention.

The following descriptions summarize a selected group of the more significant counter-terrorism treaties. They are presented chronologically and are intended only to acquaint you with the scope and application of the various conventions, with particular emphasis on their criminal provisions; no effort is made to describe them in their entirety.

§ 8–5   SAFETY OF AVIATION (1963)

The Convention on Offences and Certain Other Acts Committed on Board Aircraft ("Tokyo Convention"), Sept. 14, 1963, 704 UNTS 219, 20 U.S.T. 2941, TIAS 6768, 2 I.L.M. 1048 (1963), text available at: *http:// www.un.org/en/sc/ctc/docs/conventions/Conv1. pdf.* As of June 2013 it had 191 States Parties.

The Convention applies to acts (including but not limited to criminal acts) which jeopardize "the safety of the aircraft or of persons or property therein" or "good order and discipline on board." It specifically covers (but does not independently define) "offences committed or acts done by a person on board any aircraft registered in a Contracting State, while that aircraft is in flight or on the surface of the high seas or of any other area outside the territory of any State." For this purpose, an aircraft is considered to be "in flight" from the moment when power is applied for the purpose of take-off until the moment when the landing run ends. *See* art. 1.

The State in which the aircraft is registered has jurisdiction. Other States may not "interfere" with an aircraft in flight in order to exercise criminal jurisdiction over an offense committed on board except when the offense (a) has "effect" on the territory of that State, (b) has been committed by or against a national or permanent resident of that State, (c) is "against the security" of that State, (d) consists of "a breach of any rules or regulations relating to the flight or manoeuvre of aircraft" in force in that State, or (e) exercising jurisdiction is necessary to ensure the observance of any obligation of that State under a multilateral international agreement.

The Convention authorizes the aircraft commander to impose reasonable measures, including restraint, to protect the aircraft, maintain good order, or deliver the person to the authorities. It also lists obligations that all Contracting States must respect, including taking custody of any offenders and returning control of the aircraft to the lawful commander.

For purposes of extradition, offenses committed on aircraft registered in a Contracting State must be treated as if they had been committed not only in the place in which they have occurred but also in the territory of the State of registration of the aircraft. The Convention must be deemed to create an obligation to grant extradition.

U.S. Legislation. This treaty is primarily implemented by the Air Piracy (Destruction of Aircraft) Act, 18 U.S.C. § 32.

§ 8–6   AIRCRAFT HIJACKING (1970)

The UN Convention for the Suppression of Unlawful Seizure of Aircraft (the "Hague" or "Hijacking" Convention), Dec. 16, 1970, 12325 UNTS 860, 22 U.S.T. 1641, TIAS 7192, 10 I.L.M. 133, entered into force in the United States Oct. 14, 1971. The text is available at *http://treaties.un.org/doc/db/ Terrorism/Conv2-english.pdf.*

Under article 1, any person on board an aircraft in flight commits an offense if he or she "unlawfully, by force or threat thereof, or by any other form of intimidation, seizes, or exercises control of, that aircraft, or attempts to perform any such act, or is an accomplice of a person who performs or attempts to perform any such act." If an alleged offender is present in its territory, a Contracting States must take that offender into custody, and conduct an inquiry into the circumstances, and restore command of aircraft to the commander.

Article 4 obligates Contracting States to establish jurisdiction over the offense "and any other act of violence against passengers or crew committed by the alleged offender in connection with the offence" when the offense is committed on board an aircraft registered in that State, when the aircraft on board which the offense is committed lands in its territory with the alleged offender still on board, when the offense is committed on board an aircraft leased without crew to a lessee who has his principal place of business or, if the lessee has no such place of business, his permanent residence, in that State. They must also establish jurisdiction "where the alleged offender is present in its territory and it does not extradite him."

Under article 8, the offense must be "deemed to be included as an extraditable offence in any extradition treaty existing between Contracting States." Contracting States are also obliged to include the offense as an extraditable offense in every extradition treaty to be concluded between them. Contracting States are required to afford each other the "greatest measure of assistance" in respect of criminal proceedings.

The 1970 Convention was amended by a supplementary Protocol adopted in Beijing in 2010. It includes hijackings taking place before or after a flight (as defined in the Convention itself) and covers attempts, acting as an accomplice, and conspiracy. It also contains additional provisions on extradition and mutual legal assistance. For additional information on the 2010 Protocol, see *http://www.icao.int/publications/journalsreports/ 2011/6601_en.pdf.*

U.S. Legislation. Although the Aircraft Piracy Act, 18 U.S.C.A. § 32, had long prohibited such actions, the Hague Convention was implemented in U.S. law by the Anti-Hijacking Act of 1974, 49 U.S.C. § 1301 et seq.

§ 8–7   AIRCRAFT SABOTAGE (1971)

The UN Convention for the Suppression of Unlawful Acts Against the Safety of Civil Aviation (the "Montreal" or "Sabotage" Convention), Sept. 23, 1971, 974 UNTS 178, 24 U.S.T. 564, TIAS 7570, 10 I.L.M. 1151, text available at *http://www.mcgill. ca/files/iasl/montreal1971.pdf.*

Article 1 of the 1971 Montreal Convention targets any person who unlawfully and intentionally does any of the following:

(a) performs an act of violence against a person on board an aircraft in flight if that act is likely to endanger the safety of that aircraft; or

(b) destroys an aircraft in service or causes damage to such an aircraft which renders it incapable of flight or which is likely to endanger its safety in flight; or

(c) places or causes to be placed on an aircraft in service, by any means whatsoever, a device or substance which is likely to destroy that aircraft, or to cause damage to it which renders it incapable of flight, or to cause damage to it which is likely to endanger its safety in flight; or

(d) destroys or damages air navigation facilities or interferes with their operation, if any such act is likely to endanger the safety of aircraft in flight; or

(e) communicates information which he knows to be false, thereby endangering the safety of an aircraft in flight.

Attempts and acting as an accomplice are also covered.

States Parties must establish jurisdiction to prosecute the covered offenses when committed in their territory or against or on board their registered aircraft, and when the aircraft on board which the offense is committed lands in its territory with the alleged offender still on board. They must also cover offenses committed against or on board an aircraft leased without crew to a lessee who has his principal place of business or, if the lessee has no such place of business, his permanent residence, in that State. In addition, they must also have jurisdiction where the alleged offender is present in its territory and they do not extradite him.

The Convention also imposes duties with respect to prevention and mutual legal assistance.

U.S. Legislation. The 1971 Convention was implemented through amendments to 18 U.S.C. § 32 *et seq.* by the Aircraft Sabotage Act 1984. *See also* 49 U.S.C. § 46502.

1988 Protocol. The Convention was supplemented by the Protocol for the Suppression of Unlawful Acts of Violence at Airports Serving International Civil Aviation (the "Montreal Protocol"), Feb. 24, 1988, 14118 U.N.T.S. 1589, 27 I.L.M. 627 (1989). The text is available at *http://treaties.un.org/doc/db/ Terrorism/Conv7-english.pdf.*

The Protocol extended the scope of the Convention to include terrorist acts at international civil airports. It criminalized unlawful and intentional acts of violence against persons at international airports as well as acts of destruction or serious damage to airport facilities of such airports which are likely to endanger safety at said airports.

2010 Beijing Convention. Under the auspices of the International Civil Aviation Organization (ICAO), a diplomatic conference in Beijing has effectively replaced both the 1971 Convention and its 1988 Protocol by adopting a new instrument for the suppression of unlawful acts relating to civil aviation. Convention on the Suppression of Unlawful Acts Relating to International Civil Aviation, 50 I.L.M. 141 (2011). The text is available at *http://legacy.icao.int/DCAS2010/restr/docs/ beijing_convention_multi.pdf.*

Article 1 of the 2010 Beijing Convention on the Suppression of Unlawful Acts Relating to International Civil Aviation includes an extensive list of offenses which include and expand those in the prior treaties, for example "using an aircraft in service for the purpose of causing death, serious bodily injury, or serious damage to property or the environment." Art. 1(1)(f). It also criminalizes the release or discharge from a civil aircraft of any biological, chemical, or nuclear ("BCN") weapon or explosive or similar substance in a manner that is likely to cause death, serious bodily injury, or serious damage to property or the environment.

Paragraph 24 of the new Convention provides that, once ratified, it will prevail over both earlier instruments for those States that have accepted its obligations.

§ 8–8   INTERNATIONALLY PROTECTED PERSONS (1973)

The UN Convention on the Prevention and Punishment of Crimes Against Internationally Protected Persons (the "IPP" Convention), Dec. 14, 1973, 1035 UNTS 167, 28 U.S.T 1975, TIAS 8532, 13 I.L.M. 41 (1974). The text of this Convention is available at *http://treaties.un.org/doc/db/*

Terrorism/english-18-7.pdf. As of June 2013, 176 States were party to this Convention.

Art. 1 of the Convention defines "internationally protected persons" to include a Head of State, Minister for Foreign Affairs, representative or official of a State, any official of an international organization who is entitled pursuant to international law to special protection, and his family. Under article 2, Contracting Parties must criminalize a variety of crimes, including the murder, kidnapping or attack on an internationally protected person, an attack on the official premises of such a person, or a threat to commit such an attack.

Under this treaty, a State has jurisdiction when the crime is committed in its territory or on board a ship or aircraft registered in that State, when the offender is a national, or if the crime is committed against a person from that State who is an "internationally protected person." States Parties must cooperate in the prevention of the mentioned crimes and in following investigations. Offenses under this Convention are extraditable, and State Parties must afford each other the "greatest measure of assistance" during any criminal proceeding related to this Convention.

U.S. Legislation. Several provisions of federal criminal law are relevant to the obligations undertaken in this Convention, in particular 18 U.S.C. §§ 112, 878, 970, 1114, 1116, 1117, 1201 and 2332.

§ 8–9   TAKING OF HOSTAGES (1979)

UN Convention Against the Taking of Hostages (the "Hostage Taking Convention"), Dec. 17, 1979, 21931 UNTS 1316, TIAS 11081, 18 I.L.M. 1456. The text of the Convention is available at *http://treaties. un.org/doc/db/Terrorism/english-18-7.pdf.* As of June 2013, 170 States had ratified or acceded to this convention.

Article 1 provides that anyone who seizes or detains and threatens to kill, to injure or to continue to detain another person (hereinafter referred to as the "hostage") in order to compel a third party, namely, a State, an international intergovernmental organization, a natural or juridical person, or a group of persons, to do or abstain from doing any act as an explicit or implicit condition for the release of the hostage" commits the offense of hostage taking. Attempts and participating as an accomplice are also covered. Contracting States must make the offenses punishable by penalties that take into account their "grave nature."

Note that the Convention requires a specific *mens rea*. The Convention does not apply to acts committed during periods of armed conflict covered by the 1949 Geneva Conventions of 1949 or their two Protocols Additional. Nor does it apply in an entirely domestic situation, that is, where offense is committed within a single State, both the hostage and the perpetrator are nationals of that State, and the alleged offender is found in the territory of that State. Art. 13.

State Parties are required to take all appropriate measures to "ease the situation of the hostage, in particular, to secure his release. . . " In addition, States must cooperate in the prevention as well as the prosecution of covered offenses.

This Convention takes a narrow approach in other respects. A State has jurisdiction only if the offense was committed in its territory, by any of its nationals, or if a hostage is that State's national. The obligation to prosecute applies only to alleged offenders "present in its territory." If a State has custody of a person, it must either extradite the person or conduct criminal proceedings against him. The offense shall be considered extraditable under existing treaties between States Parties, but the individual need not be extradited when the requested State believes the request is for the purpose of "prosecuting or punishing a person on account of his race, religion, nationality, ethnic origin, or political opinion" or the "person's position may be prejudiced" for one of those reasons. Arts. 9 and 10.

U.S. Legislation. The Convention is mainly implemented by the Hostage Taking Act, 18 U.S.C. § 1203.

§ 8–10   PHYSICAL PROTECTION OF NUCLEAR MATERIAL (1980)

Convention on the Physical Protection of Nuclear Material (the "Nuclear Materials Convention"), March 3, 1980, 1456 UNTS 101, TIAS 11080; 18 I.L.M. 1419, text available at *http://www.iaea.org/*

Publications/Documents/Conventions/cppnm.html.
The treaty was amended in 2005. As of June 2013,
148 States were party.

This Convention calls for States Parties to take
various steps to ensure that nuclear material is
protected at prescribed levels during international
and domestic transport. They agree not to export or
import nuclear material unless they have received
assurances that such material will be sufficiently
protected during transport. Article 5 identifies
various levels of cooperation that State must
undertake, including if there is a robbery or theft of
nuclear material.

The treaty requires States Parties to criminalize the
intentional commission of "an act without lawful
authority which constitutes the receipt, possession,
use, transfer, alteration, disposal or dispersal of
nuclear material and which causes or is likely to
cause death or serious injury to any person or
substantial damage to property" as well as the theft
or robbery of nuclear material, embezzlement or
fraudulent obtaining of nuclear material, an act
"constituting a demand for nuclear material by
threat or use of force or by any other form of
intimidation."

A State Party must take measures to establish its
jurisdiction to prosecute when a covered offense is
committed in its territory or on board a State-
registered ship or aircraft, or when the offender is a
State national. The offense is extraditable but if the
State does not extradite the person, the case must
be submitted to its "competent authorities for the

purpose of prosecution." States Parties must afford each other "the greatest measure of assistance in connection with criminal proceedings" brought under the Convention, including providing evidence at their disposal necessary for the proceedings.

U.S. Legislation. The Nuclear Materials Convention is implemented at 18 U.S.C. § 831.

§ 8–11   MARITIME TERRORISM (1988)

The UN Convention for the Suppression of Unlawful Acts Against the Safety of Maritime Navigation (the "SUA" or "IMO Maritime Terrorism" Convention), Mar. 10, 1988, 1678 UNTS 201, TIAS 11080, text available at *http://treaties.un.org/doc/db/Terrorism/Conv8-english.pdf.* As of June 2013, it had 160 States Parties.

This Convention was adopted in the wake of the hijacking of the Italian cruise ship *Achille Lauro* to address the need for international cooperation in devising and adopting practical, effective measures to prevent "all unlawful acts" against the safety of maritime navigation. The Convention criminalizes any act to seize or exercise control over a ship by force or threat, act of violence against a person on board a ship that is likely to endanger the safe navigation of the ship, or act that destroys or damages a ship in manner that is likely to endanger the safe navigation of that ship.

The Convention applies to ships that are "navigating . . . through or from waters beyond the outer limit" of the State's territorial sea. However, it does not cover warships or vessels owned, operated or used as naval auxiliaries, or for customs, police or other non-commercial purposes.

States Parties agree to punish covered acts by penalties reflecting the "grave nature" of the offenses. A State Party must have jurisdiction when the offense is committed against or on board a ship flying its flag, in its territory or by its national. Jurisdiction may also be established over incidents in which the State's national is seized, threatened, injured or killed during the commission of a covered offense, or when the offense is "committed in an attempt to compel that State to do or abstain from doing any act."

States must take custody of alleged offenders found within their territory and notify other interested States. The offenses are extraditable and deemed included in existing extradition treaties. If the State does not extradite the accused individual, it must submit the case to its authorities for prosecution.

States must afford one another the "greatest measure of assistance" in connection with criminal proceedings, including the provision of relevant evidence. They must also take "all practicable measures to prevent preparations in their respective territories for the commission" of offenses within or outside their territories. The Convention explicitly states that it does not affect rule of international law "pertaining to the competence of States to exercise investigative or enforcement jurisdiction on board ships not flying their flag."

Fixed Platforms Protocol. In conjunction with this Convention, an optional protocol was also adopted to extend relevant obligations to acts against "fixed platforms" attached to the seabed floor. The 1988 Protocol for the Suppression of Unlawful Acts Against the Safety of Fixed Platforms Located on the Continental Shelf, 1678 U.N.T.S. 304, text available at *http://treaties.un.org/doc/db/Terrorism/Conv9-english.pdf,* currently has 148 States Parties.

It applies to acts by which individuals seize or exercise control over a fixed platform "by force or threat thereof or any other form of intimidation" or perform an act of violence against a person on board a fixed platform "if that act is likely to endanger its safety." A "fixed platform" is defined as an "artificial island, installation or structure permanently attached to the sea-bed for the purpose of exploration or exploitation of resources."

States Parties must establish jurisdiction over offenses committed against or on board fixed platforms located on their continental shelf or when committed by their nationals. They may do so when the offense is committed in an attempt to compel them to do or abstain from doing any act, or when their national is seized, threatened injured or killed during the commission of the offense. The offenses are extraditable, and States Parties automatically assume an "extradite or prosecute" obligation.

2005 Protocol. The 1988 Convention was amended in 2005 by means of a protocol, which made several changes. The text of the 2005 protocol is available

at: *https://www.unodc.org/tldb/pdf/Protocol_
2005_Convention_Maritime_navigation.pdf.*

First, new article 3*bis* added a new offense which
(among others) covers situations in which
individuals use or transport explosive, radioactive or
biological materials or weapons for purposes of
intimidating a population, compelling a Government
or an international organization to do or to abstain
from any act, or causes death, serious injury or
damage. Second, new article 8*bis* addresses
obligations of co-operation and specific procedures to
be followed in situations when a State Party has
"reasonable grounds" to suspect that a ship flying
another State's flag (or individuals on board) might
be involved in such an offense and it wants to board
that ship.

U.S. Legislation. The 1988 Convention and its
Fixed Platforms Protocol are implemented in U.S.
law primarily through 18 U.S.C. §§ 2280 and 2281.

§ 8–12   TERRORIST BOMBINGS (1997)

The UN Convention for the Suppression of Terrorist
Bombings (the "Terrorist Bombings Convention"),
Dec. 15, 1997, 2149 UNTS 256, 37 I.L.M. 249, text
available   at   *http://treaties.un.org/doc/db/
Terrorism/english-18-9.pdf.* As of June 2013, 165
States had ratified or acceded.

This Convention was prompted by various events
during 1995 and 1996, including the "sarin" poison
gas attacks in Tokyo subways, the bombing attacks
by HAMAS in Tel Aviv and Jerusalem, the bombing

attack by the IRA in Manchester, England, and the infamous Al-Khobar Towers bombing in Saudi Arabia that killed a large number of U.S. military personnel.

The Convention requires States Parties to criminalize the unlawful and intentional offense of delivering, placing, discharging or detonating an explosive or other lethal device in a public place, government facility, public transportation system or infrastructure facility with the intent of causing death, serious injury, or extensive destruction. It also covers acts by accomplices or organizers of an offense.

A State Party has jurisdiction over covered offenses committed in its territory, on board its flagged vessels or registered aircraft, or by its nationals. It may establish jurisdiction when the offenses are committed against its national, against a State or government facility abroad (including an embassy or other diplomatic or consular premises) or in an attempt to compel it to do or abstain from doing an act. It may also do so with respect to offenses committed on board an aircraft operated by the government of that State.

However, much like the Hostage-Taking Convention, the Terrorist Bombing Convention does not apply when the offense is committed within a single State, both the offender and the victim(s) are nationals of that State, the alleged offender is found in that State, and no other State has jurisdiction under the provisions described above.

Covered offenses are extraditable, and States Parties must establish "extradite or prosecute" jurisdiction. They are required to provide the "greatest measure of assistance" in connection with criminal or extradition proceedings related to covered offenses. The offenses are extraditable and may not be considered political offenses or offenses connected with or inspired by political offenses. However, States Parties may not refuse requests they consider made for the purpose of prosecution or punishment "on account of that person's race, religion, nationality, ethnic origin or political opinion" or if compliance would cause "prejudice to that person's position" on account of any of those factors.

U.S. Legislation. *See* the Terrorist Bombing Convention Implementation Act, codified at 18 U.S.C. § 2332f.

§ 8–13   FINANCING OF TERRORISM (1999)

The International Convention for the Suppression of the Financing of Terrorism (the "ICAO Terrorist Financing Convention"), Dec. 9, 1999, 2178 U.N.T.S. 197, T.I.A.S. 13075, 39 I.L.M. 270, text available at *http://treaties.un.org/doc/db/Terrorism/english-18-11.pdf.* As of June 2013, 182 States were party.

The Convention provides that a person commits an offense when he or she "by any means, directly or indirectly, unlawfully and willfully, provides or collects funds" intending or knowing they should or would be used to carry out offenses under nine multilateral treaties (listed in an annex to the treaty) or "any other act intended to cause death or serious bodily injury to a civilian, or to any other person not taking an active part in the hostilities in a situation of armed conflict, when the purpose of such act, by its nature or context, is to intimidate a population, or to compel a government or an international organization to do or to abstain from doing any act."

Each State Party must adopt domestic legislation making these offenses criminal and punishable by penalties taking into account their "grave nature." States must also adopt legislation to permit holding a "legal entity" located in its territory or organized under its laws liable when a person responsible for that entity's management or control commits a covered offense.

A State Party must establish jurisdiction over covered offenses committed in its territory, on board its flagged vessels or registered aircraft, or by its nationals. It may do so for offenses directed towards or resulting in the carrying out of an offense in its territory, against its nationals, or against a State or government facility of that State abroad, including its diplomatic or consular premises, or committed in an attempt to compel it to do or abstain from doing any act, or when the offense is committed on board an aircraft operated by the government of that State.

This Convention does not apply, however, when the offense is committed within a single State, the alleged offender is a national of that State and is present in its territory, and no other State has jurisdiction (subject to some exceptions).

States Parties assume obligations regarding the identification, detection and freezing or seizure and forfeiture of funds used for the purpose of committing covered offenses. These offenses are deemed extraditable and included in extradition treaties between States Parties. If a State with custody of an alleged offender does not extradite that offender, it must submit the case "without undue delay" for prosecution. States Parties must afford each other "the greatest measure of assistance in connection with criminal investigations or criminal or extradition proceedings" for covered offenses, including assistance in obtaining evidence necessary for the proceedings.

States Parties may not refuse a request for mutual legal assistance on the ground of bank secrecy, and none of the covered offenses can be regarded for the purposes of extradition or mutual legal assistance as a "fiscal offense" or as a political offense, an offense connected with a political offense, or an offense inspired by political motives. However, a State Party may refuse such requests when it considers them made for the purpose of prosecuting or punishing a person on account of that person's race, religion, nationality, ethnic origin or political opinion or that compliance with the request would cause prejudice to that person's position for any of these reasons. Moreover, information or evidence furnished by one State Party to another can be used for investigations, prosecutions or proceedings other than those stated in the original request without that State's prior consent.

U.S. Legislation. *See* the Suppression of Financing of Terrorism Convention Implementation Act (2002), codified at 18 U.S.C. § 2339C.

§ 8–14   NUCLEAR TERRORISM (2005)

International Convention for the Suppression of Acts of Nuclear Terrorism (the "Nuclear Terrorism Convention"), April 13, 2005, 2445 UNTS 89, text available at *http://treaties.un.org/doc/db/ Terrorism/english-18-15.pdf.* As of June 2013 it had 86 ratifications or accessions. The United States has signed but not yet ratified this Convention.

This Convention was a response to the possibility that nuclear or radioactive material might fall into the hands of terrorists. It requires States Parties to criminalize a broad range of activities involving nuclear material, including possessing radioactive material or making or possessing a device with the intent to cause death or substantial damage to property or the environment or to compel a persons, State or international organization to do or abstain from doing an act. It also covers related offenses such as threatening, demanding, organizing or directing, acting as an accomplice or otherwise contributing to a covered offense.

It does not cover activities of armed forces during an armed conflict, nor can the Convention be "interpreted as addressing, in any way, the issue of the legality of the use or threat of use of nuclear weapons by States."

States Parties must establish jurisdiction over covered offenses when committed in their territory, on board their flagged vessels or registered aircraft, or by their nationals. They may also establish jurisdiction when the offense is committed against their nationals, against their facilities abroad (including embassies or other diplomatic or consular premises), in an attempt to compel them to do or abstain from doing any act, or on board a government-operated aircraft. They must also establish "extradite or prosecute" jurisdiction.

Covered offenses are deemed extraditable and included in existing extradition treaties. States Parties must afford each other "the greatest measure of assistance in connection with investigations or criminal or extradition proceedings" in respect of covered offenses. For purposes of extradition and mutual legal assistance, none of the covered offenses can be regarded as a political offense, an offense connected with a political offense, or an offense inspired by political motives. Accordingly, a request for extradition or for mutual legal assistance may not be refused on such grounds.

On the other hand, the Convention cannot be interpreted as imposing an obligation to extradite or provide mutual legal assistance if the requested State Party has substantial grounds for believing that the request for extradition or mutual legal assistance has been made for the purpose of prosecuting or punishing a person on account of that person's race, religion, nationality, ethnic origin or political opinion or that compliance with the request would cause prejudice to that person's position for any of these reasons.

The Convention does not apply to purely domestic situations, that is, where the offense is committed within a single State, the alleged offender and the victims are nationals of that State, the alleged offender is found in that State's territory, and no other State has a prescribed jurisdictional basis.

Interestingly, the Convention requires States Parties to adopt measures to ensure that criminal acts within its scope, "in particular where they are intended or calculated to provoke a state of terror in the general public or in a group of persons or particular persons," are not justifiable "by considerations of a political, philosophical, ideological, racial, ethnic, religious or other similar nature and are punished by penalties consistent with their grave nature."

States Parties must cooperate by taking all practicable measures, including working to "prevent counter preparations in their respective territories for the commission . . . of the offences." The Convention also calls on States to work to ensure the protection of radioactive material.

§ 8–15   REGIONAL TERRORISM CONVENTIONS

In addition to the multilateral conventions listed above, a number of treaties have been adopted at the regional level to address issues of terrorism. They include:

a. The Arab Convention on the Suppression of Terrorism, April 22, 1998, text available at *https://www.unodc.org/tldb/pdf/conv_arab_terrorism.en.pdf.*

b. The Convention of the Organization of the Islamic Conference on Combating International Terrorism, July 1, 1999, text available at *http://www.oicun.org/7/38/.*

c. Council of Europe Convention on the Suppression of Terrorism, Jan. 27, 1977, text available at *http://conventions.coe.int/Treaty/en/Treaties/Word/090.doc.*

d. OAS Convention to Prevent and Punish Acts of Terrorism, Feb. 2, 1971, text available at *http://www.oas.org/juridico/english/treaties/a-49.html.*

e. OAU Convention on the Prevention and Combating of Terrorism, July 14, 1999, text available at *http://treaties.un.org/doc/db/Terrorism/OAU-english.pdf.*

f. South Asian Association for Regional Cooperation (SAARC), Convention on Suppression of Terrorism, Nov. 4, 1987, text

available at *http://treaties.un.org/doc/db/
Terrorism/Conv18-english.pdf.*

g. Commonwealth of Independent States Treaty
on Cooperation in Combating Terrorism, June
4, 1999, text available at *http://treaties.un.
org/doc/db/Terrorism/csi-english.pdf.*

IV. TERRORISM IN AMERICAN LAW

Most of the international conventions listed above
have been implemented in U.S. law by appropriate
legislation. In enacting these provisions, Congress
has relied *inter alia* on its constitutional authority
over interstate and foreign commerce and to "define
and punish Piracies and Felonies committed on
High Seas and Offences against Law of Nations."

A number of definitions of terrorism can be found in
U.S. law, adopted at different times and for
different purposes. One such provision is found in
the statute that requires the Secretary of State to
submit annual "country reports" on terrorism to
Congress. For this purpose, the term "international
terrorism" means terrorism involving citizens or the
territory of more than one country; (2) the term
"terrorism" means premeditated, politically
motivated violence perpetrated against
noncombatant targets by subnational groups or
clandestine agents; and (3) the term "terrorist
group" means any group practicing, or which has
significant subgroups which practice, international
terrorism. *See* 22 U.S.C. § 2656f(d). Those annual
country reports can be accessed at *http://www.
state.gov/j/ct/rls/crt/.*

For purposes of criminal prosecution, terrorism is mainly addressed in Chapter 113B of Title 18 of the U.S. Code. In 18 U.S.C. § 2331(1), "international terrorism" is defined to include activities that:

(A) involve violent acts or acts dangerous to human life that are a violation of the criminal laws of the United States or of any State, or that would be a criminal violation if committed within the jurisdiction of the United States or of any State;

(B) appear to be intended—

(i) to intimidate or coerce a civilian population;

(ii) to influence the policy of a government by intimidation or coercion; or

(iii) to affect the conduct of a government by mass destruction, assassination, or kidnapping; and

(C) occur primarily outside the territorial jurisdiction of the United States, or transcend national boundaries in terms of the means by which they are accomplished, the persons they appear intended to intimidate or coerce, or the locale in which their perpetrators operate or seek asylum.

The list of crimes addressed in this chapter is extensive. A number of provisions address crimes based on international conventions to which the United States is a party, such as attacks against internationally protected persons, terrorist bombings, and terrorist financing. Others deal with weapons of mass destruction, transnational terrorism, use of missile systems against aircraft, radiological dispersal devices, and other "acts of terrorism transcending national boundaries."

Three particular aspects of this statute deserve note. The first is that § 2333 provides for civil actions against terrorists over whom personal jurisdiction may be exercised (it is unusual in U.S. practice to find a civil remedy included in a criminal statute). This provision is commonly referred to at the Anti-Terrorism Act (or "ATA") and it provides for a private right of action for treble damages to any U.S. national "injured in his or her person, property, or business by reason of an act of international terrorism." 18 U.S.C. § 2333(a). It also provides for treble damages and that a criminal conviction can act as a bar to the denial of allegations related to the substance of the criminal prosecution in a civil suit. 18 U.S.C. § 2333(b).

The second is an exemption from these civil suits for (1) the United States, an agency of the United States, or an officer or employee of the United States or any agency thereof acting within his or her official capacity or under color of legal authority; and for (2) a foreign state, an agency of a foreign state, or an officer or employee of a foreign state or an agency thereof acting within his or her official capacity or under color of legal authority. 18 U.S.C. § 2337. This provision maintains sovereign immunity (both domestic and foreign) with regard to ATA suits.

Third, this statute include a range of offenses not (yet) addressed by international law, including for example harboring or concealing terrorists (§ 2339), providing material support to terrorists (§ 2339(A)) or to foreign terrorist organizations (§ 2339(B)), and receiving military training from foreign terrorist organizations (§ 2339(D)). From a prosecutorial perspective, these provisions can be critical, since they permit prosecution of the activities that precede actual/executed terrorist acts.

The same can be said, of course, about the benefits of being able to prosecute intending terrorists under the conspiracy provisions of Chapter 113B or under the "racketeering influenced corrupt organization" ("RICO") statute, see 18 U.S.C. §§ 1961–1968.

U.S. law also authorizes the imposition of various economic and other sanctions against State sponsors of terrorism, foreign terrorist organizations, and individuals who provide support to terrorists. Currently Cuba, Iran, Syria and Sudan are on the "State sponsors" list designated by the Secretary of State under section 6(j) of the Export Administration Act, section 40 of the Arms Export Control Act, and section 620A of the Foreign Assistance Act.

§ 8–16   FURTHER READING

Terry, *The War on Terror* (Rowman and Littlefield 2013); Schmid, *Routledge Handbook of Terrorism Research* (2013); Williamson, *Terrorism, War and International Law* (Ashgate 2013); Arndt Sinn, "What is Terrorism?" 13 German J. L.1013 (2013);

Jennifer Hesterman, *The Terrorist-Criminal Nexus: An Alliance of International Drug Cartels, Organized Crime and Terror Groups* (CRC Press 2013); Aviv Cohen, "Prosecuting Terrorists at the International Criminal Court: Reevaluating an Unused Legal Tool to Combat Terrorism," 20 Mich. St. Int'l L. Rev. 219 (2012).

CHAPTER 9

EXTRADITION AND RELATED PROCEDURES

I.   INTRODUCTION

This chapter summarizes the basic rules and procedure relating to extradition as well as the various alternatives to extradition, including deportation, exclusion and expulsion, transfer of prisoners and criminal proceedings, and other forms of "rendition" such as abduction.

§ 9–1   DEFINITION

In an international context, the term "extradition" refers to the formal procedure by which one State surrenders custody of an accused person or a fugitive to another State for purposes of criminal prosecution. Technically, it is one of several legal mechanisms by which an individual can be transferred (or "rendered") from one national jurisdiction to another. Deportation (sometimes called "removal" in immigration practice) is another method. The main differences are that an extradition request is premised on pending criminal charges (or an existing conviction and sentence) in the requesting State and is generally (although not always) based on a treaty or other reciprocal arrangement.

Within the United States, a distinction is drawn between domestic extraditions and international extraditions. Domestic extraditions (those between individual states of the United States) are based on the "extradition of fugitives" authority in the U.S. Constitution; Art. 4, Sec. 2, cl. 2 requires one state to deliver fugitives who have committed a "treason, felony or other crime" to the requesting state from which that individual has fled. A federal statute, 18 U.S.C. § 3182, sets the process by which such requests are made, but state law governs as well.

By distinction, international extradition is exclusively a federal function. A valid extradition treaty must be in force between the United States and the foreign country, and the governing procedures are set forth at 18 U.S.C. §§ 3181–96.

§ 9–2   PURPOSE

The availability of agreed extradition procedures helps to bring to justice those accused or convicted of crimes while promoting respect for the sovereignty and independence of the States concerned. If extradition were not possible, criminals might readily find refuge and safe haven in foreign countries. In addition, domestic law enforcement authorities might be inclined towards "self-help" measures to apprehend fugitives in other jurisdictions.

Frequently, the State in which the accused person or fugitive is found cannot prosecute the offense in question because it lacks jurisdiction over crimes committed in other countries. Even when that is not the case, it is often more practicable and more desirable for the individual to be prosecuted by the

State where the offense was committed, since that is where the evidence and witnesses are likely to be located and that State has the greatest interest in the prosecution.

§ 9–3   HISTORICAL DEVELOPMENT

The first known extradition treaty was negotiated between Ramses II of Egypt and Hittite Prince Hattusili III in the Thirteenth Century BC. The terms of that treaty were carved into the walls of the Temple of Karnak at Luxor. One of the first modern extradition treaties (and in fact one of the first post-independence American treaties) was the Jay Treaty of 1794 with the United Kingdom. Bilateral treaties proliferated throughout the 19th century with the advent of global trade and commerce.

Broadly speaking, these earlier international extradition practices have continued without significant change and reflect the nature of an international system based primarily on the interests of sovereign States. Some commentators suggest that the changing nature of the international system makes the extradition system obsolete, especially in light of the emergence of human rights norms and the establishment of international criminal tribunals. It seems likely, however, that the vast majority of criminal offenses will continue to be prosecuted in domestic courts for the foreseeable future, so extradition laws and practices will remain relevant.

II. GENERAL PRINCIPLES

No rule of customary international law requires one State to surrender accused individuals or fugitive offenders to another State. As a result, international extraditions typically proceed on the basis of a treaty or other formal agreement providing reciprocal obligations between the States concerned. In other words, the international extradition regime is founded on consent.

Besides reciprocity, the essential principle is "dual criminality," which means that the offense for which extradition is sought must be a crime in both the requesting and requested jurisdictions. Most States do not extradite people to be prosecuted elsewhere for an offense that is not a crime in their own jurisdiction.

Within each country, the specific procedures that must be followed in responding to a request for extradition are typically a matter of domestic law. Legislation may provide specific rules dictating who can be extradited, what kind of evidence may be required in support of a request, the extent of judicial review over the process, even the grounds for refusing an extradition request. The details and requirements therefore vary between national legal systems.

§ 9–4   THE TREATY REQUIREMENT

Extradition is founded on reciprocity. There is no duty under international law to extradite absent a treaty or other agreement between the States concerned. Some States may surrender persons even where no treaty exists. However, most countries, including the United States, require a valid treaty to be in force before requests for extradition can be considered.

1. *Bilateral Treaties*

Most countries extradite on the basis of bilateral treaties or agreements. The United States has traditionally conditioned its extradition laws and practices on an existing bilateral treaty with other countries. In fact, this "treaty requirement" is reflected in the extradition statutes. *See* 18 U.S.C. §§ 3181, 3184 (1996). Moreover, a bilateral treaty is almost always required. Over 100 such treaties are currently in force. They are listed at 18 U.S.C. § 3181 (1996).

U.S. courts rely on the views of the Department of State as to whether a given treaty remains in force for the United States. On questions of interpretation, the views of the Executive Branch are given substantial deference in the interpretation of treaty provisions.

2. *UN Model Extradition Treaty*

The terms of individual extradition treaties have a broad similarity but tend to differ markedly in their particulars. In 1990, to promote the adoption of modern extradition relationships by countries of differing legal cultures around the world, the UN General Assembly approved a Model Treaty on

Extradition. *See* U.N. Doc. A/RES/45/116 (Dec. 14, 1990).

3. *Extradition to Tribunals*

A recent exception to the treaty requirement in U.S. practice involves the surrender of individuals to the ICTY and ICTR. To comply with its obligations to surrender persons charged by those Tribunals, the United States concluded separate executive agreements with them in 1994 and 1995, respectively. The agreements were subsequently implemented by statute providing that the extradition laws "shall apply in the same manner and extent to the surrender of persons, including United States citizens, to [the ICTR and the ICTY]." *See* National Defense Authorization Act of 1996, Pub. L. No. 104–106, § 1342(a)(1), 110 Stat. 186 (1996).

Bishop Elizaphan Ntakirutimana, charged with acts of genocide, challenged his surrender on the ground that no "Article II" treaty existed between the ICTR and the United States. The Fifth Circuit rejected the argument, holding that it is not unconstitutional to extradite a person in the absence of such a treaty so long as Congress has authorized the action pursuant to statute. *See Ntakirutimana v. Reno*, 184 F.3d 419 (5th Cir. 1999), cert. denied, 528 U.S. 1135 (2000).

Even though the United States is not a party to the Rome Statute creating the International Criminal Court, some concerns have been expressed about the possibility of requests for the extradition of people from the United States to the ICC. These concerns are reflected in 22 U.S.C. § 7423(d), which states that

> Notwithstanding any other provision of law, no agency or entity of the United States Government or of any State or local government may extradite any person from the United States to the International Criminal Court, nor support the transfer of any United States citizen or permanent resident alien to the International Criminal Court.

In addition, subsection (f) of the same statute prohibits the use of appropriated funds to assist the "investigation, arrest, detention, extradition, or prosecution of any United States citizen or permanent resident alien by the International Criminal Court."

4. *Multilateral Treaties*

It has long been U.S. practice (strongly endorsed by the U.S. Senate) to require a separate bilateral treaty for each country. The concern has been to ensure that the United States only assumes extradition obligations with countries considered to have sufficiently reliable legal systems. By contrast, many States around the world can extradite on basis of a multilateral treaty.

Although no global extradition treaty exists, a number of regional multilateral treaties are in force. Within the Council of Europe, for example, Member

States have long based their extradition relationships on the 1957 European Convention on Extradition (for members of the European Union, this treaty has now largely been displaced by the European Arrest Warrant, discussed below). Regional extradition arrangements exist between the Benelux countries, within the Commonwealth, in the Arab League, and among the South African States.

The Organization of American States boasts two multilateral extradition treaties. The first is the 1981 Inter-American (Caracas) Convention on Extradition (entered into force in March 1992). It has six Member States: Antigua and Barbuda, Costa Rica, Ecuador, Panama, St. Lucia and Venezuela. The United States has neither signed nor ratified this treaty.

Since 1935, the United States has been party to the second, the 1933 Inter-American (Montevideo) Convention on Extradition, 49 Stat. 3097, 165 LNTS 19, to which Argentina, Chile, Colombia, the Dominican Republic, Ecuador, El Salvador, Guatemala, Mexico, Nicaragua and Panama are also parties. The United States on several occasions has relied upon its terms to accomplish extraditions in a relatively few instances where the bilateral relationship with the country in question was not sufficient.

In addition, a number of the multilateral criminal law conventions to which the United States is a party also provide a basis for extradition in respect of covered offenses, including the UN Conventions on Transnational Organized Crime, Illicit Trafficking in Narcotic Drugs and Psychotropic Substances, Maritime Terrorism, and Corruption. These are discussed *supra* in Chapter 7. These treaties operate to amend existing bilateral treaties between States Parties to include the specific offenses covered by those conventions and to provide a treaty basis for extradition for such offenses when no bilateral exists.

§ 9–5   DUAL CRIMINALITY

The general requirement of dual (or double) criminality reflects the principle that it would be repugnant to surrender someone to stand trial in another country for an act that is not considered a criminal offense in the requested State. Most extradition treaties contain an explicit dual criminality requirement. The principle is firmly established in U.S. law. "In short, an individual will be extradited under a treaty containing a [dual] criminality provision only when his actions constitute an offense in both the requesting and requested states." *United States v. Herbage*, 850 F.2d 1463, 1465 (11th Cir. 1988).

Dual criminality does not mean exact equivalence. Generally speaking, the requirement is satisfied when the relevant offenses are substantially analogous and when the conduct in question is subject to criminal sanctions in both jurisdictions. As stated in *United States v. Sacoccia*, 58 F.3d 754, 766 (1st Cir. 1995), *cert. denied*, 517 U.S. 1105 (1996)

The principle of dual criminality does not demand that the laws of the surrendering and requesting States be carbon copies of one another. Thus, dual criminality will not be defeated by differences in the instrumentalities or in the stated purposes of the two nations' laws. By the same token, the counterpart crimes need not have identical elements.

Assertions of extraterritorial jurisdiction can sometimes raise dual criminality issues. Some treaties include a specific territorial requirement, so that extradition is available only for crimes committed in the territory of the requesting State. More commonly, the treaty might provide that an extraterritorial offense will be covered if it would be prosecutable had it taken place entirely within the territory of the requested State.

§ 9–6   WHAT CRIMES ARE EXTRADITABLE?

Broadly speaking, there are two different approaches to identifying the offenses for which extradition is possible. The first is to describe them individually in the treaty itself. This enumerative or "list" approach is the traditional one. It assures dual criminality because the governments agree in advance on precisely which crimes are covered. But it has clear drawbacks. It is likely to be under-inclusive and requires constant revision to keep pace with new offenses and developments in criminal law procedure (think, for instance, of the relatively rapid emergence of cybercrime and terrorism).

The second is the more modern "no list" approach, which provides simply that all offenses are extraditable if they are punishable in both countries by a specific minimum sentence (such as one year). It is more inclusive and self-adapting but may generate difficulties in determining dual criminality in some cases. This may be the situation, for example, where prosecution in the requesting State is premised on conduct that may not be an element of the comparable crime in the requested State.

The United States occasionally confronts this problem with respect to mail and wire fraud, racketeering and continuing criminal enterprise, since most foreign legal systems do not criminalize conduct in comparable terms. Prosecution for inchoate crimes, such as attempts, conspiracy, and aiding and abetting, can also raise difficulties depending on the law of the requested State.

§ 9–7   NON-EXTRADITABLE OFFENSES

It is traditional for extradition treaties to exclude tax, fiscal and customs crimes as well as religious offenses. In recent years, however, there has been an increased willingness to narrow the fiscal offenses exception, in light of a growing consensus on the need to prosecute such practices as bribery, corruption and money laundering and to confiscate the proceeds of illegal actions (such as drug trafficking) as an effective law enforcement tool. *See, e.g.*, the Second Additional Protocol to the 1957

European Convention on Extradition, Dec. 13, 1957, E.T.S. 24, and article 18(d) of the 1990 Council of Europe Convention on Laundering, Search, Seizure and Confiscation of Proceeds of Crime, C.E.T.S. 141, reprinted at 30 I.L.M. 148 (1991).

Military crimes (i.e., offenses under military law which are not also offenses under the regular criminal law) are also typically excluded. In some cases, the exclusion covers "crimes of a military character."

The exclusion for "political crimes" is discussed in connection with the "political offense" exception, *infra* at § IV.

§ 9–8   EXTRADITION OF NATIONALS

One major issue that divides many countries concerns extradition of one's own citizens or nationals. Civil law countries traditionally refuse to do so but are able to prosecute them for crimes committed in other countries on the basis of nationality jurisdiction. By contrast, common law countries have generally rejected nationality-based jurisdiction (believing that crimes are most effectively prosecuted where they are committed no matter where the offenders come from) but have been willing to extradite their own citizens.

Historically, the United States long favored the extradition of its own nationals but was not always able to negotiate clear-cut reciprocal commitments with other countries. On occasion, ambiguous treaty language caused problems. In *Valentine v. U.S. ex rel. Neidecker*, 299 U.S. 5 (1936), the U.S. Supreme Court held that a treaty provision providing that neither State was bound to give up its nationals was an insufficient basis for extradition. As a result, for many years, the extradition of U.S. nationals to certain countries was effectively precluded by such discretionary language in the relevant bilateral treaties.

In 1992, Congress amended the extradition statute to eliminate the problem, providing that

> If the applicable treaty or convention does not obligate the United States to extradite its citizens to a foreign country, the Secretary of State may, nevertheless, order the surrender to that country of a United States citizen whose extradition has been requested by that country if the other requirements of that treaty or convention are met.

See 18 U.S.C. § 3196 (1990).

Some recent bilateral treaties deal with this issue by listing specific crimes for which extradition will not be refused solely on the basis of nationality. *See*, for example, article 3(1) the 2006 Extradition Treaty between the United States and Malta, which specifies *inter alia* participation in crimes of terrorism, trafficking in persons, computer crime, sexual exploitation of children and child pornography.

§ 9–9   GROUNDS FOR REFUSAL

In some situations, a government might have what it considers valid reasons for not surrendering the person in question. Extradition treaties and statutes typically provide a number of grounds on which extradition requests can be refused.

1. *Non Bis In Idem*

A commonly accepted basis for refusing extradition is the principle that an individual who has already been prosecuted and acquitted in the requesting State should not be re-tried for the same offense. It is sometimes referred to as *autrefois acquit*.

In the U.S. view, this principle (like its *double jeopardy* counterpart in domestic law) is not violated where the individual has been previously prosecuted and convicted elsewhere for the same or a similar offense. Thus, extradition from the United States to another country would not necessarily be refused simply because U.S. authorities had already prosecuted the individual in question for the same conduct for which the requesting State seeks his surrender. *See, e.g., Elcock v. United States*, 80 F. Supp. 2d 70 (E.D.N.Y. 2000).

Nonetheless, some U.S. extradition treaties contain provisions precluding extradition when the person whose extradition has been requested has already been tried and discharged or punished with final and binding effect in the requested State.

A more difficult situation can arise when the requested State has previously decided *not* to prosecute the individual for the conduct on which the extradition request is based. On the one hand, this may reflect a judgment that no crime had in fact been committed, or perhaps simply that the necessary evidence was lacking. On the other hand, allowing such a decision to preclude extradition can mean that the offender is effectively immune from prosecution anywhere. Some U.S. treaties include a provision permitting the refusal of extradition where the authorities have previously decided not to prosecute the person for the offenses on which the extradition is based or have discontinued such prosecutions.

2. *Lapse of Time*

Extradition may generally be refused if prosecution would be time-barred. This is sometimes referred to as "prescription." In practice, difficulties arise from the fact that different legal systems have different rules about when the "statutes of limitation" run for various crimes. Some extradition treaties provide that the relevant law is that of the requesting State, others specify the law of the requested State, and still others invoke the shorter of the two. In the United States, the general rule for federal crimes is 5 years, although more serious offenses (and some like fraud that are harder to prove) have longer periods.

3. *In Absentia Conviction*

Many countries, especially those in the civil law
tradition, are able to prosecute and convict persons
in their absence. Before agreeing to extradition,
many States require a guarantee that the individual
will have the right to challenge an *in absentia*
conviction one way or another. Typically, this means
a new trial. The United States traditionally treats
the issue as if the individual had been charged but
not convicted, and requires a trial *de novo* after
surrender.

4. *Persecution/Discrimination*

It is not uncommon for extradition treaties
(especially those involving continental European
countries) to permit denial of extradition when, in
the view of the requested State, substantial grounds
exist for believing that the prosecution or
punishment in the requesting State has a
discriminatory purpose or would be prejudicial to
the individual in question. In some of its bilateral
treaties, the United States has reserved the right to
deny extradition on this ground. See, for example,
art. 6 of the U.S.-Hong Kong bilateral agreement,
which permits either party to refuse an extradition
request which it believes is "politically motivated" or
made for the "primary purpose of prosecuting or
punishing the person sought on account of his race,
religion, nationality or political opinion." It also
permits denial when the person is likely to be
denied a fair trial or punishment for the same
reasons.

5. *Humanitarian Considerations*

Some U.S. bilateral treaties permit refusal of extradition requests when the surrender of the requested individual is considered "likely to entail exceptionally serious consequences related to age or health." *See, e.g.*, art. 7 of the U.S.-Hong Kong bilateral.

6. *Capital Punishment and Life Imprisonment*

States which have abolished capital punishment, or where a sentence of life imprisonment without possibility of parole is not permitted, are unlikely to extradite persons when such penalties are possible. Accordingly, many extradition treaties do not oblige requested States to surrender persons to States which enforce the death penalty without adequate assurances from the requesting State that it will not seek or impose capital punishment. *See, e.g.*, art.1 of the 1957 European Convention on Extradition, E.T.S. 24 (1960), and art. 9 of the 1981 Inter-American Extradition Convention.

Increasingly, these provisions have posed difficulties for extraditions to the United States when the accused would be subject to prosecution on capital charges. In its decision in *Soering v. United Kingdom*, 161 Eur. Ct. H.R. (Ser. A.) 1, 11 EHRR 439 (1989), the European Court of Human Rights held that, if it extradited a seventeen year old German citizen to the United States (where he was charged with first-degree murder), the United Kingdom would violate that individual's right to be protected against degrading treatment under the

European Convention on Human Rights and Fundamental Freedoms.

7. *Life Imprisonment*

A growing number of countries have limited or abolished not only the death penalty but also life imprisonment. For example in 2001 the Mexican Supreme Court ruled that individuals could not be extradited if they would face a potential life sentence in the requesting country.

8. *Torture*

A separate treaty basis for refusing extradition can be found in the 1984 UN Convention Against Torture and Other Cruel, Inhuman and Degrading Punishment, which entered into force for the United States on November 10, 1994, 1465 U.N.T.S. 85, 23 I.L.M. 1027 (1984). Article 3(1) provides that extradition is not allowed to a country where the fugitive would be in danger of torture. *See also* UN Model Treaty on Extradition, art. 3(1).

Specific provisions are also found in contemporary U.S. bilaterals. For example, article 6 of the Treaty on Extradition Between the Government of Canada and the Government of the United States of America (Dec. 3, 1976) provides:

> When the offence for which extradition is requested is punishable by death under the laws of the requesting State and the laws of the requested State do not permit such punishment for that offence, extradition may

be refused unless the requesting State provides such assurances as the requested State considers sufficient that the death penalty shall not be imposed, or, if imposed, shall not be executed.

Within the United States, the question of who decides whether the person whose extradition is sought faces a "substantial likelihood of torture" has occasioned a good deal of litigation. The obligation under the Torture Convention was implemented by a 1998 statute (§ 2242 of the Foreign Affairs Reform and Restructuring Act, Pub.L. No. 105–277, div. G, 112 Stat. 2681–2682, codified at 8 U.S.C. § 1231 note). The government has consistently contended that it is a determination for the executive branch, and specifically the Secretary of State, rather than the courts, *inter alia* because under the rule of non-inquiry (discussed below) courts cannot inquire into the degree of risk that the extraditee would face when returned. In *Mironescu v. Costner*, 480 F.3d 664 (4th Cir. 2007), *cert. denied*, 552 U.S. 1135 (Jan. 9, 2008), the court of appeals held that the 1998 statute precludes federal courts from reviewing a decision to extradite a fugitive despite claims that he will likely be tortured in the requesting State. *See also Trinidad y Garcia v. Thomas*, 683 F.3d 952 (9th Cir. 2012), *cert. denied*, 133 S.Ct. 845 (Jan. 7, 2013).

§ 9–10   DOCTRINE OF SPECIALTY

The doctrine of "specialty" prohibits the prosecution of a defendant for any crime other than those for which extradition has been granted. In other words, the requesting State may prosecute only for the offense for which the extraditee was surrendered and otherwise must allow that person an opportunity to leave the requesting State. Offenses committed in the requesting State following surrender are not covered by the rule.

Conceptually, the duty is owed to the requested State and thus may be waived by that State. The federal courts have tended to differ on whether an individual defendant has standing to raise a violation of the doctrine of specialty. *Compare United States v. Puentes*, 50 F.3d 1567 (11th Cir. 1995), cert. denied, 516 U.S. 933 (Oct. 16, 1995), *with United States v. Burke*, 425 F.3d 400 (5th Cir. 2005), cert. denied, 547 U.S. 1208 (2006). In *United States v. Valencia-Trujillo*, 573 F.3d 1171 (11th Cir. 2009), the court of appeals held that the specialty doctrine applies only to extraditions pursuant to treaty, with the result that a defendant whose transfer was not premised on that basis lacked standing to assert a violation.

While the question is usually framed as a treaty issue, at least one court has held that the doctrine of specialty also applies where extradition is based on customary international law. *United States v. Kaufman*, 858 F.2d 994 (5th Cir. 1988).

As a corollary to the rule of specialty, the requesting State is not able to "re-extradite" the individual to a third country, or to international tribunals, without the consent of the first State from which extradition occurred.

III. EXTRADITION PROCEDURE

The act of international extradition has been defined by the U.S. Supreme Court as "the surrender by one nation to another of an individual accused or convicted of an offense outside of its own territory, and within the territorial jurisdiction of the other, which, being competent to try and to punish him, demands the surrender." *Terlinden v. Ames,* 184 U.S. 270, 289 (1902).

In U.S. law, extradition is a formal but unique process. The purpose is criminal but the proceedings are civil. It is governed both by statute and by treaty. While the ultimate decision to surrender is a matter of discretion and lies in the hands of the executive branch, the process is governed by legal principles and requires the direct involvement and concurrence of the judiciary. Thus, the executive cannot order extradition without a judicial decision subject to certain safeguards, but the judiciary cannot order the executive to extradite a person.

§ 9–11   EXTRADITION TO THE UNITED STATES

Requests for the extradition of an individual from another country to the United States originate with the relevant federal, state or local prosecutors. These requests are necessarily based either on criminal charges or a conviction. They are coordinated in the first instance by the Office of International Affairs ("OIA") in the Criminal Division of the U.S. Department of Justice.

Working with the prosecutors in question, OIA prepares the formal extradition papers and other necessary documentation, including for example affidavits indicating the relevant facts, the charges (or judgment) on which the request is based, the evidence substantiating the allegations, information establishing the defendant's identity, and responding to other treaty requirements. The request is then reviewed by the Office of the Legal Adviser in the Department of State and, when approved, is forwarded in diplomatic channels to the U.S. Embassy in the country in question. The Embassy in turn submits the request under cover of a diplomatic note to the appropriate host government officials.

In urgent cases, a request for the provisional arrest of the individual in question may be transmitted in advance of the formal extradition request. Depending on the treaty in question, such requests can be sent through diplomatic channels, via INTERPOL, or even directly to the law enforcement authorities in the foreign country in question.

Once the necessary procedures under foreign law have been completed and the extradition request has been approved, the Department of Justice sends U.S. Marshals to take custody of the prisoner and escort him or her to the United States.

§ 9–12   EXTRADITION FROM THE UNITED STATES

By comparison, requests from foreign authorities for the apprehension and extradition of an individual in the United States are more complicated. The process is governed not only by the relevant bilateral treaty but also by the federal extradition statute, 18 U.S.C. § 3181–96, around which a great deal of interpretive case law has arisen.

Extradition requests typically arrive in diplomatic channels, for example by way of the foreign government's embassy in Washington, D.C. They are delivered to the Department of State, which conducts a preliminary review to determine that a bilateral treaty is in fact in force with the country in question, that the request falls within the terms of that treaty, and that the necessary documents have been properly authenticated so as to be admissible at trial. The request is then forwarded to the OIA at the Department of Justice, which conducts its own review and assesses the sufficiency of the evidentiary and other supporting materials.

Not infrequently, requests are found to be deficient and must be supplemented by additional materials from the requesting State in light of domestic U.S. legal requirements. Obtaining the necessary information in the proper form often takes considerable time. Once the request is complete and in proper form, it is forwarded by the Department of Justice to the Office of the United States Attorney in the judicial district where the fugitive is believed to be located. In turn, that office files a complaint in federal district court requesting the individual's extradition.

After a preliminary review, the district court may issue a warrant for the arrest of the person whose extradition is sought. Once apprehended, the individual is brought before the court for an initial appearance. Since by definition such individuals are considered flight risks, there is a general presumption against bail absent special circumstances.

Summary Extradition. It is possible at this juncture for individuals to waive their right to extradition in the formal sense and to consent to transfer without further proceedings. Some modern treaties explicitly provide for "expedited" or "summary" extradition based on the extraditee's consent.

§ 9–13   REQUEST FOR EXTRADITION

Generally, the required form and contents of an extradition request are specified in the relevant treaty. While the details vary from treaty to treaty, in all cases the requesting State must provide information concerning the identity and presumed location of the person whose extradition is sought, relevant facts demonstrating that the offense in question was committed, copies of the relevant law under which the person is charged, a copy of the foreign warrant for arrest or verdict, etc. The request must "be supported by sufficient evidence to show that the individual is the person sought for the crimes charged, that the crimes are among those listed as extraditable offenses in the Treaty and that there is sufficient justification for the individual's arrest had the charged crime been committed in the United States." *Eain v. Wilkes*, 641 F.2d 504, 508 (7th Cir. 1981).

Under 28 U.S.C. § 3181(b)(1), in making the request, the Department of Justice must certify, among other things, that sufficient evidence has been presented by the foreign government to indicate that the dual criminality requirement is satisfied and that "the offenses charged are not of a political nature."

1. *Request for Provisional Arrest*

Many extradition cases begin with requests for "provisional arrest." Most treaties provide an undertaking by the requested State to detain a person for a limited time in cases of urgency, extreme risk of flight, or extreme danger during which the requesting State can prepare the necessary formal documentation to support its extradition request. Normally, the time limit for to submission of the formal request for extradition is 45–60 days. In U.S. law, provisional arrest is authorized by 28 U.S.C. § 3187.

In addition, at the request of a member country, INTERPOL may issue a so-called "Red Notice" informing all other members that an arrest warrant has been issued for a specific fugitive. In many countries, but not in the United States, the Red Notice itself can serve as the basis for provisional arrest.

2. *Bail*

In the United States, there is a presumption against bail in extradition cases, for the reason that almost by definition the individual whose extradition is sought will properly be considered a flight risk. The Bail Reform Act does not apply in extradition proceedings, and the government will ordinarily oppose bail applications vigorously. In exceptional situations, it is possible for the person sought to establish "special circumstances" justifying release on bail. *See,* e.g., *United States v. Kin-Hong*, 83 F.3d 523 (1st Cir. 1996); *United States v. Snyder*, 2013 WL 1364275 (D. Ariz., April 3, 2013); *In re Extradition of Beresford-Redman*, 753 F.Supp.2d 1078 (C.D.Cal. 2010).

§ 9–14   THE COURT'S ROLE

The role of the extradition court is based on the provisions of 18 U.S.C. § 3184. That provision states that when an extradition treaty exists between the United States and the requesting county:

> any justice or judge of the United States, or any magistrate judge authorized so to do by a court of the United States, or any judge of a court of record of general jurisdiction of any State, may, upon complaint made under oath, charging any person found within his jurisdiction, with having committed within the jurisdiction of any such foreign government any of the crimes provided for by such treaty or convention, or provided for under section 3181(b), issue his warrant for

the apprehension of the person so charged,
that he may be brought before such justice,
judge, or magistrate judge, to the end that the
evidence of criminality may be heard and
considered.

The statutes also states:

Such complaint may be filed before and such
warrant may be issued by a judge or
magistrate judge of the United States District
Court for the District of Columbia if the
whereabouts within the United States of the
person charged are not known or, if there is
reason to believe the person will shortly enter
the United States. If, on such hearing, he
deems the evidence sufficient to sustain the
charge under the provisions of the proper
treaty or convention, or under section 3181(b),
he shall certify the same, together with a copy
of all the testimony taken before him, to the
Secretary of State, that a warrant may issue
upon the requisition of the proper authorities
of such foreign government, for the surrender
of such person, according to the stipulations of
the treaty or convention; and he shall issue
his warrant for the commitment of the person
so charged to the proper jail, there to remain
until such surrender shall be made.

§ 9–15   THE EXTRADITION HEARING

The formal extradition hearing takes place before a
magistrate or district judge pursuant to 18 U.S.C.
§ 3184. The scope of the hearing is narrowly

circumscribed. Its object is merely to confirm (1) that a valid extradition treaty exists between the United States and the requesting State, (2) that criminal charges are in fact pending in the requesting State, (3) that the offenses for which extradition is sought are covered by the relevant treaty as "extraditable offenses" and do not fall within one of the exceptions or exclusions provided by that particular treaty (such as the political offense exception), and finally (4) that probable cause exists to believe that the offenses charged were committed and that the person before the court committed them. *See Skaftourous v. United States*, 667 F.3d 144 (2d Cir. 2011).

The hearing is not a criminal proceeding and is not for the purpose of proving guilt or innocence. Indeed, the individual in question cannot defend on the merits or even present exculpatory evidence. A limited right does exist to present "explanatory evidence" by way of challenging the government's "probable cause" submission, that is, "reasonably clear-cut proof which would be of limited scope and have some reasonable chance of negating a showing of probable cause." However, a fugitive may only present evidence that explains rather than contradicts the demanding country's proof. *See In re Extradition of Azra Basic*, ___ F.Supp.2d ___, 2012 WL 3067466 (E.D. KY, July 27, 2012).

The Federal Rules of Criminal Procedure and the Federal Rules of Evidence are expressly inapplicable to extradition proceedings. *See* Fed. R. Crim. P. 1(a)(5)(A) and Fed. R. Evid. 1101(d)(3). There is no right to discovery or to cross-examination, and hearsay and otherwise excludable evidence is admissible. If properly certified, "[d]epositions, warrants or other papers or copies thereof" offered by the requesting State in support of its extradition request must be accepted and admitted as evidence. *See* 18 U.S.C. § 3190 (1948).

§ 9–16   PROBABLE CAUSE

The main objective of the extradition hearing is to determine whether probable cause exists to believe that the offenses charged were committed and that the person before the court committed them. In this context, "probable cause" is measured by the federal standard used in preliminary proceedings and means that the extradition judge's role is merely to determine whether there is competent evidence to justify holding the accused to await trial. *Hoxha v. Levi*, 465 F.3d 554, 561 (3d Cir. 2006). If these requirements are met, the judge or magistrate certifies the individual's extraditablity. *Prasoprat v. Benov*, 421 F.3d 1009, 1012 (9th Cir. 2005), cert. denied, 546 U.S. 1171 (2006).

In this narrow context, the person whose extradition is sought is not permitted to raise questions of his or her ultimate guilt or innocence, or to introduce "contradictory evidence" that conflicts with the government's probable cause evidence. By contrast, "explanatory evidence" relating to the underlying charges is admissible.

By contrast, in civil law countries, the relevant test is normally "prima facie case." In some legal systems, this can be an even lower evidentiary standard than "probable cause." Moreover, under 1957 European Convention on Extradition, Member States are not required to provide evidence of a prima facie case unless the requested State has made a reservation to that effect.

§ 9–17   RULE OF NON-INQUIRY

Another limiting feature of the extradition hearing is the so-called rule of non-inquiry, which precludes the extradition court from examining the requesting State's criminal justice system or considering claims that the defendant will be mistreated or denied a fair trial in that country. "Under the rule of non-inquiry, courts refrain from investigating the fairness of a requesting system, and from inquiring into the procedures or treatment which await a surrendered fugitive in the requesting country." *United States v. Kin-Hong*, 110 F. 3d 103, 110 (1st Cir. 1997).

The underlying principle is that assessment of such factors is the function of the executive branch, not the courts, and the decision is accordingly left to the discretion of the Secretary of State. The rule of non-inquiry "serves interests of international comity by relegating to political actors the sensitive foreign policy judgments that are often involved in the question of whether to refuse an extradition request." *Hoxha v. Levi*, 465 F.3d 554, 563 (3d Cir. 2006). *See also Skaftouros v. United States*, 667 F.3d 144 (2d Cir. 2011).

A classic application of the rule occurred in *Ahmad v. Wigen*, 726 F. Supp. 389 (E.D.N.Y. 1989), *aff'd*, 910 F.2d 1063 (2d Cir. 1990). There, the District Court rejected a political offense argument and confirmed a magistrate's order of extraditability to Israel. However, in considering the individual's claim that upon return he would be mistreated, denied a fair trial, and deprived of his constitutional and human rights, the court permitted extensive testimony from expert and fact witnesses concerning Israel's law enforcement procedures and its treatment of prisoners. The Second Circuit Court of Appeals disapproved.

A consideration of the procedures that will or may occur in the requesting country is not within the purview of a habeas corpus judge. In *Sindona v. Grant*, 619 F.2d 167, 174 (2d Cir. 1980), the court said that "the degree of risk to [appellant's] life from extradition is an issue that properly falls within the exclusive purview of the executive branch." In *Jhirad v. Ferrandina*, 536 F.2d 478, 484–85 (2d Cir. 1976), the court said that "[i]t is not the business of our courts to assume the responsibility for supervising the integrity of the judicial system of another sovereign nation." It is the function of the Secretary of State to determine whether extradition should be denied on humanitarian grounds. *Ahmad v. Wigen*, 910 F.2d 1063, 1066 (2d Cir. 1990). This view is fairly consistently held in the various appellate circuits.

Specific treaty provisions may affect the application of this rule. One prominent example of treaty-sanctioned inquiry is contained in article 3 of the 1985 U.S.-U.K. Extradition Treaty, which explicitly expanded the scope of judicial inquiry to include issues of potential discriminatory intent of the fugitive in the requesting country.

§ 9–18   DETERMINATION OF EXTRADITABILITY

If the extradition judge concludes that (i) the individual brought before the court is the person sought by the requesting State, (ii) there is, in fact, probable cause to believe that individual has committed the crimes alleged, and (iii) the crimes in question are covered by a valid treaty, that judge will issue a certificate of extraditability to Secretary of State.

Since it is not a final judgment, this determination may not be directly appealed. It is, however, is reviewable collaterally by *habeas corpus* under 28 U.S.C. § 2241. Here again, the scope of the inquiry is narrow. In the *habeas* proceeding, a petitioner may challenge whether the magistrate had jurisdiction, whether the offense charged was within the treaty and whether there was any competent evidence warranting the finding that there was reasonable ground to believe the accused guilty. The *habeas* action does not afford the reviewing court to second-guess the magistrate's findings by re-evaluating the evidence or serving in a fact-finding capacity.

If the court denies the *habeas* petition, the individual may appeal that decision. However, if the individual is found not to be extraditable, the government has no recourse. The proceeding is terminated. Since it is not a criminal proceeding, no jeopardy attaches, and the government is free to file another request for extradition.

§ 9–19   DECISION BY THE SECRETARY OF STATE

Once a court issues an order certifying extraditabilty, the decision whether to surrender the fugitive rests with the Secretary of State, who has two months to review the case. *See* 18 U.S.C. § 3186 (1948). The Secretary has final authority to extradite the fugitive, but is not required to do so. The Secretary may either sign a surrender warrant, condition the surrender on specified conditions, or surrender only after receiving assurances. Ultimately, the decision whether to surrender a person found eligible for extradition remains a discretionary one committed to the executive branch. *See In re Extradition of Hilton*, 2013 WL 1891527 (D. Mass. May 3, 2013).

Once the decision has been made, the Department of State forwards a diplomatic note to the embassy of the requesting State, indicating that the person has been found extraditable, on what charges, and the deadline for delivery. Typically, the requesting State sends its law enforcement officials to the United States to take custody of the individual from the U.S. Marshals, often at the airport.

§ 9–20   CONSTITUTIONALITY OF THE EXTRADITION STATUTE

On occasion, the fact that the ultimate decision to surrender lies within the discretionary authority of the Executive Branch has given rise to arguments that the extradition statute is unconstitutional. Specifically, the contention has been that in deciding whether to issue certificates of extraditability under 18 U.S.C. § 3184, judicial officers are exercising the "judicial power" of the United States under article III of the Constitution, and that by subjecting their judgments to the discretionary authority of the Executive Branch, the statutory scheme violates separation of powers. If, on the other hand, judicial officers are not exercising article III judicial powers when they decide extradition cases, then Congress has impermissibly required judges to act in a non-judicial capacity.

These arguments have been rejected by the courts. *See Lo Duca v. United States*, 93 F.3d 1100, 1105–10 (2d Cir. 1996); *Lopez-Smith v. Hood,* 121 F.3d 1322, 1327 (9th Cir. 1997); *cf. Matter of Requested Extradition of Artt,* 158 F.3d 462 (9th Cir. 1998). *But see LoBue v. Christopher,* 893 F. Supp. 65 (D.D.C. 1995), *vacated and remanded*, 83 F.3d 1081 (D.C. Cir. 1996). Similarly, in *Ntakirutimana*, the district court rejected the contention that, since extradition is ultimately committed to the Executive, and Congress had no right to conduct foreign policy, a statute implementing an executive agreement violated separation of powers. *See In re*

Ntakirutimana, 1998 WL 655708 at *6 (S.D. Tex. 1998).

IV.   POLITICAL OFFENSE QUESTION

One of the most important principles in international extradition law and practice is that a State is not obliged to surrender a person wanted in connection with offenses that it considers to be of a political nature. Most extradition treaties (and all U.S. extradition treaties) recognize this exception explicitly, in one form or another, using such terms as "political offense," "offense of a political character," and "offenses connected with a political offense." Exactly what circumstances qualify for this exception can be a contentious issue, and over time a considerable evolution has taken place in the doctrinal basis for the exception.

§ 9–21   ORIGINS

The origins of this exception demonstrate the conflicting interests and sensitivities of States with respect to certain kinds of crime. Historically, extradition served precisely to allow governments to obtain the return of political offenders who had fled abroad, for example those who committed crimes against the State or attempted to kill the King. During the 19th Century era of "liberal revolutions" in Europe, however, some States insisted on a right to provide asylum to those who had risen up to overthrow reactionary and repressive monarchical regimes in neighboring States and then fled across the border.

In consequence, those States began to insert a political offense exception into their treaties. The concern was that when the conduct at issue relates to political activism against the monarchy, extraditing a person who has failed in such efforts would condemn that individual to an automatic conviction and almost certain death. The United States followed suit in 1843, a decade after nations such as Belgium, France, and Switzerland first included the political offense exception in their bilateral extradition treaties.

But after Belgium refused to extradite Emperor Napoleon III's would-be assassin in 1856, States began to accept what is called the "attentat" clause, which excludes from the scope of the political offense exception attempts on the life of a Head of State or Government or members of their families.

§ 9–22   PURE VS. RELATIVE OFFENSES

A distinction is typically made between "pure" and "relative" political offenses. The core "pure" political offenses are treason, sedition and espionage. Such crimes are (in theory) perpetrated directly against the State itself and are not intended to cause private injury; they have been criminalized by the State for its own protection. "Relative" political offenses, by comparison, involve common crimes committed with a particular political motive, for example robbing a bank to finance the revolution or incidentally killing civilians shopping in the mall.

Like many other countries, the United States has traditionally limited the exception in its treaties to

purely political offenses, which have been described
as offenses of opinion, political expression, and those
which otherwise do not involve the use of violence.

In practice, "pure" political offenses are fairly easy
to identify, while "relative" political offenses depend
a more nuanced determination of the facts as well
as the underlying motives of the perpetrator.
Different jurisdictions have adopted different
approaches to the issue.

Over time, French law adopted an "objective" test,
covering only crimes directly injuring the State or
government; by contrast, the Swiss adopted a
"preponderance" test, weighing common vs. pure
aspects. For its part, the United States settled on
the "incidence test," which requires the act in
question to have taken place during an armed
uprising and be directed toward combatants, not
innocent civilians (the point being to deny terrorists
the benefit of the exception)

The incidence test thus asks whether (l) there was a
violent political disturbance or country at the time
of the alleged offense, and if so, (2) whether the
alleged offense was incidental to or undertaken as
part of that disturbance or uprising. *See Vo v.
Benov*, 447 F.3d 1235, 1241 (9th Cir. 2006).

The incidence test was based, in its origins, on the
decision in *In re Castioni*, [1891] 1 Q.B. 149, 158
(1890) (Opinion of Denman, J.), in which the court
stated that:

> It must at least be shown that the act is done
> in furtherance of, done with the intention of

assistance, as a sort of overt act in the course
of acting in a political matter, a political
uprising, or a dispute between two parties in
the State as to which is to have the
government in its hands.

The decision in *United States v. Pitawanakwat*, 120
F.Supp.2d 921 (D.Or. 2000) is illustrative. Canadian
authorities had requested extradition of James
Allen Scott Pitawanakwat, a Canadian citizen who
had violated terms of his parole by leaving Canada
without permission after serving only a portion of
his sentence for criminal mischief and gun
possession. The prosecution resulted from a
confrontation in 1995 between the Royal Canadian
Mounted Police and the Canoe Creek Band in the
Cariboo Tribal Council at Lake Gustafsen in British
Columbia. During that confrontation, Pitawanakwat
shot a rifle at a helicopter. He successfully invoked
the political offense exception to defeat the
Canadian request for his extradition. The court
found there had been an "uprising or other violent
political disturbance" and that the charged offense
was incidental to it. The court acknowledged that
applying this test in the U.S.-Canada context
seemed strange, especially since the parole
violation, which was the basis for the request, was
obviously not part of the uprising in question.
However, the antecedent crimes clearly were, as an
attempt to dislodge Canadian authorities from a
sacred burial ground.

In the words of the court of appeals in *Ordinola v.
Hackman*, 478 F.3d 588, 600 (4th Cir. 2007),

> [F]or a claimant to come within the protections of the political offense exception, it is necessary, but not sufficient, for the claimant to show that he was politically motivated. In other words, a claimant whose common crime was not subjectively politically motivated cannot come within the exception regardless of whether the offense itself could be described as an objectively "political" one.

Application of the incidence test can be difficult. For example, in *Ordinola*, the court was confronted by the question whether crimes of aggravated homicide, aggravated kidnapping, forced disappearance of persons, and inflicting major intentional injuries on innocent civilians could qualify as political offenses. The situation involved Peru and in particular the acts of a special Peruvian military unit (Grupo Colina), which had been formed by the Fujimora government to combat the Sendero Luminoso (Shining Path), a Maoist terrorist group, during the 1980s. Ordinola a former military officer active in Grupo Colina, was charged with committing his crimes as part of the campaign against Sendero Luminoso. He sought to defeat his extradition from the United States on the grounds that they qualified as political offenses.

The court of appeals upheld the district court's determination that while Ordinola's actions occurred "in the course of a violent political uprising," they were not "in furtherance of quelling the uprising." It was not sufficient, it said, that the Peruvian government had led Ordinola to believe that the victims of Ordinola's crimes were terrorists. To fall within the political offense exception, his actions had to have been in some way proportional to or in furtherance of quelling the Shining Path's rebellion. As the court noted, the "legitimacy of a cause does not in itself legitimize the use of certain forms of violence especially against the innocent."

To the same effect is the decision in *Koskotas v. Roche*, 931 F.2d 169, 171–72 (1st Cir. 1991) (quoting *Quinn v. Robinson*, 783 F.2d 776, 809 (9th Cir. 1986)), which notes that crimes "incidental to" war, revolution, or rebellion do not include "common crimes connected but tenuously to a political disturbance, as distinguished from criminal acts 'causally or ideologically related to [an] uprising.' " In *Koskotas*, the fugitive had been charged with funneling embezzled money to Greek government officials in return for political favors, and the scandal resulted in the ouster of the Greek Prime Minister and the controlling political party. The fugitive argued that the political offense exception should apply because Greece was in the midst of a violent "constitutional revolt" and his alleged financial crimes were part of the effort to eliminate political opposition to the controlling party.

See also Meza v. Holder, 693 F.3d 1350, 1358–61 (11th Cir. 2012), *cert. denied*, 133 S.Ct. 933 (Jan. 14, 2013).

§ 9–23   EXTRADITION FOR ACTS OF TERRORISM

In recent years, the increase in international terrorism has led to a narrowing of the political offense exception. It is generally no longer applicable to crimes which have been defined in multilateral conventions as offenses under international law—such as genocide, narcotics trafficking, and in particular acts of terrorism such as aircraft hijacking and hostage taking.

Within the Council of Europe, the scope of the political offense exception has been reduced by the European Convention on the Suppression of Terrorism, E.T.S. No. 90 (1977), which precluded offenses associated with terrorism from being regarded political offenses. The 1975 Additional Protocol to the 1957 European Convention on Extradition, E.T.S. No. 86 (1979) also excluded war crimes and crimes against humanity from the definition of political offense.

Article 11 of the Inter-American Convention Against Terrorism, adopted in June 2002, expressly provides that, for the purposes of extradition (as well as mutual legal assistance), "none of the offenses established in the international instruments listed in article 2 shall be regarded as a political offense or an offense connected with a political offense or an offense inspired by political motives." Inter-American Convention Against Terrorism, June 3, 2002, OAS Treaty A-66, 42 I.L.M. 19 (2003). As a result, States Parties to that Convention may not refuse a request for extradition on that ground.

Another example is article 15 of the International Convention for the Suppression of Acts of Nuclear Terrorism, which provides that none of its covered offenses "shall be regarded, for the purposes of extradition or mutual legal assistance, as a political offence or as an offence connected with a political offence or as an offence inspired by political motives."

Similar provisions have also been included in various bilateral extradition treaties. See, for example, art. 4(2)(b) of the 2006 bilateral with Estonia, which excludes among other things "an offense for which both Parties have the obligation pursuant to a multilateral international agreement to extradite the person sought or to submit the case to their competent authorities for decision as to prosecution."

V.   ALTERNATIVES TO EXTRADITION

Extradition is not the only form of international rendition. Because the formal process of extradition can be time-consuming and cumbersome, States have worked to create speedier alternatives. Several means exist as an alterantive to, or outside of, the formal extradition process.

§ 9–24   SIMPLIFIED OR EXPEDITED EXTRADITION

In some countries the law permits the person sought to consent to extradition and waive his or her rights to a judicial determination of extraditability. Typically this is done at the time of the individual's first court appearance following provisional arrest, that is, without waiting for presentation of documents. In other instances, the requesting State may first have to submit the formal extradition request with supporting documents, despite the fugitive's willingness to return immediately to the requesting State. The relevant provisions thus vary from treaty to treaty.

Such arrangements have also been adopted on a regional basis. For example, within the Commonwealth countries, which generally share a similar approach to the issues, the so-called "London Scheme" for extradition governs the extradition of a person from one Commonwealth country to another. It effectively supersedes existing extradition treaties by simplifying and expediting the process. Similarly, within the Council of Europe, the 1957 European Extradition Convention as modified by its Additional Protocols of 1995 and 1996 provided for simplified proceedings and restricted grounds for refusal.

§ 9–25   EUROPEAN ARREST WARRANT

More recently, the European Arrest Warrant has effectively replaced the traditional extradition scheme between the 27 members of the European Union. Under this system, adopted in 2002, an arrest warrant issued in one Member State must be recognized and enforced in all other Member States. In addition to removing the double criminality requirement, the EAW abolishes the political offense exception as well as the traditional exception

for surrender of own nationals. The obvious purpose
is to facilitate law enforcement in Member States by
speeding up the transfer of suspects and removing
the political dimension to extradition. The EAW
only applies to Member States of the European
Union and does not alter existing obligations under
treaties with non-EU Member States. More
information on the European Arrest Warrant is
available at: *http://ec.europa.eu/justice/criminal/
recognition-decision/european-arrest-warrant/
index_en.htm.*

§ 9–26   EXCLUSION, REMOVAL, DEPORTATION

International law generally recognizes a right to
travel, and in particular a right of every person to
leave and return to his or her own country. But
States remain free to decide whom to admit, and
there is no requirement in international law that
States must admit everyone who would like to enter
their territories. All States have their own laws,
rules and procedures regarding entry and residence.
When an individual does not qualify under a given
State's immigration laws, he or she may be denied
entry at the border. This was previously known as
"exclusion" and is now covered by the term
"removal."

Once a foreign national has entered the territory,
domestic law typically governs the procedures by
which he or she can be expelled or "removed." In the
United States, the principal method is by
deportation. The requirements, procedures, and

protections of the deportation process are spelled out in the Immigration and Naturalization Act and its accompanying regulations. In most cases, deportation proceedings are initiated as a result of the individual's violation of immigration or criminal laws.

In some circumstances, removal can be an alternative to extradition. Like extradition, deportation is a legal process, grounded in statute and involving a judicial hearing, in which the individual in question has rights and an opportunity to defend. However, the relevant standards differ: while in extradition the questions turn on the existence and applicability of a treaty and "probable cause" that the individual has committed a crime, the issue in a removal is whether the individual is ineligible to remain in the United States under statutory criteria.

In addition, naturalized U.S. citizens may subject to a process known as denaturalization. For example, where it can be established that the individual wrongly obtained citizenship, he or she can be deprived of their citizenship and then subjected to deportation. This was the process followed in the notorious case of John Demjanjuk, a former Nazi death camp guard during World War II. He had lied about his background when he was admitted to the United States; he was naturalized and lived in the country for many years. When evidence emerged about his deception, the government began proceedings to revoke his citizenship, and eventually he was deported to Germany to stand trial for war crimes.

§ 9–27   ABDUCTION AND LURING

On rare occasions a government may decide that its critical interests can only be served by using unilateral measures to obtain custody of a fugitive in another country. This is sometimes characterized as "self-help" or "irregular" or "extraordinary rendition." These actions can be taken with (or without) the knowledge and express or tacit consent of the foreign State concerned. An often-cited example of such measures is the 1960 apprehension of former Nazi official Adolf Eichmann in Argentina by individuals acting on behalf of Israel and his return to stand trial in Israel on charges of crimes against humanity. Such situations give rise to two questions (among others): (1) do such apprehensions violate international law, and if so, (2) do they deprive the courts of the apprehending state of jurisdiction to prosecute the individual in question?

The answer to the first question is fairly clear. In most situations, a unilateral cross-border apprehension undertaken *without* the consent of the other country will be considered a violation of national sovereignty and territorial integrity, for which the offending country will bear international responsibility. In the *Eichmann* case, the Government of Argentina protested on those grounds, and the Government of Israel made a formal apology. Depending on the circumstances, such an incident might become the basis for a formal complaint to an international body such as the International Court of Justice, a regional human rights court, or an international arbitral body. In almost all cases, an apprehension of an individual by a foreign government will be a violation of the criminal laws of the country in which it occurs, such as a kidnapping, exposing the responsible individuals to prosecution.

The answer to the second question is not as straightforward. Traditionally, national criminal courts have adhered to the *male captus bene detentus* rule, which means essentially that an unsanctioned cross-border rendition will not deprive the court of jurisdiction even if it took place in violation of international or domestic law. This was the holding in *Attorney General of the Government of Israel v. Eichmann* (1961), 36 ILR 5 and 277. U.S. law has long had the same approach, known as the Ker-Frisbie Rule. In *Ker v. Illinois*, 119 U.S. 436 (1886), the U.S. Supreme Court rejected a jurisdictional challenge by a defendant who had been abducted in Peru by a bounty hunter and returned to the United States to stand trial for larceny in Illinois. In *Frisbie v. Collins*, 342 U.S. 519 (1952), the forcible abduction of a fugitive from Illinois to Michigan to stand trial for murder was held not to defeat jurisdiction.

More recently, the U.S. Supreme Court adopted a somewhat narrower view of the *male captus bene detentus* rule in *United States v. Alvarez-Machain*, 504 U.S. 655 (1992), which involved the forcible abduction of a Mexican citizen from Mexico to stand trial in the United States. The defendant challenged the court's jurisdiction *inter alia* on the basis that his rendition violated the terms of the bilateral extradition treaty between the two countries. The lower courts found that U.S. officials were responsible for the abduction and that the Government of Mexico had protested the operation as a violation of the Treaty, so that the indictment was dismissed.

Relying primarily on *Ker* and *Frisbie*, the Supreme Court reversed, finding that nothing in the Treaty explicitly prohibited abductions outside its terms and declining to imply such a prohibition. Conceding that the abduction may have been "in violation of general international law principles," Chief Justice Rehnquist stated, it did not violate the Extradition Treaty, so that "[t]he fact of respondent's forcible abduction does not therefore prohibit his trial in a court in the United States for violations of the criminal laws of the United States." 504 U.S. at 669–70. Whether he should be returned to Mexico, in light of the Mexican Government's protest, is "a matter for the Executive Branch." *Id.*

Justices Stevens, Blackmun and O'Connor dissented, noting that unlike *Ker* and *Frisbie*, the case involved an officially-sanctioned abduction of another country's citizen "which unquestionably constitutes a flagrant violation of international law and a violation of the territorial integrity of that other country, with which this country has signed an extradition treaty." *Id.* at 682. In their view,

The Government's claim that the Treaty is not exclusive, but permits forcible governmental kidnapping, would transform these, and other, provisions into little more than verbiage. For example, provisions [in the Treaty] requiring "sufficient" evidence to grant extradition (art. 3), withholding extradition for political or military offenses (art. 5), withholding extradition when the person sought has already been tried (art. 6), withholding extradition when the statute of limitations for the crime has lapsed (art. 7), and granting the requested Country discretion to refuse to extradite an individual who would face the death penalty in the requesting country (art. 8), would serve little purpose if the requesting country could simply kidnap the person.

Id. at 673.

In *Alvarez-Machain*, the respondent had also argued that the U.S. court should decline to exercise jurisdiction over him because the circumstances of his abduction—the way in which he had been treated—were "shocking." In so doing, he sought to invoke the exception established (by dicta) in *United States v. Toscanino*, 500 F.2d 267, 275 (2d Cir. 1974), in which the Court of Appeals viewed the concept of due process "as now requiring a court to divest itself of jurisdiction over the person of a defendant where it has been acquired as the result of the government's deliberate, unnecessary and unreasonable invasion of the accused's constitutional rights." The court justified that conclusion not on any principle of international law but as "an extension of the well-recognized power of federal courts in the civil context to decline to exercise jurisdiction over a defendant whose presence has been secured by force or fraud." *Id.* In that case the specific allegations included deliberate misconduct by U.S. agents, including corruption and bribery of a foreign official as well as kidnapping "accompanied by violence and brutality to the person."

The so-called *Toscanino* exception has frequently been invoked but no court has found its criteria satisfied. Its continued validity has been questioned. *See, e.g., United States v. Blanchard,* 2011 WL 3423334 (D. Vt. Aug. 5, 2011); *United States v. Cournoyer,* 2012 WL 6539659 (E.D.N.Y. Dec. 14, 2012).

§ 9–28   LURES

By distinction, law enforcement authorities sometimes work to entice a suspect or fugitive to leave one jurisdiction (where he may be insulated from apprehension) for another where he can be taken into custody. In cases where defendants have urged the court to dismiss the indictment solely on the grounds that they were fraudulently lured to the United States, courts have uniformly upheld jurisdiction.

A classic example of "luring" is found in *United States v. Yunis,* 681 F. Supp. 909 (D.D.C. 1988), *rev'd on other grounds,* 859 F.2d 953 (D.C. Cir. 1988). Fawaz Yunis, a Lebanese citizen, was

accused of blowing up a Royal Jordanian airliner in
Beirut. Using the bait of a lucrative narcotics deal,
U.S. authorities successfully lured him from
Lebanon to a small boat in international waters off
the coast of Cyprus, where he was arrested. He
challenged his indictment on the basis that (i) the
circumstances surrounding the arrest were
outrageous and violated his due process rights and
(ii) the apprehension contravened U.S. obligations
under its extradition treaties with Lebanon and
Cyprus. The court rejected the first because the way
Yunis was treated did not rise to the level of
deliberate torture and abuse required by *Toscanino*.
It rejected the second because neither Lebanon nor
Cyprus had objected, and "[a]ccepted principles of
international law recognize that only sovereign
nations have the authority to complain about
violations of extradition treaties." *Id.* at 916.

In its decision in *Prosecutor v. Dokmanovic*, ICTY
95–13a–PT, Judgment, (Oct. 22, 1997), the pretrial
chamber rejected a challenge to its jurisdiction
based by stating that luring is consistent with
principles of international law.

§ 9–29   PRISONER TRANSFER TREATIES

Prolonged incarceration in a foreign country can be
a particularly difficult experience, since the
convicted person is typically far from home and in a
different culture, sometimes in difficult,
overcrowded conditions, and perhaps facing possible
mistreatment. The presence of large numbers of
foreigners can also place a strain on the resources—

financial, custodial and diplomatic—of the State in question. Over time, States have addressed these issues through consensual agreements for prisoner transfer or repatriation. While these agreements are legally distinct from extradition and work differently than the extradition process, they are nonetheless a means by which persons convicted of crimes can be transferred from one country to another.

For the United States, the first bilateral prisoner transfer treaty was with Mexico, and it came into force in 1977. Since then the program has grown, so that the United States is currently a party to 12 bilateral prisoner transfer treaties (with Bolivia, Canada, France, Hong Kong S.A.R., Marshall Islands, Mexico, Micronesia, Palau, Panama, Peru, Thailand and Turkey). In addition, the United States is a party to two multilateral prisoner transfer treaties, the Council of Europe Convention on the Transfer of Sentenced Persons (the "Strasbourg" Convention) and the Inter-American Convention on Serving Criminal Sentences Abroad (or "OAS Convention"), which together establish transfer relationships with more than eighty other countries.

The International Prisoner Transfer Program began in 1977 when the United States government entered the first in a series of treaties to permit the transfer of prisoners from countries in which they had been convicted of crimes to their home countries. The program is designed to relieve some of the hardships faced by offenders incarcerated far from home and to facilitate the rehabilitation of these offenders. Prisoners may be transferred to and from countries with which the United States has a treaty. While all prisoner transfer treaties are negotiated principally by the United States Department of State, the program itself is administered by the United States Department of Justice.

Legislation implementing the prisoner transfer treaties for the United States is found at 18 U.S.C. §§ 4100–4115. Transfers are discretionary and require the consent the U.S. Government, the foreign government and the prisoner. The individual in question must be a national of the receiving State, must have been convicted of an offense which was also punishable in the receiving State, must have completed any minimum sentence under relevant law, but must have at least six months remaining in the sentence. The sentence must be final and all appeals completed, and all fines and court costs paid. Individuals convicted of purely military offenses, and those sentenced to death, are not eligible for transfer.

Even after the transfer, the sending State retains exclusive jurisdiction over the sentence as well as the authority to pardon or grant amnesty. A transferred prisoner cannot challenge his or her sentence in the receiving country.

The U.S. Central Authority is the International Prisoner Transfer Unit, Criminal Division of the U.S. Department of Justice. *See http://www.justice. gov/criminal/oeo/iptu. See also http://travel.state. gov/law/legal/treaty/treaty_1989.html.*

Arrangements for the transfer of sentenced persons have been explicitly encouraged by some multilateral conventions. For example, article 45 of the UN Convention Against Corruption provides that "States Parties may consider entering into bilateral or multilateral agreements or arrangements on the transfer to their territory of persons sentenced to imprisonment or other forms of deprivation of liberty for offences established in accordance with this Convention in order that they may complete their sentences there."

A useful source of information is the 2012 UN Handbook on the International Transfer of Sentenced Persons, available at *http://www.unodc. org/documents/justice-and-prison-reform/11-88322_ebook.pdf.*

§ 9–30   RECOGNITION OF FOREIGN CRIMINAL JUDGMENTS

While in some cases individual prisoners may be transferred to serve the remainder of their sentences in another State, States do not as a general rule enforce foreign criminal law or give effect to the criminal judgments or sentences of other countries. Certainly, no rule of customary international law requires them to do so. As Chief Justice Marshall noted in *The Antelope*, 23 U.S. 66, 123 (1825), "[t]he Courts of no country execute the penal laws of another." *See also Restatement (Third) of Foreign Relations Law of the United States* § 483, Reporters' Note 3 (1987): "Unless required to do so by treaty, no state enforces the penal judgments of other states."

Domestically, this is occasionally called the "Penal Law Rule" and is frequently addressed as a component of the broader "Revenue Rule," under which U.S. courts typically decline to enforce foreign laws or judgments regarding tax, customs or other revenue laws or liabilities. Both rules reflect a general reluctance to give effect to the "public policy" rules of foreign governments. Recent decisions have given a cautious interpretation to the broader rule. *See, e.g., Pasquantino v. United States*, 544 U.S. 349 (2005) (upholding prosecution under federal wire fraud statute for smuggling liquor into Canada to evade Canada's alcohol import taxes).

Some countries do, however, give effect to criminal sentences and related judgments (for example, awarding damages) rendered by foreign governments. A few treaties exist for that purpose, such as the 1970 European Convention on the International Validity of Criminal Judgments, E.T.S. No. 70, which permits one Contracting State to enforce a "sanction" (meaning a punishment or other measure expressly imposed on a person in connection with a criminal offense) which has been imposed in another Contracting State and is enforceable in the latter State. The Convention only applies in certain cases and subject to certain conditions; the obligation to give effect to a foreign sanction arises only at the request of another Contracting State; and requests may be refused *inter alia* on various grounds such as lack of jurisdiction, conflict with "fundamental principles," *non bis in idem*, political offense, or discrimination on basis of race, religion, nationality or political opinion.

§ 9–31   TRANSFER OF CRIMINAL PROCEEDINGS

In some cases, arrangements exist for the transfer of the actual criminal case (as opposed to the sentenced person) from one State to another.

Under the 1972 European Convention on the Transfer of Proceedings in Criminal Matters, E.T.S. No. 73, for example, one State may ask another to undertake prosecution of an accused person on its behalf. Such a request may be made if the suspected person is a national of, or normally resident in, the requested State, if the transfer of proceedings is warranted in the interests of a fair trial, or if the enforcement of an eventual sentence in the requested State is likely to improve the prospects of his/her social rehabilitation. The requested State may not refuse acceptance of the request except in specific cases and in particular if it considers that the offense is of a political nature or that the request is based on considerations of race, religion or nationality. This convention is currently in force between twenty-four members of the Council of Europe.

Within the European Union, a framework decision on the transfer of criminal proceedings was adopted in 2008, and EU Member States were required to implement its provisions into their national law.

Provisions related to transfer of proceeding can also be found in a number of international criminal law proceedings, including the 1988 UN Convention Against Illicit Trafficking in Narcotic Drugs and Psychotropic Substances Convention (art. 8), the UN Convention Against Corruption (art. 47) and the UN Convention on Transnational Organized Crime (art. 21).

A model UN treaty on the transfer of proceedings in criminal matters was adopted in 1990. *See* UN Doc. A/RES/45/118 (Dec. 14, 1990).

§ 9–32   FURTHER READING

William Magnuson, "The Domestic Politics of International Extradition," 52 Va. J. Int'l L. 839 (2012); Robert Iraola, "Due Process, the Sixth Amendment, and International Extradition," 90 Neb. L. Rev. 752 (2012); Jones and Davidson, *Extradition and Mutual Legal Assistance Handbook* (Oxford 2011); Michael John Garcia and Charles Doyle, *Extradition To and From the United States: Overview of the Law and Recent Treaties*, Congressional Research Service (7–5700 98–958) (March 17, 2010); Christophe Paulussen, *Male Captus Bene Detentus? Surrendering Suspects to the International Criminal Court* (Intersentia 2010); Bassiouni, *International Extradition: United States Law and Practice* (Oceana 5th ed. 2007).

CHAPTER 10
MUTUAL LEGAL ASSISTANCE

I. INTRODUCTION

Because criminal activity is increasingly transnational, both prosecutors and defense counsel face a growing need to obtain evidence from foreign jurisdictions. But different legal systems have different rules about what evidence can be gathered when, in what form, and by whom. What is normal or necessary procedure in one country may well be unusual, unknown, or even illegal in another. As a result, it can be difficult to gather the necessary evidence quickly and in a manner that makes it admissible in the relevant proceedings.

States have no general obligation under customary international law to furnish evidence to a requesting State for use in criminal proceedings in that State. The corollary is also true: States have no unilateral right to gather evidence in other States for purposes of criminal prosecutions. In many countries, such functions are reserved to governmental authorities. In some, it is a crime for anyone but those authorities to interview witnesses, take depositions, or gather documents and other evidence for use in a foreign criminal proceeding. Like extradition, therefore, cooperation in such matters depends on consent, agreement, and cooperation.

This chapter discusses the various ways in which evidence and other forms of "legal assistance" can be obtained for use in foreign criminal proceedings. For reasons of simplicity, the orientation is largely on issues arising when evidence is sought from other countries for use in a U.S. criminal proceeding.

II. THE LIMITATIONS OF DOMESTIC PROCEDURES

In a criminal case with transnational aspects, neither the prosecution nor the defense can assume that the ordinary rules and procedures (state or federal) will apply to efforts to collect information, statements, documentation, and other potentially probative or exculpatory evidence located abroad. It may be difficult, if not impossible, to obtain that evidence in a form that complies with the relevant admissibility requirements (chain of custody, to give one illustration). Even attempting to gather such evidence may violate the law in the foreign jurisdiction.

Consulting local counsel in the foreign jurisdiction may be the best course for defense counsel. Government prosecutors have more options, including compulsory process.

By way of example, a prosecutor may attempt to subpoena the information from a defendant (for instance, as part of the grand jury's investigation) when it is in that defendant's control abroad. Sanctions can be imposed for non-compliance. This method can also be used with regard to third (foreign) parties who are subject to the court's jurisdiction. Clearly, no compulsory measures can be applied to individuals or entities outside the court's jurisdiction (in most cases, the state or federal district in which the court sits).

Even when the court has jurisdiction, however, difficulties arise when the subpoena seeks to compel an action which would either violate foreign law or place the defendant or third party at risk of foreign sanctions, including prosecution. This situation can arise, for example, when the prosecution seeks to compel a defendant or the U.S. branch of a foreign bank to produce records and other information located abroad which they claim is subject to bank secrecy laws in the foreign country.

In such instances, U.S. courts typically engage in a balancing of the competing interests, considering among other things the importance of investigating and prosecuting criminal violations, the need to respect foreign law and policy, the evident good faith and cooperation of the person or institution subject to compulsion, the right to privacy, and the availability of alternative methods of obtaining the information. In conducting this analysis, they frequently refer to the international principle of comity as reflecting the recognition which one nation allows within its territory to the legislative, executive or judicial acts of another nation, having due regard both to international duty and convenience, and to the rights of its own citizens or of other persons who are under the protection of its laws. *See, e.g., Linde v. Arab Bank P.L.C.*, 706 F. 3d 92, 114–115 (2d Cir. 2013); *In re Grand Jury Subpoena*, 696 F. 3d 428 (5th Cir. 2012); *In re Grand Jury Proceedings (Bank of Nova Scotia)*, 691

F.2d 1384 (11th Cir. 1982), cert. denied, 462 U.S. 1119 (1983).

III. LETTERS ROGATORY

One alternative to unilateral action and compulsory measures is to seek the assistance of foreign judicial authorities. The classic method for doing so is through "letters rogatory." These are simply formal requests from the courts in one country to the courts of another asking for direct assistance in providing the necessary evidence or information.

Letters rogatory have long been recognized in international practice and rest on the principle of comity or mutual respect for the judicial systems of other countries. The system is most widely used in civil and commercial cases, but letters rogatory can be used in criminal cases as well, for example in locating witnesses, arranging for statements to be taken, obtaining copies of public documents, and even in conducting searches and seizures or seizing, freezing and forfeiture of property and assets in the other country. Defendants may use letters rogatory, pursuant to Fed. R. Crim. P. 15, to take testimony and obtain evidence in foreign countries.

Letters rogatory involve both positive and negative considerations. Because there are no "qualifications" or requirements as to form, they can be broad and flexible, and they can provide an opportunity for the requesting party (through the court) to explain (in appropriate detail) what information is sought, why, and in what form it is needed. On the other hand, they are discretionary in the sense that the requested court is under no obligation to respond. They typically travel in diplomatic channels and may follow a circuitous and lengthy route (e.g., from court to embassy to foreign ministry to justice ministry to court). Execution is subject to foreign law and procedures, and there is no guarantee that the requested evidence, if and when it arrives, will be a form that is admissible in U.S. courts.

Finally, in many civil law countries, courts will generally not provide assistance at the investigatory stage (in their view a grand jury is not a court). Some interject a dual criminality requirement, declining to consider letters rogatory in respect of proceedings involving activities that would not be considered crimes in the requested State.

In the United States, the Department of State's authority to transmit letters rogatory both from foreign tribunals (incoming) and to them (outgoing) is set out in 28 U.S.C. § 1781 (1948). Note that the statute by its terms does not preclude direct requests in either direction.

Under 28 U.S.C. § 1696, a federal district court may order service on a person in connection with a proceeding in a foreign or international tribunal, based on a letter rogatory from the tribunal or any interested person. Under 18 U.S.C. § 3512, a federal judge may issue such orders as may be necessary to execute a request from a foreign authority for assistance in the investigation or prosecution of criminal offenses, or in proceedings related to the prosecution of criminal offenses, including proceedings regarding forfeiture, sentencing, and restitution.

For a recent discussion of these authorities, *see In re Premises Located at 840 140th Ave. NE, Bellevue, Washington*, 634 F.3d 557 (9th Cir. 2011); *In re Doulours Price*, 718 F.3d 13 (1st Cir. 2013).

IV. MUTUAL LEGAL ASSISTANCE

In recent years, law enforcement authorities have sought to establish direct cooperative relationships with counterparts in other countries in order to facilitate the exchange of information, especially at the investigative stage. Police-to-police ("cop-to-cop") communication can be a very useful way of acquiring information, especially in the early phases of investigations. Such assistance is informal and voluntary, and it typically involves such activities as obtaining public records, locating persons, serving documents, executing investigative requests, setting up interviews, conducting joint investigations, and assisting investigations.

Police agencies have established networks of liaison officers throughout the world as well as lines of communication and protocols with foreign colleagues. For example, the Federal Bureau of Investigation stations "legal attachés" at many U.S. embassies abroad, and other U.S. law enforcement agencies (such as the DEA, Customs, and Secret Service) are represented as well. In addition, the INTERPOL network can be used for this purpose.

The international community has recognized and endorsed this development. For instance, recent multilateral conventions typically require States Parties to "afford one another the widest measure of mutual legal assistance in investigations, prosecutions and judicial proceedings" in relation to their covered offenses. *See* art. 7(1) of the 1988 UN Convention Against Illicit Traffic in Narcotic Drugs and Psychotropic Substances and art. 18(1) of the 2000 UN Transnational Organized Crime (UNTOC) Convention; *see also* art. 38 of the UN Convention against Corruption and art. 14(1) of the International Convention for the Suppression of Act of Nuclear Terrorism Convention.

The 1988 Illicit Traffic and 2000 UNTOC conventions contain some of the most detailed requirements, spelling out the specific types of assistance that can be provided (even in the absence of a request from another State Party), eliminating bank secrecy as a grounds for refusal, permitting the transfer of persons in custody for purposes of identification or giving testimony, and requiring States Parties to establish "Central Authority" for this purpose.

These provisions are the product of a concerted effort which began in the 1970's to establish and formalize cooperative arrangements on a transnational basis. In the United States, the project initially involved case-specific undertakings, in the form of executive agreements, between the Department of Justice and its foreign counterparts to share information in bribery, corruption and securities fraud cases. They eventually matured into more formal commitments called "mutual legal assistance treaties" or MLATs. Where they exist, these treaty arrangements effectively eliminate the need for the government to use letters rogatory. They are not, however, generally available to non-governmental parties.

§ 10–1   MUTUAL LEGAL ASSISTANCE TREATIES

For the United States, the first bilateral MLAT was with the Swiss Federation, signed on December 15, 1973. Entitled a treaty on "mutual assistance in criminal matters," this agreement obligated the two countries to undertake to afford each other assistance in investigations and court proceedings within their respective jurisdictions. Over time, the number and sophistication of these treaties has grown significantly. Today, the United States has entered into nearly sixty bilateral MLATs with foreign countries, as well as an umbrella treaty with the European Union (which covers its twenty-seven Member States).

The United States is also a party to the Inter-American Convention on Mutual Legal Assistance (a multilateral MLAT) as other multilateral criminal law agreements which contain significant mutual legal assistance provisions, such as the UNTOC, UNCAC, and Terrorist Financing Conventions.

In addition, the United States has reached other types of agreements for sharing relevant information, for example a Mutual Legal Assistance Agreement with the People's Republic of China and forfeiture cooperation and asset sharing agreements with Singapore, Canada, the Cayman Islands, Colombia, Jamaica, and Mexico, among others. The Department of the Treasury's Financial Crimes Enforcement Network has also established formal relationships with the financial intelligence units of many countries to facilitate the exchange of information.

1. Types of Assistance

While the specific provisions of MLATs vary, they generally obligate treaty partners to take agreed steps on behalf of the requesting State when certain conditions are met. MLATs typically contain broad "scope" provisions obligating the parties upon request to collect and share specific kinds of information (for example providing originals or certified copies of documents such as bank, financial or corporate records), to examine sites or objects and to collect physical evidence, to locate and identify persons and potential witnesses within their territory, to take their statements, depositions or testimony, and to serve judicial documents such as subpoenas *duces tecum*.

They may also include the obligation to execute searches and seizures, to freeze and forfeit assets, to collect fines, and possibly to share proceeds or instrumentalities of offenses. They might even provide for transferring persons in custody to testify as witnesses in the requesting Party. Most treaties are open-ended in this regard, providing for example that the Parties may afford each other any other forms of mutual legal assistance allowed by their domestic law.

The key obligation under the MLAT is for the requested State to execute the request promptly, in accordance with its own law and (to the extent possible) in the manner specified in the request. This latter consideration is often critical to ensuring that the information obtained will be deemed admissible in the courts of the requesting Party.

2. Contents of Requests

MLATs specify the arrangements for making and receiving requests for assistance. Requests typically must contain the identity of the authority making the request and specify the subject matter and nature of the investigation, prosecution or proceeding to which the request relates, and the name and the functions of the authority conducting such investigation, prosecution or proceeding. They must include a summary of the relevant facts, a description of the assistance sought, details of any particular procedure the requesting Party wishes to be followed, the identity, location, and nationality of any person concerned (where it is known), and the purpose for which the evidence, information, or action is sought.

3. Central Authorities

Normally, parties to an MLAT must designate a "Central Authority" (such as the Ministry of Justice) to be responsible for handling the requests. Central Authorities serve as the main channels of communication and decide whether requests comply with the treaty's requirements.

4. Benefits

Clearly, the main benefit of an MLAT is that it establishes an agreed, obligatory and expeditious means for obtaining information related to criminal proceedings. As a practical matter, having a direct channel of communication between the parties' respective law and prosecutorial communities is critical. Not only does it eliminate the need to go to a court and to correspond through diplomatic channels, it also provides for more effective acquisition of evidence and testimony in a manner compatible with the admissibility requirements of the requesting State's courts.

It also helps to avoid confrontations and misunderstandings. A few MLATs contain "first resort" undertakings. For example, article 18 of the 2006 US.-Bermuda MLAT requires each party to attempt in good faith to use the treaty mechanisms to obtain information before enforcing "any compulsory measure requiring an action to be performed by any person located in the territory of the other Party."

§ 10–2   GROUNDS FOR REFUSAL

As in the case of extradition, requests for mutual legal assistance can be (and sometimes are) declined because they do not meet the agreed requirements of the treaty (improper form, insufficient information, etc.). They may also be denied when, in the view of the requested State, execution of the request is likely to prejudice its sovereignty, security, public order (*ordre pubic*), or other essential interests. Finally, a party need not act on any request which would be prohibited by its domestic law or contrary to its legal system. Provisions containing such rules can be found both in many bilateral treaties as well as in some of the most important multilateral treaties, such as art. 7(15) of the 1988 Illicit Trafficking Convention and art. 19(21) of the UNTOC Convention.

Most mutual legal assistance treaties and agreements require the requested State to consult with the requesting State before refusing a request, in order to consider whether assistance might still be given under conditions.

1. Dual Criminality

Unlike extradition treaties, bilateral MLATs typically do not require dual criminality. Multilaterals are more cautious. Article 46(9)(b) of the UN Convention Against Corruption, for instance, provides that States Parties may decline to render assistance on the ground of absence of dual criminality, but not for "assistance that does not involve coercive action." Article 18(9) of the UN Convention on Transnational Organized Crime allows a State to decline a request in the absence of dual criminality but gives it the option of waiving the requirement of dual criminality and providing the assistance in any situation it sees fit.

The U.S-China bilateral follows the UNTOC approach: art. 3(1)(a) permits refusal of requests related to offenses that would not be serious crimes under the law of the requested State but permits parties to agree to provide assistance for particular offense or categories of offenses "irrespective of whether the conduct would constitute an offense under the laws in the territory of both Parties." Agreement with the People's Republic of China on Judicial Assistance, June 19, 2000, TIAS 13102. Article 3 of the U.S.-Malaysian bilateral also invokes dual criminality but excludes from this rule a number of offenses listed in an annex, but then refers to some exceptions where dual criminality will apply.

2. Bank Secrecy

Generally, requested States cannot refuse requests on the grounds that the offense in question is a "fiscal offense" or that the requested information is covered by bank secrecy laws. In many cases, however, military offenses are not subject to MLAT obligations. Article 4 of the U.S.-Russia bilateral, for example, excludes requests relating to "a crime under military law that is not a crime under general criminal law" but excludes denial on the grounds of bank secrecy. Article 46(22) of the UNCAC provides that States Parties "may not refuse a request for mutual legal assistance on the sole ground that the offence is also considered to involve fiscal matters."

3. Political Offense

The majority of bilateral MLATs permit refusal of requests that relate to "political offenses." *See, e.g.,* art. 3(1)(a) of the U.S.-Malaysia bilateral. The U.S.-China agreement has a broader formula, permitting in art. 3(1)(d) refusal when the request relates to "a political offence or the request is politically motivated or there are substantial grounds for believing that the request was made for the purpose of investigated, prosecuting, punishing, or otherwise proceeding against a person on account of the person's race, religion, nationality or political opinions."

Most of the multilateral terrorism conventions specifically exclude "political offense" grounds. For example, article 15 of the Terrorism Financing Convention states that none of its covered offenses shall be regarded, for mutual legal assistance purposes, "as a political offence or an offence connected with a political offence or as an offence inspired by political motives." At the same time, it goes on (in art. 16) to permit refusals when the requested party has "substantial grounds for believing that the [request for information] has been made for the purpose of prosecuting or punishing a person on account of that person's race, religion, nationality, ethnic origin or political opinion or that compliance with the request would cause prejudice to that person's position for any of these reasons."

4. Double Jeopardy

Some treaties permit denial on *non bis in idem* (double jeopardy) grounds. Article 3(1)(f) of the U.S.-China bilateral agreement, for instance, permits refusal if the requested Party has already rendered a final decision on the same suspect or defendant for the same offense referred to in the request. Article 4(2)(h) of the Bermuda bilateral requires a statement from the requesting Party that none of the persons being investigated has previously been tried, convicted or acquitted for the same conduct that is under investigation (or a statement indicating why a retrial would be proper).

5. Interference With Other Cases

Most treaties permit postponement of the execution of a request on the ground that compliance would interfere with an ongoing investigation, prosecution or proceeding in the requested State. In such a situation, the requested Party is required to consult with the requesting Party to determine if the assistance can still be given subject to such terms and conditions as the requested Party deems necessary.

6. Limitations on Use

In addition to these limited grounds for refusing to comply with a request for mutual legal assistance, most treaties contain some limitations on the manner in which they can be used as well as the purposes for which information itself can be used.

7. Specific Use

A standard provision states that information and evidence provided by the requested State shall not be used for purposes other than those specified in the original request except with the prior consent of the requested State. *See, e.g.*, art. 9(1) of the U.S.-Russia bilateral.

8. Governmental Use

MLATs are intended for the use of governmental authorities. Many provide specifically that private parties have no right under the treaty to "obtain, suppress or exclude any evidence or to impede execution of a request." *See, e.g.,* art.1(4) of the U.S.-Bermuda bilateral. Article 1(3) of the U.S.-China bilateral agreement states that "[t]his agreement is intended solely for mutual legal assistance between the Parties" and that it "shall not give rise to a right on the part of any private person to obtain, suppress, or exclude any evidence, or to impede the execution of a request."

9. Confidentiality

Most multilaterals and bilaterals permit the requesting State to require the requested State to keep the fact and substance of the request confidential, except to the extent necessary to execute the request. *See*, for example, art. 7(3) of the U.S.-Malaysia bilateral. Article 18(20) of the UNTOC Convention contains a similar provision.

§ 10–3   REGIONAL MECHANISMS

The global mutual legal assistance network is complicated and expanding. Besides the major multilateral treaties, many countries today have (like the United States) entered into a network of bilateral agreements. A model bilateral MLAT was adopted by the UN General Assembly in 1990, *see* UN doc. A/RES/45/117 (Dec. 14, 1990). In addition, a number of regional mechanisms have come into existence.

Among the first were those adopted within the Council of Europe. For many years, the basic multilateral instrument was the 1959 COE Convention on Mutual Assistance in Criminal Matters, to which Additional Protocols were added in 1978 and 2001. Within the European Union, the 2000 Convention on Mutual Assistance in Criminal Matters, amended by protocols in 2001 and 2011, covers broad range of cooperative measures between EU Member States.

For practical purposes, this treaty-based system is being replaced by the adoption of the European Evidence Warrant, adopted by the European Council in a Framework Decision in December 2008. Like the European Arrest Warrant, it seeks to establish a single set of procedures for the issuance and execution of requests (warrants) valid in all Member States. The European Evidence Warrant ("EEW") is a judicial decision issued by a competent authority of a Member State with a view to obtaining objects, documents, and data from another Member State in certain kinds of criminal proceedings.

Other measures of regional integration had already been taken. In 1998, the European Council had created the European Judicial Network (EJN) to improve standards of co-operation between judicial authorities in criminal matters. In 2002, it established the European Judicial Co-operation Unit ("Eurojust") to facilitate co-operation between the judicial authorities of the Member States, supporting criminal investigations and assisting with the co-ordination of prosecutions for serious cross-border crimes.

Within the OAS, the Hemispheric Information Exchange Network for Mutual Assistance in Criminal Matters and Extradition (called the "Network") has been established. Like its European counterpart, it aims to improve the exchange of information among OAS Member States in mutual assistance in criminal matters. The Network consists of three components: a public website, a private website, and a secure electronic communication system.

The public component is a virtual library containing information related to mutual assistance and extradition for the thirty-four OAS Member States, including descriptions of national legal systems as well as the texts of mutual legal assistance treaties to which those countries are party. The private component contains information points of contact in member countries. The Secure Electronic Communication System facilitates the exchange of information between central authorities in member countries by means of secure instant email service to central authorities. For additional information, consult *http://www.oas.org/juridico/mla/en.*

§ 10–4   U.S. AUTHORITY TO EXECUTE MLAT REQUESTS

Within the U.S. legal system, MLATs are generally considered "self-executing" treaties (and therefore directly applicable as federal law) but they also rest on existing statutory authority. Recently, some questions have arisen about whether the treaties themselves provide sufficient authority to compel the production of evidence in certain circumstances, particularly whether they authorize or compel federal courts to issue subpoenas and under what circumstance.

In 2000, Congress passed and the President signed the Civil Asset Forfeiture Reform Act, Pub.L. No. 106–185, § 15, 114 Stat. 202, 219–21 (2000). That Act included most of what is now codified at 28 U.S.C. § 2467. That section grants federal district courts jurisdiction to enforce "foreign forfeiture or confiscation judgment[s]" and to "enter such orders as may be necessary to enforce the judgment on behalf of the foreign nation." 28 U.S.C. § 2467(c)(1), (d)(1). It allows the U.S. Government to forfeit assets based on the existence of a foreign court judgment, so that there is no need to institute independent forfeiture proceedings based on violations of U.S. law in order to seize such property.

In 2001, the Patriot Act was adopted and included what is now 28 U.S.C. § 2467(d)(3), authorizing federal district courts to issue temporary restraining orders to "preserve the availability of property subject to a foreign forfeiture or confiscation judgment." § 2467(d)(3)(A). By its text, § 2467(d)(3) allows U.S. courts to issue temporary restraining orders to preserve property "subject to a foreign forfeiture or confiscation judgment."

In 2009, the Foreign Evidence Request Efficiency Act, Pub. L. No. 111–79, 123 Stat. 2086, was enacted to supplement the authority given to U.S. courts by 28 U.S.C. § 1782 to respond to letters rogatory from foreign courts or international tribunals. New § 1783 allows the federal courts to issue subpoenas requiring the appearance of a U.S. national or resident before a foreign court or the production of a specified document in a proceeding in such a court.

The relationship of this new statute both to § 1782 and to a decision by the executive to act on a mutual legal assistance request has given rise to some recent decisions. In *In re Premises Located at 840 140th Ave. NE, Bellevue, Washington,* 634 F.3d 557 (9th Cir. 2011), the Court of Appeals held that notwithstanding the new statute, a federal court retains discretion to enforce subpoenas issued pursuant to MLATs, since enforcement of a subpoena is an exercise in judicial power, and that MLATs like statutes are subject to separation of powers limits.

More recently, the courts have had to consider issues raised by the effort of the United Kingdom to use its bilateral MLAT with the United States to gain access to information in the files of the Belfast Project at Boston College. UK authorities sought (among other things) taped interviews with members of the Provisional Irish Republican Army, as well as documents, notes, and computer records, in conjunction with an investigation of alleged violation of UK law. The objects of the request challenged the U.S. Attorney General's decision to execute the request.

In *United States v. Trustees of Boston College*, 831 F. Supp. 2d 436, 452 (D. Mass., 2011), the District Court held *inter alia* that in assessing such an MLAT request, "the appropriate standard of review is analogous to that used in reviewing grand jury subpoenae." In upholding that ruling, the First Circuit in In re Request from the United Kingdom, 718 F.3d 13, 23 2013 WL 2364165 *6 (1st Cir. May 31, 2013), observed that "the enforcement of subpoenas is an inherent judicial function which, by virtue of the doctrine of separation of powers, cannot be constitutionally divested from the courts of the United States. Nothing in the text of the US-UK MLAT, or its legislative history, has been cited by the government to lead us to conclude that the courts of the United States have been divested of an inherent judicial role that is basic to our function as judges."

The Court of Appeals had earlier ruled, in *In re Request from the United Kingdom*, 685 F.3d 1 (1st

Cir. 2012), that the bilateral mutual legal assistance treaty had not created any rights to suppress evidence or to impede execution of requests.

V. CONSTITUTIONAL AND OTHER CONSTRAINTS

Outside the context of agreed mutual legal assistance procedures, efforts by law enforcement to obtain evidence in other countries have also raised some important constitutional issues.

Nothing in the U.S. Constitution directly addresses whether, or to what extent, its provisions apply outside U.S. territory. In *Reid v. Covert*, 354 U.S. 1 (1957), the Supreme Court established that at least some constitutional protections apply when the government acts with respect to American citizens abroad. In that case, the Court found that the overseas trials by military commission of two civilian dependents of U.S. service members violated the Constitution.

To some extent, following agreed MLAT procedures will reduce or eliminate such problems, since by definition the requests are executed by foreign authorities in accordance with their domestic laws. In the absence of a specific treaty provision, however, no specific statutory provision indicated the mechanism whereby U.S. authorities can obtain evidence abroad.

§ 10–5   FOURTH AMENDMENT—SEARCH AND SEIZURE

Generally, the actions of foreign law enforcement authorities within their own countries are governed by the laws of those countries. Neither the Fourth Amendment to the U.S. Constitution nor the exclusionary rule under it applies to acts of foreign officials within their own territory. Neither do such domestic statutes as the Omnibus Crime Control and Safe Streets Act of 1968. As a result, evidence obtained by searches and seizures carried out by foreign law enforcement officers in their own countries can be admissible even if the circumstances and methods would not have been permissible under U.S. law. This is true even if the persons from whom the evidence is taken are U.S. citizens. *United States v. Cotroni*, 527 F.2d 708 (2d Cir. 1975).

Does the involvement of U.S. law enforcement personnel change the legal analysis, and if so, in what way? The answer appears to be no, when the object of the search is not a U.S. national, even if that individual is in the United States at the time. In *United States v. Verdugo-Urquidez*, 494 U.S. 259 (1990), the U.S. Supreme Court held that the Fourth Amendment does not apply to the search and seizure by U.S. agents of property owned by a foreign non-resident located in a foreign country. In that case, a Mexican citizen and resident, who was the alleged leader of a significant drug smuggling ring, had been expelled to the United States by Mexican police officers and was incarcerated pending trial. In preparation for the trial, the DEA sought to obtain evidence by means of a search of defendant's residence in Mexicali, without first obtaining a warrant from the U.S. district court where the trial was pending.

Overruling the district's suppression order, the Supreme Court reversed, holding that because the defendant was an alien and a resident of Mexico with "no previous significant voluntary connections with the United States," and because the place searched was in Mexico, the Fourth Amendment did not apply. Several Justices filed sharp dissents.

But if the target is a U.S. national, the rule is different. Several courts have held that the Fourth Amendment's warrant requirement does not govern searches conducted abroad by United States agents, so that searches even of United States citizens need only satisfy the Fourth Amendment's requirement of reasonableness. *See In re Terrorist Bombings of U.S. Embassies in East Africa (Fourth Amendment Challenges)*, 552 F.3d 157, 168–176 (2d Cir. 2008), cert. denied *sub nom. El-Hage v. United States*, 130 S. Ct. 1050 (Jan. 11. 2010). *See United States v. Stokes*, 710 F. Supp. 2d 689 (N.D. Ill. 2009).

Over time the courts have adopted several interpretations of this rule. One is to judge the degree of involvement by the U.S. officials. Where the evidence is collected by foreign officials on their own territory acting under their own law and subsequently turned over to U.S. authorities, it is not barred under the Fourth Amendment even if gathered in a manner which would not have been permissible if the evidence had been located in the United States. Some have referred to this as the "international silver platter" doctrine.

On the other hand, if the conduct of the foreign officials "shocks the conscience" of the court, or where the involvement of U.S. officials is intended to evade otherwise applicable constitutional requirements or is such that the foreign officials become their "virtual agents," then the evidence may be deemed inadmissible. Some courts use a "joint venture" test. *See United States v. Barona*, 56 F. 3d 1087 (9th Cir 1995); *United States v. Peterson,* 812 F.2d 486 (9th Cir. 1987). The question is largely factual.

For a recent decision on these issues, *see United States v. Lee*, 723 F.3d 134, 2013 WL 2450533 (2d Cir. June 7, 2013), holding that the circumstances of surveillance conducted by Jamaican officials did not make them "virtual agents" of the United States. In footnote 3, the Second Circuit noted that while there had been criticism of the silver platter doctrine in its domestic context, its holding "is demonstration anew of the substantive validity of the international silver platter doctrine, if not of its moniker." See also *United States v. Getto*, __ F.3d __, 2013 WL 4779622 (2d Cir. Sept. 9, 2013).

§ 10–6   BORDER SEARCHES

Traditionally, an exception to the warrant requirement under the Fourth Amendment has applied to searches conducted at the border (airports, ports of entry and other land crossings, etc.). *See United States v. Flores-Montano*, 541 U.S. 149 (2004). Recent developments in information technology have put this rule under some strain.

Recently, the Ninth Circuit addressed the "reasonableness" requirement in this context. In *United States v. Cotterman,* 709 F.3d 951 (9th Cir. 2013), it held that reasonable suspicion was in fact required for the forensic examination and analysis of the hard drive of a traveler's laptop computer. Authorities had taken an image of the individual's hard drive and subjected it to specialized analysis, which uncovered information from deleted files on the unallocated space of the computer's memory. The court described this as "essentially a computer strip search." 709 F.3d at 966. Because today's personal electronic devices often contain sensitive and confidential information, the court held that such a search requires "reasonable suspicion." *See generally* Janet Hoeffel and Stephen Singer, "Fear and Loathing at the U.S. Border," 82 Miss. L. J. 833 (2013).

§ 10–7   FIFTH AMENDMENT

Generally speaking, statements obtained by foreign officers conducting interrogations in their own nations under their own law have been held admissible in U.S. courts despite a failure to give *Miranda* warnings to the accused. *See, e.g., United States v. Frank*, 599 F3d 1221 (11th Cir. 2010), cert. denied, 131 S.Ct. 186 (Oct. 4, 2010); *United States v. Yousef*, 327 F.3d 56 (2d Cir. 2003).

By distinction, questioning by U.S. authorities is subject to the Fifth Amendment privilege against self-incrimination, even when the subject is a non-resident alien and the questioning takes place abroad, if that individual faces a criminal trial in the United States. *See, e.g., United States v. Bin Laden*, 132 F. Supp. 2d 168 (S.D.N.Y. 2001), aff'd *sub nom. In re Terrorist Bombings of U.S. Embassies in East Africa*, 552 F. 3d 177 (2d Cir. 2008), cert. denied *sub. nom. Al 'Owhali v. United States*, 129 S.Ct. 2778 (June 8, 2009).

See generally David Henek, *Ensuring Miranda's Right to Counsel in U.S. Interrogations Abroad*, 57 N.Y.L. Sch. L. Rev. 557 (2012/13).

1. *Compelled Consent*

May an individual invoke his or her Fifth Amendment privilege against self-incrimination in refusing to consent to the release of foreign bank records which would otherwise be protected under foreign law? This issue was addressed in *United States v. Ghidoni*, 732 F.2d 814 (11th Cir. 1984), where in its pursuit of tax evasion charges, the government sought to compel Ghidoni's waiver of bank secrecy protections under foreign law. The court of appeals rejected Ghidoni's argument, holding that the act of signing the consent form does not itself incriminate, even if the information contained in the documents might do so. The U.S. Supreme Court agreed that compelled consents do not violate the Fifth Amendment in *Doe v. United States*, 487 U.S. 201 (1988).

2. *Fear of Foreign Prosecution*

The privilege against self-incrimination has sometimes been asserted in a different context, where the individual claims that testimony in a U.S. proceeding might be used against him in foreign proceedings. Within the United States, aliens and citizens alike are entitled to the same protections against self-incrimination from U.S. prosecutions. But in *United States v. Balsys,* 524 U.S. 666 (1998), the Supreme Court rejected such a Fifth Amendment claim based on fear of foreign prosecution.

In so doing, it said, even though concerns about possible foreign prosecution were beyond the scope of the privilege, cooperative conduct between the United States and foreign nations might develop to a point at which such a claim could be made.

> If it could be said that the United States and its allies had enacted substantially similar criminal codes aimed at prosecuting offenses of international character, and if it could be shown that the United States was granting immunity from domestic prosecution for the purpose of obtaining evidence to be delivered to other nations as prosecutors of a crime common to both countries, then an argument could be made that the Fifth Amendment should apply based on fear of foreign prosecution simply because that prosecution was not fairly characterized as distinctly "foreign." The point would be that the prosecution was as much on behalf of the

United States as of the prosecuting nation, so that the division of labor between evidence gatherer and prosecutor made one nation the agent of the other, rendering fear of foreign prosecution tantamount to fear of a criminal case brought by the Government itself.

524 U.S. at 698–699.

INDEX

References are to Pages